GLOBAL FAMILIES

D1566419

NATION OF NEWCOMERS: IMMIGRANT
HISTORY AS AMERICAN HISTORY
General Editors: Matthew Jacobson and Werner Sollors

Global Families

A History of Asian International Adoption in America

Catherine Ceniza Choy

NEW YORK UNIVERSITY PRESS
New York and London

NEW YORK UNIVERSITY PRESS
New York and London
www.nyupress.org

References to Internet websites (URLs) were accurate at the time of writing.
Neither the author nor New York University Press is responsible for URLs that
may have expired or changed since the manuscript was prepared.

Library of Congress Cataloging-in-Publication Data

Choy, Catherine Ceniza, 1969-
Global families : a history of Asian international adoption in America / Catherine Ceniza
Choy.
pages cm. — (Nation of newcomers : immigrant history as American history)
Includes bibliographical references and index.
ISBN 978-0-8147-1722-6 (cl : alk. paper) — ISBN 978-1-4798-9217-4 (pb : alk. paper)
1. Intercountry adoption—United States. 2. Intercountry adoption—Asia. 3. Adopted
children—United States. 4. Adoption—United States. 5. Asian Americans. I. Title.
HV875.5.C47   2013
362.734—dc23   2013016966

New York University Press books are printed on acid-free paper, and their binding materials
are chosen for strength and durability. We strive to use environmentally responsible
suppliers and materials to the greatest extent possible in publishing our books.

Manufactured in the United States of America
10 9 8 7 6 5 4 3 2 1

Also available as an ebook

*This book is dedicated to
my husband, Greg Choy,
my amazing partner in life and work*

CONTENTS

ILLUSTRATIONS

ACKNOWLEDGMENTS

These acknowledgments must begin with my gratitude for the presence of Asian American adoptees in my University of Minnesota classes. Their belief that Asian American adoptees' history, art, and contemporary issues matter to Asian American Studies, and vice versa, has been a major source of inspiration. While I was an assistant professor of American Studies at the University of Minnesota, I had the privilege of being a cofounding member of the Asian American Studies Initiative and working with a dynamic group of colleagues, especially Josephine Lee, Richard Lee, Greg Choy, Jigna Desai, and Erika Lee. In the Department of American Studies, Elaine Tyler May and Lary May instilled confidence in me that this project would be meaningful for the region, the nation, and beyond. I completed this book while I was an associate professor of Ethnic Studies at the University of California, Berkeley, where the mentorship of Evelyn Nakano Glenn and Tom Biolsi helped me strike a delicate balance among research, teaching, and service.

I am grateful for funding sources that affirm the critical role of the humanities in the twenty-first century. A Mellon Foundation Project Grant provided crucial support for the completion of *Global Families*. A UC Berkeley Institute of International Studies Manuscript Mini-Conference Grant enabled me to receive constructive critical feedback from Ellen Herman, Mark Jerng, Hertha Sweet Wong, Barbara Yngvesson, Beth Piatote, and Sarah MacDonald. A UC Berkeley Townsend Center for the Humanities Initiative Grant provided course relief as well as stimulating conversations with humanities faculty from various departments. Hertha Sweet Wong graciously served as my faculty mentor during the tenure of the grant. UC Berkeley research fellowships and grants in the form of a Committee on Research Faculty Research Grant, Humanities Research Fellowship, and a Research Assistantship in the

Humanities as well as an American Association of University Women Postdoctoral Research Leave Fellowship offered much-needed funding support during the earlier research and writing stages.

Global Families would not have existed if not for the skillful work of curators, archivists, and librarians who have sustained archival collections and guided researchers with critical insight, especially Dave Klaassen and Linnea Anderson of the University of Minnesota Social Welfare History Archives; Gary Handman of the UC Berkeley Media Resources Center; Corliss Lee of the UC Berkeley Library; Lillian Castillo-Speed of the UC Berkeley Ethnic Studies Library; Mark Quigley of the UCLA Film and Television Archive; Anne Garrison of the Swarthmore College Libraries; Wendy Chmielewski of the Swarthmore College Peace Collection; and Jane Nakasako of the Japanese American National Museum. John Dougherty and Jennifer Jue-Steuck were dedicated and diligent research assistants. I am also grateful to the Armstrong Foundation project manager Jan Biagio; the photographer Cho Seihon; Jane Nakasako, the Japanese American National Museum digital asset and research coordinator; and the filmmakers Deann Borshay Liem and Marlon Fuentes for providing permission to use archival and film images.

I thank Julie Rosicky, the executive director of the International Social Service-United States of America Branch (ISS-USA), for helping me to secure permission to conduct research in the ISS-USA case files. The historical records of the ISS-USA Branch (located in Baltimore, Maryland) on which this study is based are held by the Social Welfare History Archives at the University of Minnesota. Permission for their use in this research project was granted by the ISS-USA. For more information, see http://www.iss-usa.org and http://special.lib.umn.edu/swha. Points of view in this book are mine. They do not necessarily represent the official position or policies of the ISS-USA. When referencing adoptees and their families in the case files and organizational records, I have used pseudonyms to maintain their confidentiality.

As I conducted research in the ISS-USA organizational records, I developed a fascination and admiration for the life histories and work of the ISS-USA's assistant director, Susan T. Pettiss, and the Major League Baseball pitcher and author Jim Bouton. Lynne Taylor, Tammy Gerhart, Jane Weston, and especially Greg and Susie Leatherbury generously shared memories and materials about Susan Pettiss, who passed away in 2006. Kim Park Nelson, Sasha Aslanian, and Ochen Kaylan located a lovely photo of Susan Pettiss demonstrating her dedication to working with children. Jim Bouton offered assistance regarding a feature story about his family in *Signature* magazine.

Parts of this book were published as earlier versions in various publications. Earlier versions of sections of chapter 1 appeared in "Race at the Center: The History of American Cold War Asian Adoption," *Journal of American-East Asian Relations* 16, no. 3 (2009): 1–20, and earlier versions of sections of chapter 3 appeared in "Institutionalizing International Adoption: The Historical Origins of Korean Adoption in the United States," in *International Korean Adoption: A Fifty-Year History of Policy and Practice*, edited by Kathleen Ja Sook Bergquist, M. Elizabeth Vonk, Dong Soo Kim, and Marvin D. Feit (Binghamton, N.Y.: Haworth Press, 2007), 25–42. An earlier version of chapter 5 was coauthored with Gregory Paul Choy and appeared in "Memory Works: Reimagining Loss in *First Person Plural, Bontoc Eulogy,* and *History and Memory*," Second International Symposium on Korean Adoption Studies, Seoul, Korea, August 2010, 129–145. In the conclusion, my discussion of Yngvesson's book first appeared in my book review of *Belonging in an Adopted World* that was published in *Adoption Quarterly* 14, no. 3 (2011): 218–220. I thank the editors and anonymous readers for their insightful comments and suggestions.

Book chapters also emerged from presentations of works in progress at various venues, such as a keynote lecture at the Alliance for the Study of Adoption and Culture conference. There were also invited talks at Kyoto University's Institute for Research in Humanities; the Asian American Studies Lecture Series at the University of Maryland, College Park; the Asian American Studies Workshop Series at the University of Illinois at Urbana-Champaign; the Ohio State University Center for Historical Research Program, and UC Berkeley's Beatrice Bain Research Group. Lastly, there were panel presentations at meetings of the Society for the History of Childhood and Youth, Childhood and Migration Working Group, and the American Historical Association. I am grateful to Susan Castagnetto, Yasuko Takezawa, Yoshiyuki Kido, Larry Shinagawa, Kent Ono, Allan Gallay, Riitta Hoegbacka, Miroslava Chavez-Garcia, Sam Yamashita, and Sid Lemelle for organizing, facilitating, and/or publicizing these generative opportunities.

Writing coaches and editors helped me prioritize and improve my writing. Thank you to Nanou Matteson for getting me to move the book project forward at a time when I felt my writing was at a standstill. Academic Ladder coaches and group members made regular writing an enjoyable habit. After having admired the writing of Cheri Register and assigning *Are Those Kids Yours?: American Families with Children Adopted from Other Countries* in one of my classes at the University of Minnesota, it was a privilege to have her work on this project as an editor.

At NYU Press, the editor-in-chief, Eric Zinner, was steadfast in his enthusiasm for *Global Families* over many years. Thank you, Eric, for remaining "bullish" about this project. I am also grateful to the assistant editors Ciara McLaughlin and Alicia Nadkarni and the production editor, Alexia Traganas, for their professionalism. I greatly appreciated two earlier readers' endorsement of this book project, and I am indebted to the two readers of the final manuscript for their astute and detailed constructive critique.

This book also emerges from a community of scholars who cared enough to take the time to tell me about a book, article, or film that was related to my project; to give me feedback on my work in progress; and, above all, to offer encouragement and collegiality. Thank you, Naoko Shibusawa, Evelyn Nakano Glenn, Tom Biolsi, Michael Omi, Beth Piatote, Sau-ling Wong, Judy Yung, K. Scott Wong, Shelley Fisher Fishkin, Barbara Posadas, Vicki Ruiz, Rudy Guevarra, Eiichiro Azuma, Madeline Hsu, David Yoo, Gladys Nubla, Joshua Troncoso, Joanne Rondilla, Jordan Gonzales, Ariko Ikehara, Jason Oliver Chang, Julie Thi Underhill, Amy Shen, and Wei-Chi Poon. I feel so privileged that this community also includes many individuals who are at the forefront of adoption studies: Richard Lee, Amanda Baden, Kim Park Nelson, Jane Jeong Trenka, Tobias Hubinette, Jennifer Kwon Dobbs, Carol Singley, Caroline Levander, Deann Borshay Liem, Ellen Herman, Cheri Register, Lee Herrick, Jared Rehberg, Lorial Crowder, Kathleen Jo Sook Bergquist, Sara Dorow, Mark Jerng, Josephine Lee, E. Wayne Carp, Peter Selman, Hosu Kim, Soojin Pate, Sarah Park, Anne Jin Soo Preston, Kimberly McKee, Rebecca Hurdis, Daniel Schwekendiek, Eleana Kim, and Kim Su Rasmussen. My deep thanks to Max Leung, Jeanette Roan, Anne Garrison, Mike Magoolaghan, Victoria Haas Choy, Walt

Jacobs, Valerie Minor, Jeannie Wang, Milton Tong, Leighton Fong, Anna Presler, Barbara Yasue, and the late Yuji Yasue for conversations and dinners that sustained me.

As soon as I started researching this book, my mother, Patria Ceniza, immediately shifted gears from clipping newspaper and magazine articles about Filipino nurses (the topic of my first book) to stories about international adoption. I am so grateful for her unwavering support. The commonsense wisdom of my sister Caroline Ceniza-Levine continues to be inspirational. And the awesome ability of my children Maya and Louis to work hard *and* to have lots of fun keep me going everyday. Finally, I dedicate this book with great love and respect to my husband, Greg Choy. Thank you for walking beside me and for being my friend.

International Adoption Nation

"Where did your little girl come from?"

I was finishing my lunch and was about to get my one-year-old daughter ready to visit another part of the Minneapolis Institute of Arts, when I was taken off guard. Judging by the woman's age—early to mid-sixties—I doubted she needed a lesson on the birds and the bees. Thus, I thought I had been asked a variation of the question that has been posed to virtually every Asian in the United States, whether they be newly arrived immigrants or fourth-generation Americans: "Where are you from?" This is a question for which New York City, the place of my birth, is not the right answer. "My family is originally from the Philippines," I explained. "My daughter is a third-generation Filipino American as well as a fourth-generation Korean and Chinese American on her father's side."

When the woman drew a blank look, it struck me that I had completely misinterpreted her question. She wanted to know *from where in Asia I had adopted* my daughter. She explained that her daughter had recently adopted a baby girl from China. It was then that I realized that the paradigm of the adopted Asian child had become so strong that it overrode common sense; even though I'm "Asian looking," there was still the assumption that my daughter was adopted.

* * *

International adoption from Asia has transformed the racial and ethnic landscape of the heartland of America to the point where—as in the situation I just described—it has become a social norm.[1] According to a 2009 local news story, more than thirteen thousand Korean adoptees live in Minnesota; this is the largest number of Korean adoptees in any one place in the world.[2] In the Twin Cities of Minneapolis and St. Paul, the phenomenon of Asian international adoption is especially visible because of its predominantly transracial nature, with primarily white parents adopting Asian children. During one visit with my daughter to our neighborhood playground, I observed that I was the only *nonwhite* parent of an Asian child.

Asian international adoption in America is not solely a regional phenomenon, however. It has contributed to the transformation of the United States into an international adoption nation. The United States is the top recipient of internationally adopted children. According to the Evan B. Donaldson Adoption Institute, international adoptions in the United States have more than doubled between 1991 and 2001. In the new millennium, Russia, Guatemala, Romania, and Ukraine are among the top sending countries of adoptive children to the United States. However, Asian children have comprised the majority of children internationally adopted by U.S. citizens. Between 1971 and 2001, U.S. citizens adopted 265,677 children from other countries; 156,491 of those children were from Asian countries.

Since the late 1990s, China has been a major sending nation of adoptive children to the United States. In 2000, it led the list of the top twenty primary sending countries, with 5,095 children from China being adopted by U.S. citizens. South Korea provided 1,794 adoptive children, making it third on the list. Vietnam, India, and Cambodia also placed in the top ten of primary sending nations.[3]

Asian international adoption has also made a mark on our national culture. It has become a powerful way to imagine contemporary U.S. multiculturalism because it shapes one of the most intimate, emotionally laden, and cherished institutions: the family. The publicity about celebrities adopting internationally has made the American public highly aware of the possibility of families becoming transracial. In the early twenty-first century, for example, the omnipresent publicity of Angelina Jolie and Brad Pitt's "world's most beautiful" family—formed through the international adoptions of a Cambodian boy, an Ethiopian girl, and a Vietnamese boy in addition to their three biological children—has contributed to a popular perception of international and transracial adoption as a socially acceptable, if not desirable, way to create a family.[4]

International adoptions by celebrities are not solely the product of recent media hype; they have also been shaped by the celebrities' lived experiences. For example, the actress Katherine Heigl named her adopted Korean baby girl after her mother and her sister, who was also adopted from Korea.⁵ The positive portrayal of international and transracial adoption appears onscreen as well as off. The adoption of a Chinese baby girl by Kristin Davis's character Charlotte York is the happy ending to her struggle against infertility in the final episode of the iconic HBO sitcom *Sex and the City*.

Mainstream news media further illuminate how Asian international adoption has become a prominent example of contemporary multicultural family formation. A 2007 *New York Times* photo essay on the Jewish rites of passage of adopted Chinese girls illustrates how international and transracial adoption adds yet another layer of diversity to American cultural pluralism. The photo essay features Fu Qian, renamed Cecelia Nealon-Shapiro, completing bat mitzvah, the rite of passage into Jewish womanhood. A lesbian couple, Mary Nealon and Vivian Shapiro, had adopted "Cece," who was abandoned at an orphanage because of China's one-child rule. Although Nealon was raised as a Roman Catholic, and Shapiro was raised by atheistic Jews, they were drawn to Judaism after they met and decided to give Cece a relatively traditional upbringing.

Six Chinese adoptees from Cece's orphanage flew in from different parts of the United States to attend her bat mitzvah. And the writer Andy Newman reports that while Cece is one of the first Chinese adoptees in the United States to go through the rite of passage, "she will not be the last. Across the country, many Jewish girls like her will be studying their Torah portions, struggling to master the plaintive singsong of Hebrew liturgy and trying to decide whether to wear Ann Taylor or a traditional Chinese outfit to the after-party."⁶ These stories and images present Asian international adoption as the newest chapter in an increasingly progressive American mosaic.

A darker, more problematic side of international and transracial adoption of Asian children lurks alongside these celebratory narratives. The specter of American racism and nativism toward Asians haunts the joyous imagery of these adoptive families. In *Sex and the City*, Charlotte York's desire to adopt a Chinese baby is met with her mother-in-law's disapproval of having a Chinese member in their MacDougal clan. "Me no like Mandarin baby," the mother-in-law succinctly explains. And while this specific example of popular culture might be easily dismissed as a dark, humorous vestige of an American racist past in contrast to its postracial present, since the late 1990s a growing body of memoirs, documentary films, and anthologies by Korean American adoptees who have come of age underscore the theme of their numerous mundane encounters with American racism. In doing so they present a more nuanced, if not ambivalent, picture of Asian international adoption. In the first published anthology by and about Korean adoptees, entitled *Seeds from a Silent Tree*, a Korean adoptee named Mi Ok Song Bruining writes about her American childhood:

> Adolescence is traumatic enough without being targeted for being racially different, culturally identified as "alien" & looking like no one else—peer, child, or adult. I was stared at, harassed, bullied, called names, insulted, threatened & verbally abused by other kids—younger & older—on a daily basis—on the school bus, in school, stores, restaurants, & many other public places in Rhode Island.[7]

These works remind us that the historical legacies of anti-Asian sentiment in the United States—codified, for example, in U.S. immigration legislation, which targeted Asians for exclusion during the late nineteenth century and the first half of the twentieth century; in U.S. naturalization law that rendered Asian immigrants ineligible for citizenship until the 1940s and 1950s; and in antimiscegenation laws in fourteen states that prohibited interracial sex and marriage between Asians and whites until the U.S. Supreme Court made such laws unconstitutional in 1967—persist in more recent times.

The increasing popularity, since the 1960s, of the seemingly positive stereotype of Asian Americans as "model minorities" in relation to negative ("less than model") stereotypes of African Americans adds an additional layer of complexity regarding how race informs the phenomenon of Asian international adoption. Although positive and negative stereotypes of these communities are dehumanizing and dangerous, they have influenced both international and domestic adoption in the United States. Some scholars, such as the sociologist and adoption studies expert Sara Dorow, have argued that these stereotypes undergird a racial preference for Asian children over African American children.[8] In her pioneering book about contemporary transnational adoption between the United States and China, Dorow claims that these attitudes reflect popular images and ideologies of a "flexible Asian difference" that can be successfully integrated in American families and communities in contrast to a "less assimilable" African American difference.

Furthermore, the decreasing supply of white babies in the United States in the late twentieth century—a result of the creation of the birth control pill, the legalization of abortion, and the increasing social legitimacy of single parenting—contributes to the commodification of Asian children for an international adoption market. The process highlights the way in which profit motives as well as a broader context of unequal social, political, and economic relations within and across nations create specific flows of adoptable children from one country to another. In a *Los Angeles Times* article in September 2009, Barbara Demick reported that in some rural areas in China "instead of levying fines for violations of China's child policies, greedy officials took babies, which would each fetch $3,000 in adoption fees."[9] Several scholars have strongly criticized international adoption by documenting and highlighting a global market that transports babies from poorer to richer nations, likening it to a form of forced migration and human trafficking.[10] Thus, Asian international adoption is simultaneously highly celebrated and deeply controversial.

But these international and transracial sensibilities about family making, and the heated debates that they generate, are not as new as they seem. They have a history.

*   *   *

This book explores the historical origins of this highly visible and growing phenomenon of international adoption from Asia. Although an emergent scholarly field of American adoption studies combined with in-depth journalistic accounts have forcefully illustrated that the United States is—to use the book title by the journalist, adoption advocate, and adoptive parent Adam Pertman—an "adoption nation," the history of the international turn in this phenomenon and the formative role that adoption from Asian countries has played in it are not well known.[11]

My study seeks to move beyond one-dimensional portrayals of Asian international adoption as a progressive form of U.S. multiculturalism on the one hand or as an exploitative form of cultural and economic imperialism on the other. Rather, its major objective is to move toward a nuanced, complex understanding of its history as a history of race, foreign relations, immigration, and labor as well as intimacy.

This study was primarily inspired by the six and a half years I spent living and teaching in Minnesota—first, accompanying my husband, Greg, when he taught at Gustavus Adolphus College in St. Peter, and then working as an assistant professor of American Studies at the University of Minnesota—in the late 1990s and the first few years of the new millennium. Gustavus Adolphus College and the U of M had hired us primarily on the basis of our professional expertise in Asian American Studies, a relatively young interdisciplinary scholarly field created out of social protest movements in the 1960s and 1970s, which emphasizes the study of the history, artistic expressions, and contemporary concerns of Asians in the United States. Neither Greg nor I are part of families in which adoption has played a major role. However, we were immediately struck by the presence of Korean American adoptees in our undergraduate classes. They sought to learn more about their personal histories in a larger sociohistorical context through Asian American Studies. However, in the late 1990s, little research had been conducted about Asian international adoption in the context of the field.[12] Most of the scholarly studies on Asian international adoptees in the United States were psychological and medical studies that focused on the adjustment of the adoptees.[13] These were important, pioneering studies, but they also framed international adoption as a problem to be rectified rather than as a dynamic phenomenon to be studied on its own terms.[14] In addition to the desire to write a groundbreaking work in Asian American Studies, I was also moved to undertake a study of Asian international adoption because of the Asian American Studies commitment to create knowledge that is relevant to the Asian American communities in which we live and serve. While a resident of Minnesota and a professor at the U of M, I recognized that Asian American adoptees were important members of that community.

I am also a trained historian and, upon embarking on a study of Asian international adoption in the United States, I learned that the

University of Minnesota housed the records of the International Social Service-United States of America Branch (ISS-USA) in its Social Welfare History Archives. Organizational records and in-depth oral interviews have been vital resources for recent historical and ethnographic studies of U.S. domestic adoption, adoption in the Americas, and international adoption. *Global Families* complements these works through its close reading of the ISS-USA organizational records. While several scholars have utilized the ISS-USA records alongside those of the Child Welfare League of America, U.S. Children's Bureau, United Nations agencies, and various Korean government agencies among others, their focus on U.S. domestic adoption and Korean international adoption misses the broader trajectory of ISS-USA work over time and in other parts of Asia.

The ISS-USA records were a gold mine in many ways. The scope of the collection was large, including fifty-six linear feet of general administrative correspondence and history files; minutes and reports from annual meetings, board of directors meetings, and administrative committee meetings; financial reports and budgets; and organizational statistics. The ISS-USA records also include five hundred linear feet of case records and case record indexes dating from 1929 to 1995.[15] An especially rich feature of these records was its correspondence about adoption, both that concerning programs and services that the ISS offered and that between the ISS-USA and prospective adoptive parents, independent adoption agencies, state social service agencies, and ISS branches in other countries. Taken together, these records enable us to see the key roles that an international social service agency, local social workers, independent adoption agencies, humanitarian organizations, and individual adoption advocates from many different walks of life have played in this history. These interactions were not always cooperative. Indeed, conflict over how international adoption should be facilitated was a major theme of the correspondence.

Interestingly, the historical origins of the ISS-USA were not rooted in the world of adoption. Rather, the early history of the ISS-USA was linked to the growing social awareness of family problems related to international migration more broadly. Early twentieth-century problems that plagued family members who were separated by national borders and, at times, by vast distances led to the creation of an international, independent, and nonsectarian organization in 1924 that could coordinate social welfare casework across national boundaries. Initially called the International Migration Service, the organization changed its name in 1946 to the International Social Service to reflect the breadth of its casework. Although such casework was varied—including, but not limited to, the separation of families; desertion and child support; child custody; paternity claims; and legal questions concerning deportation, repatriation, and immigration—by the late 1950s, casework related to international adoption constituted the major activity of the ISS.[16]

In contrast to the more well-known singular divine mission of the Oregon farmer Harry Holt and his Holt Adoption Program to save Korean war orphans through adoption by born-again Christians in the United States and the work of the celebrated Nobel Prize–winning writer Pearl S. Buck, who founded the international and interracial adoption agency Welcome House, the records reveal that ISS social workers (in Europe and Asia as well as the United States) expressed ambivalence as well as advocacy regarding the phenomenon of Asian international and transracial adoption. During the formative Cold War period of Asian international adoption, the ISS concluded that international and transracial adoption was a viable, indeed a beneficial, form of making a family. Yet its official publications strongly noted that it could also work against the best interests of the children—even wreaking havoc on their personal development, the lives of their biological and adoptive families, and the effectiveness of social welfare work in Asia and America—if not handled professionally and ethically. As a result of studying these records, I was able to glean the complexity of international and transracial adoption, its radical and progressive possibilities of a world profoundly united across national, cultural, and racial divides through family formation, as well as its strong potential for reifying the very national, cultural, and racial hierarchies it sought to challenge.

A profound lesson I learned from this collection was that, while the mainstream news reports of the time period exalted the efforts of charismatic individuals like Harry Holt and Pearl Buck, a comprehensive and more accurate history of Asian international adoption needed to capture the collective—albeit chaotic on many occasions—effort made by many different groups and individuals to enable its practice. And although state governments in Asia and the United States played important roles in this history through immigration laws and adoption regulations, many nongovernmental organizations and individual citizens were at the center of the creation of this international phenomenon. This collective effort speaks to the heart of the inspirational intellectual project outlined by a distinguished historian of international relations, Akira Iriye:

> If what is at the heart of our historical inquiry is the human condition, then it makes sense to go beyond the nation or the state as the sole framework of analysis and deal with human affairs, human aspirations, human values, and human tragedies. States do play a role, but only a partial role in all of these. The task that challenges historians of international relations is to devise a new transnational perspective that takes into account both states and non-state actors.[17]

This study takes up this task by presenting a history of Asian adoption as an international and, above all, human story comprised of the efforts of many seemingly ordinary people.

My premise is that the history of Asian international adoption is best understood as a unique but also increasingly normative type of family formation in our self-consciously global age. It is one important form of what I call "global family making." I define "global family making" as the process involving the decisions made and actions taken by people who create and sustain a family by consciously crossing national and often racial borders. In contrast to a state-centered or "top-down" approach to such a process—such as the South Korean government's recent official attempt to incorporate overseas Korean adoptees into the state's "global family"[18]—my concept of global family making calls for more attention to the nonstate actors, such as the international workers, adoptive parents, and adoptees and their birth families who participate in the global family-making process from the bottom up.

The international adoption community has struck me at times to be an insular world with its own membership and outlets of communication and expression by and for the community. This insularity is due in no small part to the marginalization, if not exclusion, of adoptive

families because of the tendency to see racially matched and/or biologically formed families as "normal" or "real."[19] But the history of international adoption is a significant part of Asian American history, and by
extension Asian and U.S. histories, that is important for all of us, not
just those directly involved in adoption, to learn. The history of international adoption speaks to the way in which family formation needs to
be understood on a global social, political, and economic scale, and not
solely a personal or local one.

The concept of global family making connects the seemingly uncom-
mon world of adoption to the broader forces of international migration that bind so many of us. For example, global family making is not
solely applicable to international adoption, but it involves the growing phenomenon of international marriage. The sociologist and Asian
American Studies scholar Hung Cam Thai's recent study of Vietnamese
international marriages points out that marriage is a major reason why
people migrate to the United States.[20] And the research of the feminist
studies scholar Felicity Amaya Schaeffer on international marriages
between American men and Mexican and Colombian women illuminates that these international marriages often cross racial as well as
national borders.[21]

Finally, while it is important to acknowledge that global family making can result and has resulted in the breaking down of racial divides,
and while some might interpret the increasing popularity of international, transracial adoption as proof of our "postracial" society, my
research urges us to take seriously the historical and present-day significance of race in the lives of global families and in the process of global
family making. Race, I argue, is fundamental to understanding the
demographics, discourses, and institutions of early Asian international
adoption history as well as the lived experiences of Asian American
adoptees. It is an analytical category that is historically linked but not
always inextricably tied to racism. This is a lesson obtained from the
ISS-USA records, which demonstrates that ISS workers were sensitive
to the difference between race as a socially constructed category and
the practice of racism in both Asian countries and the United States.
But the lesson is most powerfully felt in the cultural productions—the
memoirs, creative writing, visual art, and documentary films—by and
about adult Asian adoptees, most of whom are of Korean descent. In

these works we learn that the absence of an acknowledgment about race is not necessarily a socially progressive or liberatory move. Rather, to ignore or to reject any critical engagement with race can be and has been detrimental. Thus, we must not conflate race and racism but must instead recognize that a discussion about race in the history of international and transracial adoption is productive for all of our families, our societies, and our world.

* * *

The book is organized chronologically and thematically. Chapter 1, "Race and Rescue in Early Asian International Adoption History," challenges the popular notion that international adoption in America is the newest face of U.S. multiculturalism by connecting this phenomenon to the post–World War II and Cold War presence of the United States in Asia through the establishment of military bases and the fathering of mixed-race children (popularly known as Amerasians) overseas by U.S. servicemen with Asian women. The origins of Asian international adoption were inextricably linked to the adoption of mixed-race Japanese, Korean, and Vietnamese children by American families in the 1950s through the 1970s. U.S. news media, social welfare agencies, and independent adoption organizations represented the mixed-race children from Japan, Korea, and Vietnam as an Asian social problem due to restrictive Asian traditions and values based on patrilineal bloodlines. While these images racialized Asia as a backwards place in contrast to a progressive United States, social critics also complicated the East-West divide by invoking the moral responsibility of the United States in Asia. The ISS believed that this international problem—a problem of racial mixture, Asian social discrimination, and U.S. accountability abroad—required a transnational solution. It could only be resolved through stronger social service in the Asian countries as well as international adoption by American families.

Chapter 2, "The Hong Kong Project," presents an earlier history of Chinese international adoption from Hong Kong in the 1950s and 1960s, which has been overshadowed by the more recent phenomenon of Chinese international adoption that began in the 1990s. It also links this earlier history of Asian international adoption to refugee resettlement. While, at first glance, the pairing of adoptees and refugees may appear odd, the histories of Asian international adoption and Asian refugee resettlement in the United States share several similarities. These include their emergence in the chaotic aftermath of war, the migration of Asian adoptees to the United States under the auspices of refugee policies, and several discursive similarities such as the depiction of Asian adoptees and refugees by scholarly studies and the mainstream media as objects in need of rescue by the United States. As an increasing number of white Americans expressed interest in international *and* transracial adoption, their adoption of "full-blooded" Chinese children presented social workers with another problem of race: assessing racial tolerance among potential adoptive parents and their communities.

Chapter 3, "A World Vision," explores the central role of international and local social service agencies and independent adoption organizations in facilitating Asian international adoption. It acknowledges the significance of individual efforts in this history—most notably Harry Holt and Pearl S. Buck—but also attempts to broaden our understanding of the increasing popularity of this phenomenon beyond the efforts of charismatic individuals. The participation of many different agencies and organizations illustrates that the history of Asian international adoption is rooted in a collective past. Sadly, competition between social service agencies and individuals dominated the discourses of how international adoption should work. The collaboration between the screen siren Jane Russell and the ISS-USA provides one example of how a famous and religiously motivated individual could work effectively with a nonsectarian organization. Well known for starring in Howard Hughes's 1943 film *The Outlaw*, Russell should also be remembered for her leadership and dedication to the WAIF (World Adoption International Fund), which became the fund-raising arm of the ISS-USA's adoption division in the 1950s.

The emotional ups and downs of pioneering American adoptive families are featured in chapter 4, "Global Family Making." In the 1950s and 1960s, many news stories popularized Asian international adoption to the general public by representing these families' experiences with wonderful beginnings and happy endings. In doing so, the writers of these stories also obscured the serious challenges that accompanied creating a family through international adoption. Although the ISS-USA archival records primarily depicted the perspectives of social service workers, some documents illuminated the experiences and viewpoints of American adoptive parents. In contrast to mainstream news stories, they put forward more complex narratives that highlighted spousal disagreements, financial stress, adjustment difficulties, and racial anxieties. When taken together, these challenges as well as joys of global family making present a more accurate portrayal of the history of Asian international adoption in the United States.

A notable absence from the archival records are the voices of adoptees. However, since the 1990s, the emergence of a sizable body of artistic work by and about Asian American adult adoptees has challenged the representation of Asian international adoption as a "quiet migration."[22] The final chapter, "To Make Historical Their Own Stories," calls attention to the sociohistorical as well as aesthetic contributions by Asian American adult adoptees for adoption studies and for Asian American history. The chapter features close readings of the documentary films *First Person Plural* and *In the Matter of Cha Jung Hee*, which were both written and directed by Deann Borshay Liem, a Korean international and transracial adoptee whose adoption was arranged by the ISS-USA. The memories and contemporary reflections of Borshay Liem, her Korean and American families, and other Korean women and men whose lives transformed and were transformed by international adoption constitute an alternative and much-needed archive for the study of adoption.

The chapter analyzes *First Person Plural* and *In the Matter of Cha Jung Hee* in relation to two experimental films. Marlon Fuentes's *Bontoc Eulogy* explores the relationship between U.S.-Philippine colonial history and contemporary Filipino immigrant identity through one Filipino American's search for the whereabouts of his Bontoc Igorot grandfather who participated in a live display at the 1904 St. Louis World's Fair. Rea Tajiri's *History and Memory* contemplates the impact of Hollywood's and the U.S. government's renditions of World War II on her Japanese American family members' fading memories of their internment.

Finally, given that the presence of adoptees in my Asian American Studies classes inspired this study, the chapter emphasizes that the artistic work by and about Asian American adoptees is important for Asian

American history and not solely for adoption studies. *Bontoc Eulogy* and *History and Memory* do not address the subject of Asian international adoption, but, when studied alongside *First Person Plural* and *In the Matter of Cha Jung Hee*, the films expose the multilayered difficulties of documenting the histories of Americans of Asian descent. These challenges include bumping up against the presumed authority of social workers, individual adoption advocates, adoptive parents, museum directors, and government officials, and confronting the predominantly sentimental and chauvinistic depictions of Asian international adoption, U.S. colonization of the Philippines, and Japanese American internment. The filmmakers Borshay Liem, Fuentes, and Tajiri subvert popular understandings of these histories by reclaiming their historical agency and the historical agency of their families and specific communities—that is, their ability to tell and to document their own stories with complexity, humanity, and dignity.

1

Race and Rescue in Early Asian International Adoption History

When the January 12, 2010, earthquake in Haiti brought renewed attention to the international and transracial adoption of Haitian children by white American families, much of the media coverage was controversial and, unfortunately, one-dimensional. The story of ten white Americans who were detained at the Dominican border for "kidnapping" thirty-three Haitian children soon after the worst natural disaster in Haiti's history dominated U.S. news coverage. Some observers began immediately taking sides for the Americans who, they claimed, had good intentions to rescue the children through international adoption, while others harshly criticized them for infringing on Haitian national sovereignty. There was little mention of previous attempts in our nation's history to rescue children abroad in the wake of catastrophe by adopting them, of the complexity of processing sound and ethical international adoptions, or even of the significance of racial difference in transracial adoptions. Given the decades-long history of international and transracial adoption in the United States, we can and should have a more informed and productive discussion.

Beginning in the 1950s, American families began adopting children of different racial backgrounds from countries abroad in significant numbers. These pioneers of global family making adopted Japanese and Korean war orphans and Korean "mascots."[1] However, mixed-race Asian and American children in these countries soon captured the hearts and minds of the American public and became a focal point for the work of international nongovernmental organizations such as the International Social Service (ISS).

The post–World War II U.S. occupation of Japan (1945–1952) and U.S. Cold War involvement in the Korean War (1950–1953) created a population of mixed-race children produced by American servicemen and Japanese and Korean women. Although war had a devastating impact on all sectors of Japanese and Korean societies, the lives of these children were especially bleak. Japanese and Korean societies rejected these children as "improper" because many of them were conceived outside of wedlock, they looked physically different, and even more importantly they embodied the unequal political relationship between occupied and occupying nations. Although an American military presence in Japan and Korea was responsible for these children's births, the U.S. government bore no official responsibility for the children's or their mothers' welfare. Nongovernmental organizations and concerned individuals stepped in to provide some relief to the children and their mothers. Thus, international adoption and humanitarian rescue were inextricably linked during this time period.

As in the recent Haitian crisis, white American individuals rushed to rescue these children via international adoption. And critical concerns about the trafficking of these children also soon emerged. The International Social Service (ISS) was not an adoption agency, but it reasoned that international adoption was a form of immigration necessitating coordinated social welfare work across national borders. Beginning in the 1950s, the ISS focused more of its welfare work on international adoption, with the creation of an adoption division, WAIF-ISS. The international adoption of mixed-race Asian and American children led to the establishment of ISS units in Japan in 1955 and in Korea in 1957. The ISS collaborated with American and Asian government officials as well as nongovernmental organizations to study and to implement practices that benefited the children first. These practices included an investment in social welfare work that focused on the integration of the children within the Asian countries. Simply put, ISS work in this area shows us that humanitarianism does not always have to take the form of the white American savior.

At the same time, ISS workers also successfully placed mixed-race Asian and American children in, primarily, adoptive homes of white Americans. The workers approached this process with caution and restraint, raising thoughtful questions about the meaning of racial, cultural, and national differences for the child and his or her American adoptive parents, and considering the most effective process through which an adoptive child of a different racial background could become a real part of a new family in a new setting. The United States is the world's leading recipient of adoptive children from many different countries within Asia, Latin America, and Africa, so these questions continue to be relevant today. Contemporary analyses of international and transracial adoption should go beyond stories of adoption rescue attempts gone awry. They need to acknowledge the complex history of our international adoption nation, a history in which race and rescue have played central roles.

The Interracial Ties That Bind: Rescuing Mixed-Race Asian and American Children

In the 1940s and 1950s, Europe was a major sending region of adoptive children, primarily German, Greek, and Italian children, to the United States.[2] The destructive and chaotic aftermath of World War II in these European countries had left children orphaned and impoverished, while the United States had been largely untouched by war damage.[3] By the mid-1950s a demographic shift had occurred. The supply of European children had dwindled, but an increasing number of children from East Asia were available for adoption.[4]

While both European and Asian international adoption arose in the historical contexts of war and U.S. military involvement overseas, race informed early Asian international adoption history in distinct ways. In the 1950s, interracial intimacy between American men and Asian women was a well-known feature of U.S.-Asian relations.[5] Hollywood films such as *Sayonara* popularized these interracial relationships to the American masses with hopeful antiracist messages about the possibility of a peaceful coexistence and the integration of East and West. The 1957 Warner Brothers film, which garnered four Academy Awards and received a nomination for Best Motion Picture, starred Marlon Brando as Major Lloyd Gruver, a Korean War pilot who is reassigned to Japan. Initially a staunch supporter of the U.S. military's opposition to marriages between American soldiers and Japanese women, Gruver falls in love with a Japanese actress, Hana-ogi, portrayed by Miiko Taka. In the film's conclusion, Gruver and Hana-ogi defy American and Japanese social conventions by deciding to marry one another, but not before Hana-ogi expresses anxiety over the fate of their mixed-race children.

"We live in different worlds, come from different races," she laments, then adds worriedly, "What would happen to our children? What would they be?" Gruver allays her fears matter-of-factly: "They'd be half Japanese, half American. They'd be half yellow, half white. They'd be half you. They'd be half me. That's all they're going to be."[6]

A radio broadcast expressed similar optimism in Japan. Sawada Miki, a Japanese heiress and philanthropist and the founder of the Elizabeth Saunders Home for children of unmarried Japanese women and American servicemen, first learned about these children while listening to the early-morning news on June 28, 1946. According to her biographer, Elizabeth Anne Hemphill, Sawada "heard the announcer say that a child of mixed Japanese and American parentage had been born that morning. He said it was the first time that the two countries had shaken hands, and he called the child a symbol of love to bind the two shores of the Pacific."[7]

These utopian visions were important because they enabled current and future generations to imagine an interracial world. However, the situation of children born to U.S. servicemen and Japanese or Korean women, also referred to as "Occupation babies" and "GI babies," was precarious.[8] The ISS-USA collected magazine and newspaper clippings from Asian countries as well as the United States about various child welfare issues, and the plight of mixed-race Asian and American children figured prominently in print media. According to one American magazine article, these children were "destined, if they remain in Asia, to a life of degradation and misery."[9] A Japanese news article characterized the future of these children as "bleaker than that of almost any children in the world."[10]

The distinctive racial features of these mixed-race children made them visible targets for discrimination and abuse. Although the children of American white servicemen and European women also suffered from neglect and abandonment, as the writer Norman Lobsenz noted, "no external sign sets them apart."[11] By contrast, "in the Orient, where their Eurasian features brand them like the mark of Cain, the children are rejected and ostracized."[12] The discrimination against these children in Japan and Korea, the lack of U.S. and Asian governmental support, and desertion by their American fathers influenced their mothers' decisions to abandon them, creating a group of children in need of rescue *and* available for adoption.[13]

Separate orphanages for mixed-race children in Japan, such as the Elizabeth Saunders home in Oiso and Our Lady of Lourdes Baby Home in Yokohama, and special wings of orphanages in Korea, such as the Choong Hyun Baby Home near Seoul, offered better care for these children.[14] Yet the possibility of leaving institutional care was minimal at best. In Japan, discrimination against mixed-race children discouraged their domestic adoption. One news article reported that "a Japanese couple who daringly adopted an Eurasian baby returned it after a few

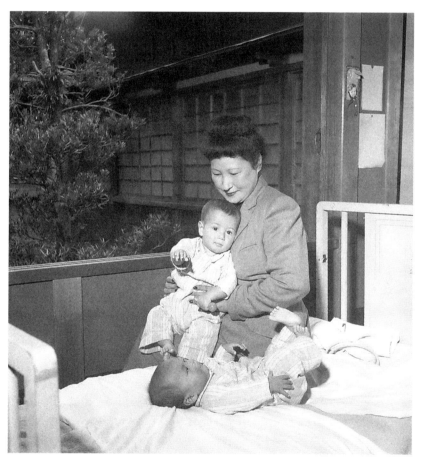

Figure 1.1. Philanthropist Holding Infant at Orphanage. Japanese philanthropist Miki Sawada holds an Amerasian infant at the Elizabeth Saunders Home. Another baby lies on a bed next to her. She established the orphanage to care for babies of Japanese women and American servicemen. (© Horace Bristol / CORBIS)

weeks. They could not stand up to the pressure of resentment and prej-udice from their neighbors."[15]

Correspondence among ISS workers corroborated news reports and detailed the critical situation of mixed-race children in Korea. Reports noted the "intense prejudice" in addition to poverty that pressured Korean mothers to give up their children to the Korean Child Place-ment Service or "any foreign welfare agency who will take them in."[16] The discrimination faced by mixed-race children in institutional care was compounded by the already "deplorable" state of the care facili-ties for the estimated fifty thousand homeless children in Korea. One report claimed that these children may have been deprived of food and clothing in orphanages that were already lacking adequate heat, water, clothing, and staff. It concluded dismally that their situation was one of life and death: "Doubtless many of these children will perish during the winter months for lack of food, shelter and mothering."[17]

The plight of mixed-race Asian and African American children was deemed especially tragic. In 1952, the local PTA of Oiso opposed the enrollment of seventeen mixed-race Japanese and American children from the Elizabeth Saunders Home, and the matriculation of the three half-black children in particular. In addition to Japanese parents' preju-dicial claims that the mixed-race children were intellectually inferior disease carriers, their fears that the Japanese and African American children were especially violent fueled their protest.[18] An *Ebony* maga-zine feature article on mixed-race Japanese and African Americans was titled "Japan's Rejected." Its author, Era Bell Thompson, noted that "in Japan today there are some 20,000 mixed-bloods who were fathered by American servicemen, both white and black. The children of con-querors, and mostly illegitimate, all are unwelcome aliens in the land of their birth. First to be abandoned and last to be adopted, the 2,000 or so who are half-Negro are thrice damned."[19]

A 1957 report claimed that "among the Korean children of mixed parentage, the Korean-American Negro orphans are the most pitiful. Usually Negro physical characteristics predominate and they are very noticeable."[20] Daniel Quinn, the chairman of the Ad Hoc Children's Committee on Adoption of the American Council of Voluntary Agen-cies for Foreign Service, described the problem of mixed-race children in East Asia as "acute." According to Quinn, "It is quite evident from firsthand observation and experience in the field that a Negro child, particularly in Korea, would never be accepted into the Korean society and there is no future for the child."[21] Given this information, Susan Pettiss, the assistant director of the U.S. branch of the International Social Service (ISS-USA) concluded that "the neediest children are the Korean-Americans, especially those of Negro fathers. Although a number of these half-Negros have been placed there are still some in institutions in the Far East, where they are misfits and often discriminated against. Although we recognize the scarcity of Negro adoptive homes in the United States, we cannot help but consider the meager alternatives for those in foreign countries."[22]

Place as well as race informed the tragedy of these children's lives. A 1959 Manual on Intercountry Adoption noted that the mixed-race background of some children, "unfortunately, makes them unacceptable in their present locality."[23] This was not the case in Europe where, the writer Norman Lobsenz noted, "virtually no stigma of any kind attaches to an illegitimate child in Europe. The continent has been a battlefield too long to view war babies as part of a problem in morals, and its normal peacetime illegitimacy rate is high."[24] By contrast, social workers as well as journalists conceptualized and represented Japan and Korea as closed, impenetrable places, which encouraged discrimination against mixed-race children. Era Bell Thompson referred to "an inherent Japanese prejudice against those who are 'different.'" Despite its "unparalleled postwar leap from commercial impotence to the world's sixth industrial power," Japan, as Thompson concluded, was still a "racially monolithic nation; its people a closed society."[25] In a paper presented at the 1957 National Conference on Social Welfare about the discriminatory treatment faced by mixed-race Korean and American children, an ISS-USA senior case consultant, Margaret Valk, described Korea as a country "unique and isolated among the countries of the Far East, priding itself on the purity of its racial lineage."[26]

Such characterizations about Europe as well as Asia were exaggerated and sensational. They erased the brutal stigmatization of French, German, Czech, and other European women who were suspected of having intimate relationships with occupying soldiers, a censure leveled against Japanese and Korean women as well.[27] They also grossly downplayed the highly politicized situation of French-German and German–African American children in post–World War II Europe.[28]

Instead these depictions overemphasized a stereotypical backwardness of Asian countries, masking the diverse beliefs Asians held toward these children. Japanese responses to the plight of mixed-race Japanese and American children ranged widely and included acceptance as well as ostracism.[29] By December 1952 Japan's Ministry of Education supported integrated schooling.[30] In 1953, the Ministry of Welfare issued a statement claiming that various government agencies would pay special attention to mixed-race children who remained in Japan, supporting them to become respectable Japanese citizens. And while some Japanese called for increasing American adoptions of mixed-race children, others urged Japan to work on overcoming its own racism toward these children as well as other minority groups in Japanese society.[31]

Finally, these generalizations about Japan and Korea glossed over racism in the United States against Asian Americans, African Americans, and mixed-race people. They did not acknowledge how an American military presence contributed to the hardships of these children. In the history of antimiscegenation laws in the United States, thirty-eight states banned black-white relationships and fourteen states prohibited Asian-white marriages.[32] The U.S. military actively discouraged marriages between American servicemen and Japanese and Korean women. And American servicemen commonly deserted their children.[33]

In other words, Japanese, Korean, *and* American prejudices contributed to the social ostracism of mixed-race children in Japan and Korea, a phenomenon exacerbated by the immediate historical context. The chaos of war and its aftermath in these countries produced not solely an emergency situation in the present but also new categories of people seemingly without a future. As John Dower writes in his Pulitzer Prize–winning history of Japan under U.S. occupation, "Many of the most pathetic Japanese war victims now became the country's new outcasts. . . . It was an especially conspicuous phenomenon in Japan at war's end, when whole new categories of 'improper' people felt the sting of stigmatization. These included . . . war orphans and street children, forced to live by their wits outside 'proper' society."[34]

A common fear was that mixed-race children would be social out-casts and would have little opportunity to contribute positively to Jap-anese society as they grew up. They encountered a hopeless situation because they would be unable to marry or to secure decent employ-ment. Many of these "improper children" became street "women," though some prostitutes were as young as fourteen years old. War orphan boys earned pocket money by leading GIs to prostitutes.[35]

With few exceptions, Korean mixed-race children who survived the immediate aftermath of the Korean War faced similar circum-stances.[36] In her correspondence with American social workers, Susan Pettiss noted that "the child of mixed racial parentage is a complete outcast in Korea, socially and culturally. He cannot attend school and would have no employment possibilities."[37] "There is absolutely no future for them in Korea," she emphasized.[38] Another ISS report based on the observations of General Lyman Lemnitzer, the commander of United Nations forces in South Korea, described the situation of the increasing numbers of mixed-race children in the mid-1950s as "a new kind of time bomb that had been quietly ticking away." The report warned that as "a generation dispossessed and rejected, these children could become adults ripe for any kind of criminal activity or subversive leadership."[39]

A 1958 case study of a four-and-a-half-year-old mixed-race Korean and African American boy illuminated the multiple levels of neglect that such children suffered. The boy with "brown wavy hair," "large brown eyes," and an "olive" complexion was found abandoned in the street, his parents' whereabouts unknown. Social workers characterized him as a "deprived, frightened, and sickly little boy." Admission into the Choong Hyun Baby Home's section for mixed-race children resulted in better attention, but the researchers surmised that while "he lost his fears, and has developed very well mentally . . . his early treatment and neglect have left their marks upon him in that for sometime to come he will need careful building up under medical supervision." And they recommended that "he be brought to his adoptive home in the United States as soon as possible."[40]

This race against time was exacerbated by the absence of perma-nent immigration legislation in the United States that could facilitate international adoption, as well as a decades-long history of policies excluding immigration from Asia.* Social workers depended on ad hoc U.S. refugee policies to facilitate American families' adoption of mixed-race Asian and American children.[41] In the early 1950s, American military families stationed in Japan who had adopted children there were able to bring these children to the United States only after the passage of private bills that gave congressional authority for the immigration of each child.[42]

Nineteen fifty-three was a watershed year for international adoptions on a larger scale. The passage of Public Law 162 created five hundred nonquota immigration visas that enabled the admission of alien adopted children. And the Orphan Section of the Refugee Relief Act of 1953 provided an additional four thousand nonquota immigrant visas to eligible orphans under the age of ten. According to a study by a former American serviceman and social worker, Lloyd Barner Graham, by June 30, 1957, 3,571 alien children had used the visas issued to them under this law, and 1,222 of these were children from Japan who had been adopted by American families.[43]

Although new ad hoc policies were expected to facilitate international adoption, their scope and time frames were unpredictable. The most important piece of legislation to enable the immigration of internationally adopted children, the Refugee Relief Act, was set to expire on December 31, 1956. These short temporal windows of opportunity further intertwined rescue with international adoption. As one piece of legislation was about to expire, the ISS-USA advocated for the passage

---

*Although the United States prides itself on being a "nation of immigrants," the exponential increase in Asian immigration to the United States is a relatively recent phenomenon and is the result of the liberalization of U.S. immigration policy in 1965 with the passage of the Hart-Celler Act. Before 1965, the restriction of Asian immigration to the United States was a prominent feature of immigration policy, beginning with the 1882 Chinese Exclusion Act, which banned the immigration of Chinese laborers, and followed by the 1907 Gentlemen's Agreement, which restricted the immigration of Japanese laborers; the 1917 creation of the Asiatic Barred Zone, which denied entry from most Asian countries; and the passage of the nation's first comprehensive restriction law, the 1924 Johnson-Reed Act, which further prohibited most Asian immigration. According to the 1924 Act, a child who was one-half of a race that was ineligible for U.S. citizenship, such as the Japanese, was also ineligible for U.S. citizenship and barred from entry to the United States. It was not until the passage of the McCarran-Walter Act in 1952 that Japanese became eligible for U.S. citizenship.

of new laws. Thus, their officials arranged international adoptions with a fervor stemming from unforeseeable time constraints. In 1957, Susan Pettiss wrote to the supervisor of the state of Michigan's casework department: "As you will see, we are trying to move ahead with applications from Negro families and from Caucasian families interested in the mixed-blood children from the Far East. . . . However, we have a much smaller number of homes approved for the placement of half-Korean children, and are trying to build up a large enough group of these to give us a wide selection when there is a new law. The need of these Korean-Caucasian children is so great, and their future so very uncertain, that we think it urgent to be prepared in advance so that no time need be lost."[44] During the same year, Margaret Valk urged her colleagues to find more African American adoptive families for mixed-race Korean and African American children, emphasizing that "we therefore need to find *11 more Negro families immediately* and should therefore be following up on individual PAPs [prospective adoptive parents] to state agencies previously."[45]

In the broader history of U.S. expansionism in Asia, mixed-race children were not a new people. U.S. colonialism in the Philippines beginning in 1898 had produced mixed-race children of U.S. military men and Filipino women. In the opening section of Evangeline Canonizado Buell's stunning memoir of growing up Filipino in the United States, she recounts how her grandfather was among six thousand African American soldiers, known as "Buffalo Soldiers," who were sent to the Philippines in 1898 to fight in the Spanish-American War as part of the Ninth Cavalry of the U.S. Army. According to Canonizado Buell, "during this conflict, the Buffalo soldiers had benefited from the solidarity of Filipinos, who refused to shoot African American soldiers because they felt an affinity with them. The Caucasian soldiers had referred to both groups as 'savages.'"[46] A group of these men, including her grandfather, remained in the Philippines after the Spanish-American War, forming families by marrying Filipino women and having children with them.

After the death of his Filipina wife, Maria, Buell's grandfather had his three daughters stay with his wife's relatives while he completed his army service. While one daughter found love and acceptance in her new home, a different set of relatives treated the other two daughters "like servants because they were half black and did not look like their cousins with straight hair and fairer skin."[47] Although these children did not fare well, there was no outcry from the American public, and the U.S. colonial government did not assume responsibility for these children. The overt racism against both African Americans and Filipinos during this time period was partly responsible for the lack of response. Furthermore, the U.S. colonial government's major objective of preparing Filipinos and the Philippines for gradual independence involved American tutelage, but not integration into the U.S. nation and by extension American families.[48]

By the 1950s, however, decolonization movements in Africa and Asia and the escalation of the Cold War posed fundamental challenges to American racism. The image of the United States at home and abroad became a cause for alarm.[49] Communist governments challenged U.S. claims of democracy and freedom by pointing to the social realities of racial segregation, violence, and protest in the United States. Although the Soviet Union led the communist world, the role of Asian nations in the Cold War was a major concern of the U.S. government, especially after the victory of the Chinese Communist Party in the Chinese Revolution of 1949. This international politics of race heightened debates about U.S. accountability for the population of mixed-race Asian and American children and informed the moral urgency to rescue them.

Thus, in the 1950s, U.S. news reports couched the situation of Asian children fathered by U.S. military men overseas in a new language of moral responsibility directed to the American masses. In a 1956 *Redbook* article, the writer Norman Lobsenz described the lack of U.S. action on the part of these children as "shocking." According to Lobsenz, when asked what was being done about the "war babies" a U.S. State Department official referred to "a committee looking into that."[50] The committee had not met, however, in more than a year. Lobsenz quoted the official as saying, "Well, aren't those kids just another kind of war damages, anyway?"[51] Lobsenz acknowledged the hard work of many individuals and social welfare organizations to address the critical situation but noted that "their resources are simply too small to cope with so large and complicated a problem. Thus, except for a few devoted persons, no one is particularly interested in the children as individuals. No one cares that they are in a legal and emotional limbo, imprisoned by red tape and averted eyes."[52] He characterized these children as "ghost children" created by "the sins of the fathers," poignantly highlighting American responsibility for these children. Lobsenz provided readers with a different, humanitarian approach offered by Albert Schweitzer who said, "The time must come when one can expect the former occupying country, which cannot avoid a share in the responsibility for these children, to help open for them a way in the world."[53] Lobsenz then concluded that "for children whose status as war babies is branded on their features, adoption by Americans is perhaps the best solution."[54]

International Adoption: The Best Solution?

In the 1950s and 1960s, representations of Asian international adoption in America were dominated by the emphasis on the contrast between East and West. A phenomenon popularly viewed as breaking down racial and national divides and hierarchies could just as powerfully reify them. News media represented the Far East as a stagnant, homogeneous place of backward-thinking people in contrast to a progressive and dynamic United States. It popularized international adoption to the United States as the best hope for mixed-race children by publicizing the welcoming arrivals and life-altering circumstances of those who had already been adopted. For example, a January 1955 article in the *New York Times* announced that five orphans from Japan—"all are children of American fathers and Japanese mothers who are dead or unable or unwilling to care for them"—had received homes in the United States: "Tekio Muto, 8-year-old adopted daughter of Mr. and Mrs. Philip Pedley of Glen Ellen, Calif., cried, 'I'm going home!' Eight-year-old Diane and 3-year-old Barbara Pedley, the couple's own children welcomed their new sister with an armful of dolls."[55] A 1963 *Sacramento Bee* news article, entitled "Hearts across the Sea: Korean Orphans Find Happy Homes Here," featured this adoptive parent's observation: "You should have seen the children. Remember, most of them come to this country, love-starved and food-starved. Now they're healthy and so responsive."[56]

News reports also represented the United States as a place of liberation for mixed-race Korean and African American children. A 1956 *Kansas City Times* news article described the excitement of the adoptive parents of five newly arrived Korean–African American children from Seoul. One mother commented that when the children arrived in Chicago, they had lacked warm clothes but, upon arrival, were wrapped in blankets and later had sufficient clothes purchased for them.[57] A 1964 *Muncie Evening Press* article featured Martha Gwyn's reflection on her child's transformation after his adoption:

> Nick's mother was Korean and his father was an American Negro G.I. . . . If he had to stay in Korea it would have been terrible for him. Koreans simply reject all children of mixed racial backgrounds even to the point of physical abuse. He was in one of the best orphanages in Korea before we got him, but when he got here there was a bad rash all over the front of his legs and he had some sort of scalp infection. And he was starved—not just for affection, but physically starved. We couldn't fill him up. . . . For a few weeks after he got here . . . even when

Figure 1.2. Author Pearl Buck sitting on window seat in her library with granddaughter Susan on her lap and flanked by adopted daughters Joanna (R) and Mary Chieko, at home [taken in 1965]. (Photo by Reginald Davis/Pix Inc./Time Life Pictures/Getty Images)

he had eaten all he could hold and there was food left, he'd hold that food in his hands and not let anyone take it away from him. He's over that now. He knows he's safe, that there's plenty to eat and he's getting more secure.[58]

Studies conducted by the ISS during the 1950s also claimed that international adoption was the best solution for mixed-race Japanese and Korean children in the aftermath of occupation and war. Between 1955 and 1957, the Japanese branch of the International Social Service (ISS-Japan) placed 279 children of mixed parentage in adoptive homes of Americans stationed in Japan and of Americans in the United States.[59] Midori, a six-and-a-half-year-old Japanese and African American girl, was one of these placements. According to the ISS, she was found "abandoned in a railroad waiting room in Japan." The case study featured this happy ending:

> With no future before her in Japan where children of mixed blood have no place in the Japanese community, the orphanage was anxious to find a good Negro family in America for her before she would have to go to school and be ostracized by the other children. With the assistance of the local US adoption agency, the [Pattersons] were found to be a thoroughly dependable couple who had given a great deal of thought to the adoption and all that it would mean to them and a child from Japan. They are in their 40's and have no children of their own. Midori seemed just the child for them and the "match" was made. . . . Midori was met by delighted parents who say she is the "sweetest little girl in the world."[60]

In 1957, Margaret Valk posed thoughtful, open-ended questions about what was ultimately best for the mixed-race Korean and American child:

> A most understandable question has been: Is it sound to uproot children from so far away and of so different a cultural background and racial composition; wouldn't such drastic transplantation, in addition to the painful deprivations experienced by the child, be too great a burden for him? Wouldn't it be wiser, or a happier solution, to seek some way of caring for these children in their country of birth?

Yet, she concluded that one response to the situation was clear: "To us, the only solution for the children of mixed parentage is their placement outside their own country in good Caucasian and Negro homes. In the absence of such placements, they will not live or will have nothing to live for."[61]

Valk's visit to Korea in November 1956 forged her conviction. In her correspondence to a New York state adoption worker, she related, "I was over myself for a brief period in Korea during November and brought back nine of our children. It was a most memorable experience for me. Conditions in Korea must be seen to be believed, and I think it is true to say that probably little [Philip's] life has been saved by this placement for adoption."[62] A 1958 study sponsored by the ISS-USA and the Child Welfare League concurred: "Many children are the illegitimate offspring of American servicemen stationed overseas. In Japan and Korea, for example, there are an unknown number of children of mixed racial background for whom adoption by American families may offer the best hope for a useful, happy future."[63]

Television helped publicize the solution of international adoption and the work of the ISS-USA in this area to the American public. In 1957, *Armstrong Circle Theatre*, one of the longest-running anthology series in television history, presented an episode entitled "Have Jacket, Will Travel."[64] Written by the postwar American novelist Vance Bourjaily, who served as an Army infantryman in Japan during World War II, "Have Jacket, Will Travel" featured three stories of international adoption coordinated by the ISS-USA's adoption division, WAIF.[65] Douglas Edwards, a CBS news anchor and the *Armstrong Circle Theatre* host, introduced the episode as follows: "Every day on the front pages of the newspapers we read of the world's mighty—kings, presidents, dictators, ambassadors, generals. There is another group affected by the mighty, sometimes tragically. These are the world's children. Their stories seldom appear on page one. This episode tells a small part."

"Have Jacket, Will Travel" featured the adoption stories of three children: Petro Andros, a nine-year-old boy from Greece; Gina Biko, an eight-year old girl from Italy; and Kim, a five-year-old mixed-race Korean American boy, who "was among thousands of these orphans of American-Korean parentage." Edwards informed viewers that although world wars and international economics and politics created orphans, the global distribution of orphans was not well balanced: "In some parts of the world, families are large, homes are full, money is short, and orphanages are overcrowded, whereas in other countries, like the United States, homes are available, but children are not." He pointed out that the United States was the chief receiving country of international adoption and that, although international adoption was not an easy process, it was also not much more difficult than local adoption.

Armstrong Circle Theatre, which premiered in the summer of 1950, aired for more than fourteen seasons. According to the writer Susan Gibberman, some contemporary critics characterized *Armstrong Circle Theatre*'s programming as sentimental stories that communicated a "pleasantly related moral." "Have Jacket, Will Travel," which aired on November 11, 1957, exemplified the shift in *Armstrong Circle Theatre* beginning in 1955, when the series presented an early form of the docudrama, or fact-based dramatization. The executive producer David Susskind and the producer Robert Costello deemphasized the role of actors in order to make the story the "star." According to Costello, their aim was "to combine fact and drama—to arouse interest, even controversy, on important and topical subjects." Another objective was to present some solutions for viewers.[66]

In "Have Jacket, Will Travel," the story about Kim's adoption features Sergeant Walter and Harriet Duff, a handsome couple in their mid- to late twenties, who are stationed in Osaka, Japan. They have been married for five years but are childless. Walter encourages Harriet to consider adopting a mixed-race Korean and American child by highlighting the U.S. military's accountability: "We're responsible for these kids in Korea. They're the sons and daughters of GIs like me." Walter's connection to Korea is also personal, because his brother had died there. While he was alive, he had written to Walter about the abysmal situation of the children and had let him know that he donated half of his paychecks to help the Korean children and refugees.

In line with the new docudrama format of *Armstrong Circle Theatre*, the episode highlighted two important, topical issues: the first was the plight of mixed-race Asian and American children in Korea and Japan. During a visit to Korea, Walter meets Kim. Television viewers learn that although there are orphanages in Korea, the problem is more pressing for those of mixed heritage because no nation accepts responsibility for these children. In Korea, some mothers even dye their children's hair so that neighbors will not identify them as "half-GI." Kim's mother tried to hide him from neighbors but then committed suicide. Kim's Korean caretaker tells Walter that Kim does not play and he does not eat. Meanwhile, in Japan, Harriet learns about the situation of mixed-race Asian and American children from her conversations with Chizuko, the Duff's Japanese domestic helper. Chizuko makes the historical connection between Japan and Korea when she refers to these children as "very sad babies, half American, half Korean. Korean people, just like Japanese people, do not want sad, half-blood babies."

This dramatization of the tragedy of mixed-race Asian and American children echoed the story of their critical situation that had been publicized in the print media. Its depiction of the humanitarian largesse of American servicemen against a backdrop of Japanese and Korean prejudice toward women and children resonated with American viewers in the 1950s. As the scholarship of Christina Klein and Naoko Shibusawa has persuasively shown, cultural productions—magazine and news articles, Hollywood movies, and Broadway musicals—during this time were not solely vehicles for entertainment. Their narratives about U.S. moral responsibility in Asia (especially toward women and children) made the U.S. occupation of Japan and U.S. Cold War involvement in Asia justifiable, palatable, and even desirable to the American general public.[67] By presenting adoption as the only solution for Kim's tragic situation, "Have Jacket, Will Travel" pulled on viewers' heartstrings and continued this line of thinking.

However, the second topical issue raised by the episode was that of American racism against Asians. "Have Jacket, Will Travel" presented some of the challenges regarding racial difference that potential adoptive parents of international and transracial children faced in the 1950s. As Walter's interest in the adoption grows, Harriet expresses reluctance about adoption in general and about the adoption of a mixed-race Korean and American boy in particular. Her doubts stem from the provincial attitudes in their small town in the United States "in a state who never saw a Korean." Harriet wonders, "Who would the child have for friends? You can't tell me they wouldn't be prejudiced." Describing Kim as "a child whose place I'd have to fight for," she confesses, "Walt, I'm not that strong." Walter insists, "I'd like to see anyone pull that stuff on my kid that I adopted," but he acknowledges the social reality behind Harriet's fears by suggesting the possibility of their living in the more diverse state of California.

This particular story line resonated with the ISS-USA belief that American adoptive families needed to directly confront the possible discrimination that their Asian adoptive children would encounter outside the home. As Valk explained:

> It has seemed to us that if an American family who wish to adopt a Korean child, particularly a half-Korean child, and to make him a part of their family are ready to face the fact that he may inevitably sometimes face discrimination and prejudice in his life outside the home and are prepared to work out the results of this with him and to understand what this must mean for him, then such a family will have or find the strength to be able to give the child the assurance, warmth and security he will need when coming up against these difficulties. In preparing a family to receive an Asiatic orphan we have found that it is very helpful to discuss this question with them and to be able to show them that it will be of no help to the child if the adoptive parents simply try to close their minds to the painful facts of discrimination and cannot recognize its existence. The discrimination will be real for the child and they must be prepared to meet it with him and to understand what it will mean for him.[68]

In "Have Jacket, Will Travel," the specter of American racism continues to haunt the Duffs after they begin the adoption process. When Walter's father learns about their plan, he writes to say that Walter should forget about building a house in their hometown, castigating Walter for yet "another soft-headed idea" with "this one beat[ing] them all." His confidence wavering, Walter asks Harriet if she wants to change her mind. This time she responds steadfastly that she wants to do what he wants to do, which is to adopt a mixed-race child from Korea.

Harriet prefers a girl, whom she thinks she might get along better with, and she wants as young a child as possible, but Walter wants to see Kim again: "I saw this kid in Korea who will die unless someone takes care of him. I've got to do something." When he reunites with Kim in Korea, he says, "I shouldn't do this, but you know something, I couldn't forget you." Walter brings Kim back to Japan, but instead of reciprocating

Figure 1.3. Walter and Harriet Duff embrace their adopted son, Kim, at the conclusion of "Have Jacket, Will Travel." (UCLA Film and Television Archive/Permission granted by Armstrong Foundation)

Walter's affection, Kim refuses to talk. Walter says regretfully, "This isn't what my wife ordered. I just took him. It's a bad deal for Harriet." But then he sees Harriet lovingly embrace Kim and hears her tell him, "You're Kim and Walt wanted you. And that's enough to make me love you. Chizuko, help me put *my son* to bed." Walter, Harriet, and Kim embrace in the final scene, leaving viewers with the message that, in spite of several, serious challenges, Kim's adoption is indeed the best solution.

If this message was unclear, Douglas Edwards explains in the closing "real-life" segment of the episode that, for the last three years, WAIF had played a part in more than four thousand adoptions by families in the United States. He introduces two adoptees, Deborah and Johnny, who had arrived in the United States from Korea within the past two years and had been adopted by a couple in New York. Edwards tells audience viewers that Johnny, who spoke only Korean when he came to the United States, attends kindergarten and now says he speaks "American."

Figure 1.4. After the broadcast of "Have Jacket, Will Travel," Douglas Edwards introduces viewers to Deborah and Johnny, who had arrived from Seoul, South Korea, and had been adopted by a family in New York. (UCLA Film and Television Archive/Permission granted by Armstrong Foundation)

Edwards describes the younger Deborah as "a doll" who "doesn't speak very much yet." Noting that these are two of the many children who find families through ISS-USA and WAIF, he concludes, "Every child in this world is entitled to a home and loving parents."

Beyond Rescue: From International to Indigenous Social Services

During this early period, ISS reports and correspondence prominently featured ambivalence about as well as advocacy of the practice of international adoption. One of the organization's guiding principles was the careful consideration of possible alternatives before the child is removed from his or her relatives for adoption. The ISS believed that a parent should have sufficient opportunity to consider the full range of legal and psychological consequences involved in the decision to relinquish a child for adoption.[69] Doubts about the ethical implementation of Asian international adoption arose from the concern that Asian relatives' opportunities to fully consider the impact of adoption were grossly insufficient. In his study of the adoption of children from Japan by American families between 1952 and 1955, Lloyd Barner Graham observed that only a minority of Japanese mothers of mixed-race children received social casework help when making decisions regarding adoption. They often made the decision to relinquish their children under great social and economic duress. He suggested that such decisions might have been reversed if recourse had been possible in Japanese courts for civil actions against members of the Occupation forces and if a social service system, such as Mothers' Allowances or Aid to Dependent Children, had been available in Japan. Graham concluded that "once committed to institutional care, the tendency was for adoption decisions to be made by default, rather than after careful consideration of the mother. . . . The child-centered principle might have been much more wisely implemented than it was."[70]

ISS officials also recalled that in European countries after World War II, international agencies took children too quickly from mothers in refugee camps.[71] Thus, the reports of children being forcibly removed from their mothers for adoption overseas were a cause of alarm for ISS workers. In 1958, Susan Pettiss reported that a Korean pediatrician criticized independent adoption organizations in Korea, in particular "the efforts in Korea to force mothers of mixed blood children to give up these children. [The physician] had witnessed on three different occasions the mothers actually being physically forced to give up their children."[72]

ISS-USA workers considered the potential problems of uprooting Asian children for adoption and weighed them against the alternatives for them in the children's home countries. In the mid-1950s they expressed a range of opinions. In a 1955 letter, Margaret Valk related, "These questions are ones to which the Child Welfare Advisory Committee of our organization has given a great deal of hard thought and is continuing to give much thought. The opinions expressed differ very much and we feel that there is probably no 'right' and no one definite answer."[73]

While some ISS officials strongly advocated for the international adoption of mixed-race children because of reports of their social ostracism and abuse in Japan and Korea, others began, by the late 1950s, to question the severity of attitudes toward mixed-race children in these countries and to link changing local attitudes to the strong desires of mothers to keep their children. In 1958, Virginia Baumgartner, an ISS representative in Korea, wrote to the ISS-New York office:

> About your question of the mother not wishing to give up their chil-dren for adoption. This as you realize cannot be put down to any one factor as they are many and varied. However it is my impression that a major factor is the fact that attitudes toward these children are changing. It is difficult to perceive in most cases any discrimination against these children on the part of family or friends or other children. Of course this is in the villages where this mixed blood child is no longer a rarity and when the villages are in relatively close contact with the nearby army installations.[74]

ISS officials also cautioned against large-scale international adoption from these countries. As Valk explained, "Until now ISS has been explor-ing each such request on a case by case basis with the different program representatives in Korea, but with no real conviction ourselves that it was the wisest plan for a Korean child (unless he was of mixed racial parent-age which wasn't often in this type of case) to encourage his emigration and adoption overseas."[75] She outlined a range of critical considerations regarding the ISS's ability to process Korean international adoptions in a sound and ethical manner such as the difficulty of obtaining sufficient and reliable information concerning the adoptive children's health histo-ries, personalities, and behaviors, as well as the inadequate preparation of the children for joining their new American families.*

Even in the special case of mixed-race abandoned children, the ISS continued to advocate for the careful consideration of alternative plans for a child within his or her own country. Some ISS officials were

* As I will discuss more fully in chapter 3, individual adoption advocates and indepen-dent adoption organizations harshly criticized the ISS for upholding these principles through time-consuming bureaucratic practices, but the significance of thorough investigation of an adoptive child's history and of adequate preparation for his or her integration in an American family is clear even in more recent times with the well-publicized April 2010 case of a Tennessee mother returning her seven-year-old adopted son to his native Russia because of his alleged psychological and behavioral problems.

concerned that the use of international adoption as a solution for the plight of mixed-race children detracted from the process of racial integration in Japan and Korea as well as the development of effective indigenous social service for all Japanese and Korean children. For example, in a 1957 meeting, Eugenie Hochfeld, an ISS-USA supervisor, observed that the ISS had initially conceptualized international adoption as a "temporary phenomenon" in the aftermath of World War II. However, by the mid-1950s, partly "due to an abnormally large number of illegitimate children," it had become clear that it was a continuing trend. Yet, an ISS-Geneva official, Greta Frank, warned, "we all talk about educating . . . in our countries. By taking children away we don't educate."[76] Furthermore, by focusing on the international rescue of children, the "solution" of international adoption may have inadvertently contributed to perpetuating global inequalities. Greta Frank continued that "the child is free for adoption, but [the mother] would not have given up the child [if] she would have had food and shelter. . . . It is just a question, a warning voice."[77]

ISS-USA workers questioned the impact of cultural and national differences on the internationally adopted child. In a 1957 workshop on international adoptions, their broad and open-ended questions illuminated the new and uncharted cultural landscape created by the phenomenon: "What do the cultural and national differences mean in general? What inherent values have they for the child which should be preserved? How fast can a child be expected to become a real part of a new family in a new setting?"[78] The workshop's attendees—who included representatives from the ISS-USA, the Child Welfare League of America, and children's service departments from Connecticut, New York, New Jersey, Pennsylvania, and Iowa—thoughtfully questioned whether international and transracial adoption was advantageous for the child, and they acknowledged sociohistorical as well as contemporary barriers to assimilation in the United States:

> What is the meaning of placement in the United States to the older child who wants to be "American," when there are pressures to keep him identified with his own nationality group? Is it best for the child to be placed with adoptive parents of the same ethnic background? Can a child really feel he belongs to both cultures and nationalities at the same time? How does this possible conflict affect his sense of identity?[79]

Such questions hinted at the broader and longer-term limitations of international adoption as a form of rescue and of the United States as an emancipatory place.

In the 1960s, the ISS continued to facilitate Asian international adoptions, but it increasingly emphasized the important role of indigenous social services to alleviate the plight of mixed-race children. In a 1964 report based on her visit to Korea, Letitia Di Virgilio, a supervisor of the WAIF division of the ISS, charged that "ISS efforts should not be narrowly focused on intercountry adoption of racially mixed children, but should relate to a program of broad service to all children in need in Korea. The program of foster family care started by ISS is both a demonstration of a better method of orphan care and a way of overcoming prejudice against the racially mixed child."[80] This foster family care program was called the Han River Project because it focused on the Han River area of Seoul, the most depressed part of the city. It responded to the tragic conclusions of Lloyd Barner Graham's study and the cautionary words of Greta Frank regarding the trauma of Japanese and European mothers after World War II by giving more attention to Korean mothers and to "the problems that force a mother to give up her child." The program included forty-five Korean families who cared for mixed-race children awaiting adoption by American families, demonstrating that some Korean families were accepting of mixed-race children.[81] Another hopeful sign of racial integration in Korea in the mid-1960s was the Korean government's decision to admit mixed-race children to the middle and upper schools in Korea.[82]

Similarly, the ISS-USA associate director Sidney Talisman, visited Korea and wrote a 1968 report that related how Korean government officials called for more strategies of racial integration in Korea and less reliance on international adoption as the best solution. For example, Talisman met with Choo Chung-Il, the director of the Women and Children's Bureau of the Ministry of Health and Social Affairs, who believed that "children belong with their families. . . . Although younger racially-mixed children may be better off outside of Korea, Korean society must eventually change attitudes towards these children."[83]

The 1968 Talisman report emphasized that, although mixed-race Korean and American children continued to suffer from unequal status in Korean society, "most responsible and enlightened Koreans whom we

spoke to think along the following lines. If a country of 30 million people which is aspiring to be a democratic modern society cannot absorb
a few thousand racially-mixed children, then what hope is there for the
total society?" Talisman quoted one prominent social welfare leader,
Mr. Kim, the director of the Korean National Red Cross, who suggested
that international adoption hindered the process of racial integration:
"Since inter-country adoptions tend to drain off the most attractive and
intelligent children, by pursuing inter-country adoption as a goal for
racially-mixed children we are depleting that particular group of exactly
those members who might in the future help to alter their image in the
society and to mitigate against prejudicial attitudes toward them."[84]

Talisman concluded his report by citing the work of Charles Chake-
rian, the social development advisor to the Korean Ministry of Health
and Social Affairs:

> The Korea of 1968 is not the Korea of 1963 when the country was just
> beginning to embark on its first five-year economic plan, and it is cer-
> tainly quite different from the war-torn country of 1953. Dr. Chakerian
> sees Korea as being ready now to move from the use of emergency mea-
> sures to deal with immediate pressing problems to more coordinated
> and longer range social planning, to a concentration on services rather
> than, as he terms it, "rescue."[85]

The Persistence of Race and Rescue

The plight of "GI babies" persisted into the 1960s and 1970s in the context of war in Vietnam and the U.S. military presence there. A 1972
New York Times article attributed the critical situation of mixed-race
Vietnamese and African American children to Vietnamese racial bias,
implying that international adoption in the United States would be the
best solution: "The Vietnamese are usually prejudiced against dark-
skinned races, and they do not like foreigners. Any child who grows up
without a family which is the focus of Vietnamese life, and is also black,
confronts obstacles that a Westerner cannot imagine. . . . After a visit,
Rev. Hosea Williams wanted to hire two jet planes to take all the black
children to the United States to place them in homes."[86]

The mainstream news media also perpetuated stereotypical representations of a homogeneous Asia and its peoples' inability to care for abandoned children in general. As one 1973 *Newsweek* article explained: "In
part, the tragic condition of Vietnamese orphanages stems from an Oriental belief that it is the responsibility of relatives—not strangers—to care
for parentless children."[87] It suggested that American rescue might be the
only option for the well-being of these children by concluding that "if that
help does not come from the United States, it may not come at all."[88]

By contrast, ISS-USA officials presented a more complex account of
the situation in Vietnam. A 1971 report entitled "The Special Needs of
Vietnamese Children—A Critique" by Wells Klein, the general director of the ISS-USA, acknowledged Vietnam's history of contact with
other racial or ethnic groups, including the French, Chinese, Khmer,
and Indians. Given the history of French colonialism in Vietnam, the
"Caucasian-Vietnamese" child was not a new phenomenon. Klein's
report described distinct levels of race consciousness in different Asian
countries, illuminating that "unlike Korea and, to some extent, Japan,
Vietnamese culture does not place great emphasis on racial purity."[89]
Klein did not deny the presence of racism in Vietnam, but he cautioned
that, given its colonial history, the futures of mixed-race Vietnamese
and white American children were difficult to predict. On the one hand,
the general societal belief that "white is beautiful" in Vietnam and that
light-skinned infants were attractive suggested that the successful racial
integration of mixed-race Vietnamese and white American children
was possible. On the other hand, troubling reports of discrimination
against these children emerged when they were old enough to attend
school. According to Klein, these social problems stemmed not solely
from racial difference but from the stigmatization of these children
because they were illegitimate or the children of prostitutes. Another
factor to consider was their partial American nationality. Klein suggested, "It is possible that a growth of anti-Americanism in South Vietnam will adversely affect these children."[90] Klein also drew a comparison between the situation of mixed-race children of African American
descent in Japan and Korea with those in Vietnam:

> There is unanimity among Vietnamese that the part-black child will
> encounter many difficulties because of his color. The experience, and

present social position, of children fathered by French-Senegalese troops during the 1945–1955 period bears out this prediction. Stated simply, the part-black child in Vietnam faces dim prospects because of his color. Furthermore, because there is no black community in Vietnam, he will grow up and live in relative social isolation.[91]

Klein emphasized, however, that, even given the critical situation of mixed-race Vietnamese and American children, international adoption could benefit only a small number of children. Large-scale international adoption from Vietnam was unrealistic given the relatively small numbers of these children in orphanages, the existence of close relatives who placed the children in these institutions primarily because of economic duress, and restrictive Vietnamese laws that made international adoption a difficult, time-consuming process. He concluded, "Thus, concern for children—including this special group—must by and large be exercised through programs of assistance in Vietnam."[92]

Conclusion: Toward Social Service Solutions

One noteworthy exception to the ahistorical coverage of Haitian international adoption after the January 12, 2010, earthquake was John Seabrook's personal history essay, entitled "The Last Babylift," in the May 10, 2010, issue of *The New Yorker*. Seabrook importantly connected the phenomenon to a broader history of orphan-rescue missions in the United States, beginning with the post–World War II airlift of German and Japanese orphans and followed by other rescue attempts after the Korean War, the Bay of Pigs invasion, and the Vietnam War. Seabrook also acknowledged the work of the ISS, which is characterized in the essay as a "prominent children's aid organization," like UNICEF and Save the Children, that emphasizes "improving social conditions within sending countries, rather than facilitating international adoption."[93]

However, the ISS's work to improve social conditions within the Asian sending countries did not translate into a rejection of international adoption. By the mid-1960s, the number of children referred to the ISS-USA for international adoption from Japan had declined as the result of improved economic conditions and an increase in local adoptions, but the problem of mixed-race children in Korea persisted.[94]

And the ISS continued to endorse international adoption as a remedy. A 1966 presentation to the Child Welfare League of America about international adoptions featured ISS's work on Korean international adoption:

> At the present time, most of the children referred to ISS for adoptive placement are from the Orient . . . but I'd like to elaborate a little, on the present picture regarding Korea. . . . Nearly all the children referred to ISS for adoptive placement are the "mixed blood" children [of] Korean mothers and Caucasian fathers. The problem of racial discrimination has created many difficulties for this group. Although efforts are being made to help their acceptance in the community, through supervised foster home placements, admission into public schools, etc., still, large numbers face a dreary future with little hope for true integration.[95]

The ISS expressed optimism about international adoption overall, noting in particular the resilience of the adoptive children and parents: "Nevertheless we now have considerable evidence of an impressive degree of success in these inter-country placements despite the usual problems involved."[96] Successful international adoption placements by the ISS gave rise to the organization's belief in the possibility of one world united in the recognition of diversity and dignity across cultures, races, and nations:

> The adoption of the child from a foreign land requires the greatest of understanding and identification. The acceptance of cultural difference and today with the preponderant number of children coming who are racially and therefore patently different, this surely requires basic respect for our fellow man with a true recognition of his dignity, whatever his origin, race, or culture. In a shrinking world, where continents are only several jet hours away, ISS continues to build bridges to surmount barriers of language, to create avenues of communication and understanding, to help a little bit in the creation of "one world."[97]

In the early 1970s, specific ISS units continued to focus on the problems of mixed-race children, and they had developed a more nuanced analysis regarding the discrimination and prejudice these children

encountered in Asia. ISS workers noted that historical contexts of war, U.S. military occupation, and the unequal relationships between nation-states figured prominently into the plight of mixed-race children. At the First Asia-Oceania Conference of the ISS in Tokyo, Japan, in 1973, a work study group for the "protection of children across national boundaries" with a focus on international adoption observed that "bi-racial children born to parents of unequal relation (social, economic, or political) tend to face more discrimination and prejudice, especially when the children live in the group of the parent who is of the inferior status."[98]

Referring to the histories of international adoption from Japan and Korea, the work study group presented contrasting views on international adoption as the best answer for mixed-race children without family ties:

> As certain historical developments have occurred, ISS intercountry adoption programs have shifted their locale. The Korean War, for example, produced an emergency situation where there were many orphaned children, and also many racially-mixed children being born into a society, which, at that point, was unable to assimilate them. The same situation had existed after World War II in Japan. . . . There are some who would argue that intercountry adoption can be, at best, a solution for a relatively small number of children, and that the use of such a program relieves the pressure on governments to give priority to social development programs which will, in the long run, benefit larger segments of the population. Others believe that intercountry adoption programs can be developed parallel to local programs and may even speed up or stimulate the development of local solutions.[99]

On the one hand, the work group strongly stated that "without a question, inter-country or international adoption is an area where we can play effective roles for protection of the best interest of a bi-racial adoptive child." Yet it also advocated that the ISS simultaneously work on the integration of mixed-race children within the local communities: "Because of the nature of ISS service we have had the most frequent contacts with the largest numbers of bi-racial children than any other welfare organization. For this reason, ISS organizations could best understand the children and eventually build up rich knowledge and skill in dealing with the integration of the racially mixed children."[100] The paper concluded with the recommendation to provide local social services, including domestic adoption, suggesting that a singular plan to resolve the problems of mixed-race children was untenable. In other words, the commitment to indigenous social services, racial integration, and improved social conditions in Asian countries *as well as* the belief in the possibility of sound and ethical international adoptions were not mutually exclusive.

2

The Hong Kong Project

Chinese International Adoption in the United
States in the 1950s and 1960s

Without a doubt, China plays a key role in the American public's understanding of international adoption in the United States. Newspaper and magazine articles about the phenomenon abound. Although Americans also adopt large numbers of Eastern European, Latin American, and other Asian children, Chinese girls have become the poster children of international and transracial adoption, if not contemporary American adoption in general. In the twenty-first century the image of American families adopting from China has become increasingly mainstream.[1] In the April 2007 issue of *O: The Oprah Magazine*, a photograph of Chinese adoptees is featured in the article "Speak Easy: What Never to Say to an Adopted Child." At the White Swan Hotel in Guangzhou, where many American adoptive families stay in China to complete visa paperwork, one can purchase "Going Home Barbie," a Barbie who is cradling a Chinese baby.[2]

Adoption from China is a powerful visual example of contemporary American multiculturalism because it is predominantly transracial with white American parents adopting the majority of Chinese children. Published in 2000, Rose Lewis's children's picture book *I Love You Like Crazy Cakes* features an American woman who travels to China to adopt a baby girl. Based on Lewis's personal experiences as an adoptive mother, the book became a *New York Times* best seller and garnered several awards, including a *Child Magazine*'s Best Books of the Year 2000 award and a Children's Crown Gallery Award. In 2006, the book was adapted into an animated feature for a Scholastic video collection about different families entitled *I Love You Like Crazy Cakes . . . and More Stories about Families*.

In most accounts, the history of international adoption from China begins in the late 1980s and early 1990s with the concurrent emergence of China's "one-child policy" and its increasing standardization of international adoption. The policy may have eased some of the pressures of a rapid population increase within Chinese communities. One source estimates that the Chinese population has been reduced by at least 250 million. The major criticism of the policy is that it motivates Chinese families, living in a patriarchal society with a marked cultural preference for boys, to discriminate against female infants, who may be aborted, abandoned, or unregistered.[3] Abandonment created a supply of baby girls available for adoption. This demographic coincided with the implementation of China's first adoption law in 1991 and the Chinese government's creation of institutions such as the China Center for Adoption Affairs, which connected it with the demand for adoptive babies in the United States by projecting an image of organization and transparency that is attractive to potential adoptive parents from the United States.[4]

In the United States, multiple social phenomena converged to increase the popularity of international adoption from China. The accessibility of birth control pills beginning in 1960, the legalization of abortion in 1973, and the increasing social legitimacy of single parenthood decreased the supply of white American babies available for adoption.[5] Racial tensions over the adoption of African American children by white American families that had culminated in the 1972 National Association of Black Social Workers' public opposition to transracial adoption; the legal barriers deterring the adoption of Native American children by non–Native Americans erected by the passage of the 1978 Indian Child Welfare Act; and the stigmatization of children in the U.S. foster-care system motivated potential American adoptive families to consider adopting children available overseas.[6] Furthermore, after the highly publicized North Korean criticism of South Korea's "export" of children vis-à-vis international adoption during the 1988 Olympics in Seoul, the South Korean government created incentives to encourage domestic adoption and implemented a plan to eliminate international adoption by 2012.[7] Thus, social developments in Asia as well as in the United States turned American potential adoptive parents toward the possibility of adopting from China.

This history of Chinese international adoption is generally understood to be distinct from that of Japan, Korea, and Vietnam. While the histories of the latter are inextricably linked to the aftermath of war,

U.S. military involvement, and the rescue of war orphans and mixed-race children, by contrast Chinese adoptees are hardly perceived as war orphans in the U.S. public imagination. Rather, international adoption from China is cast as one of the most socioeconomically privileged forms of modern family formation with solidly middle-class if not wealthy Americans adopting Chinese girls.

This popular narrative of the history of Chinese international adoption has overshadowed an earlier period of Chinese adoption in the United States. My research in the archival records of the International Social Service-United States of America (ISS-USA) branch reveals that beginning in the late 1950s, Chinese American and white American families adopted Chinese children in increasing numbers. The ISS-USA facilitated the adoptions of Chinese refugee children from Hong Kong under the auspices of what their social workers called "the Hong Kong Project."

The deplorable, severely overcrowded living conditions of Chinese refugees who fled from communist mainland China to Hong Kong resulted in the increasing abandonment of their children. Beginning in 1958, the ISS-USA collaborated with Hong Kong agencies to facilitate the international adoption of Chinese orphans in the United States. Initially, the project targeted Chinese American communities for the recruitment of potential adoptive parents, but the ISS-USA considered families of any ethnic group. The majority of these placements involved the adoption of "known" children by Chinese American families, meaning that the adoptive parents either knew of the child through a friend or other intermediary in Hong Kong or were even related to the child. However, American social workers observed with surprise that white American families were also eager to adopt these children. By the early 1960s, more than five hundred Chinese children had been adopted under the auspices of the Hong Kong Project. In 1962, a special flight of forty-eight Chinese orphans arriving in the United States for adoption received significant national publicity in mainstream and local newspapers. Yet, despite recent media attention to other historical international airlifts of children such as Operation Babylift during the Vietnam War, this airlift of Chinese orphans has been forgotten today.

The history of this earlier period of Chinese international adoption in the United States is significant in two major ways. First, it illuminates some striking resemblances between this earlier Chinese adoption and adoption from other Asian countries. The historical context of war—in this case, the Cold War against communist China—as the condition that makes children available for adoption connects the histories of international adoption from these countries. Furthermore, as with previous waves of mixed-race Japanese American and Korean American adoptive children, U.S. refugee legislation and special bills facilitated the immigration of Chinese children in the absence of a permanent provision in U.S. immigration law regarding international adoption. Narratives of the rescue and liberation of Chinese adoptive children, similar to the stories about other adopted mixed-race Asian American children, appeared in American news reports. Despite such stories, the problematic issues of visible racial difference and racism also haunted the international adoption of Chinese children by white American families.

Second, despite a myriad of problems ranging from the difficulty of determining the guardianship of children and of obtaining official documentation to social workers' anxieties over physical and cultural differences in transracial adoption, ISS-USA reports maintained that ultimately such challenges could be overcome. Emphasizing the flexibility and resilience of Chinese adoptive children, they concluded that Chinese international and transracial adoption in the United States could indeed work. Given that the practice of racial matching had dominated domestic adoption in the United States and also influenced social workers' processing of international adoptions, ISS-USA's conclusion was a watershed in the history of Asian international adoption and in the transformation of the United States into an international adoption nation.

The Hong Kong Project

The ISS-USA began arranging Chinese international adoptions in the United States beginning in the 1950s, but the numbers were initially small. In 1955, it provided assistance to American families who adopted four Chinese children from Hong Kong.[8] The high level of publicity devoted to the plight of Japanese and Korean mixed-race children overshadowed adoption from Hong Kong. Within a few years, however, interest in adopting children from Hong Kong had increased significantly, even exceeding interest in adoptions from Japan and Korea. By January 1, 1959, the ISS-USA was processing 139 cases of children from Hong Kong for adoption in the United States, exceeding the numbers of cases from Japan (26) and Korea (49).[9]

The change derived from the introduction of the Hong Kong Project and the active recruitment of adoptive families in the United States by the ISS-USA in collaboration with Hong Kong social welfare agencies. The project illustrates that transnational adoption cannot be understood solely on the basis of supply and demand without taking into account the specific transnational linkages created by organizations and individuals, in this case a project undertaken by the ISS-USA that inspired family making across national borders and facilitated formal adoption.[10]

In 1958, an ISS newsletter announced that the Hong Kong Project was a new two-year ISS program, which involved opening an ISS branch office in Hong Kong in the hope of finding homes for several hundred abandoned and orphaned Chinese children.[11] The announcement featured plans for stimulating interest in adoption from residents in several cities, beginning with San Francisco and then moving to Los Angeles, New York, Seattle, Portland, and Chicago.[12]

Although the project targeted Chinese American communities throughout the United States, the ISS-USA expressed an openness to transracial adoption: "Placements will be considered for families of any ethnic group, but it is thought probable that Chinese families would be most interested." It also considered potential adoptive families who had not originally applied for "Oriental" or part "Oriental" children (as they were referred to in the literature of that time) as possible families for the children.

My findings reveal that the initial focus on Chinese communities in the United States was primarily a strategic move to facilitate adoptive placements and less an attempt at racial matching, a prominent practice in U.S. domestic adoption. ISS officials noted that "while it is anticipated that a large number of children will be placed for adoption with Chinese American families who know at first hand the appalling conditions under which they live and who wish to provide a chance in life for these children who share their culture and heritage, applications are acceptable from U.S. citizen families of any ethnic group."[13]

Such was the case for the Bing family of California. Even prior to Mr. and Mrs. Bing's adoption of their goddaughter Belinda's four children from Hong Kong, Mr. and Mrs. Bing provided financial support to the children and their parents. After the children's birth father passed away, Belinda and her children encountered further hardship, which led to the Bing family's adoption of the two oldest sons followed by the younger brother and sister. A 1958 "Social History" report by a Hong Kong caseworker named Wynne Chan described Belinda and her children as "undernourished." According to Chan, one of the younger sons "had only two proper meals a day. He had either bread or pudding in the morning. He stated that the family took a lot of porridge during summer time." Although Chan's report also highlighted the mother's sensitivity and capability—noting that she took care of her children, while stitching gloves at a factory and sewing at home—Chan concluded that their living conditions were "not at all up to standard."[14] After the Bing family adopted Belinda's two oldest boys, the birth mother asked if they would also adopt her two remaining children. An ISS–Hong Kong caseworker named Ho Kam Fai detailed their poor living conditions in a 1962 social study:

> The widowed mother is living with the children-in-question and a 16-year-old sister-in-law in a cubicle on the sixth floor of a resettlement building. The cubicle measures about 12 feet square. It is partitioned into a bed-room, a sitting room and a kitchen. The bed-room is just large enough for a bed in which the children-in-question and the mother share. The sister-in-law sleeps on a canvas bed which is placed in the sitting room at night. The kitchen is just a tiny place which is crammed with 2 kerosene stoves, a container for storing water and other cooking utensils. . . . The sitting room, jammed with everything, from sewing machine to old broken shoe boxes and broken chairs, looks more like a store room. Accommodation is evidently inadequate, house-keeping standards are poor. As there is in the cubicle only one window which is tightly closed, ventilation is bad, especially in the hot summer. As this area is mainly a resettlement area, the whole place is covered by numerous resettlement buildings which are identically alike in design and which are uniformly of seven storeys. Each building houses about 420 families.[15]

Another case described equally, if not more, dire living conditions. In 1959, the Lee family of Seattle, Washington, began adoption proceedings for a three-year-old boy from Hong Kong. The Lees knew the boy because his mother and Mrs. Lee had been close friends since childhood. The boy's father died, leaving the mother to care for the young boy and his two older brothers. In her social study of their living conditions, Valeen Pon, another ISS-Hong Kong caseworker, observed:

> They live in a squatter area of huts. . . . During floods in June of this year, some of these huts collapsed and there were fatalities. . . . The hut is made from salvaged tin, lumber and cardboard. The hut belongs to fellow-villagers who allow the family their small living area. It is not even 3 ft. wide, 6 ½' high, and about 7 ft. long. Two wooden shelves about 5 ft. long on which they sleep, take up almost all the space. They eat on a small table with a collapsible leaf and there is not more than 2 sq. ft. of floor space. . . . Water is carried from a street tap several blocks away. There are no toilet facilities. The mother cooks on an old kerosene drum with wood. Their accommodation is very poor, even on Hong-kong standards.[16]

In both these cases, social workers at the ISS-Hong Kong branch noted the formidable challenges that the birth mothers faced in order to provide basic housing and nutrition for their children. As Pon wrote in her evaluation of the adoption plan, "The mother is struggling alone to keep the children fed." These observations harken back to Greta Frank's warning in 1957 about using international adoption to provide better opportunities for adoptive children: "[The mother] would not have given up the child [if] she would have had food and shelter. . . . It is just a question, a warning voice."[17]

U.S. national and local press publicized the availability of Chinese children for international adoption.[18] ISS-USA workers also solicited advice from Chinese Americans on how to target the Chinese American community. In 1958, when a Chinese American colonel from Washington, D.C., visited the ISS-USA office in New York on behalf of friends who were interested in adopting a Chinese boy from Hong Kong, Dorothy Sills utilized the opportunity to get his insight on the Hong Kong Project:

Figure 2.1. Shacks of refugees from Red China, in Hong Kong. May 1, 1962. (Photo by Larry Burrows/Time & Life Pictures/Getty Images)

Since he showed a great deal of interest in the Hong Kong project in the course of our discussion of procedure for his friends, I asked if he had a few minutes to look at the pictures of our Hong Kong children and talk briefly with Mrs. Valk about the project. This appealed to him and he made a few suggestions about ways in which we might reach the professional Chinese group in the United States. He implied that this group would probably not keep up with the Chinese newspapers, but would keep up with the alumni bulletins of their colleges and universities. He mentioned particularly that there are many Chinese physicians, engineers, and attorneys and thought these groups would be interested in the project and might also be a resource of families or homes. He suggested Massachusetts Institute of Technology, Columbia College and University, the University of Michigan, and the Universities of California and Southern California as having had particularly large groups of Chinese-American students. He was very much in agreement with the steps that had already been taken and offered to help us at any time he could in developing this project.[19]

Soon after the Hong Kong Project commenced, the ISS-USA mentioned receiving "a sprinkling of applications from all over the country and from many kinds of people, both Chinese and Caucasian, and mixed couples."[20] The first child processed under the auspices of the Hong Kong Project was a two-and-a-half-year-old orphan boy whose prospective adoptive parents were American-born Chinese. According to the ISS-USA, the prospective father was a World War II veteran with a Master of Science degree. He and his wife tried to adopt an American-born Chinese child but were told there were none.[21] Thus, the appeal to the Chinese American community coincided with the scarcity of Chinese children available for adoption in the United States, a historical product of the predominantly male composition of Chinese American communities in the late nineteenth century and first half of the twentieth century. Chinese social customs favoring the emigration of men greatly contributed to this demographic as did the passage and implementation of U.S. immigration restriction, specifically the 1875 Page Law, which stereotyped Chinese women as prostitutes and barred them from entry.

The Hong Kong Project reached its peak with much fanfare and publicity over two events. The first was the arrival in the United States of the five hundredth Hong Kong orphan for adoption. A 1961 news article characterized the child as lucky: "Shirley, as she is now named, was met by her new parents, Mr. and Mrs. Chen Foo Wong of Forest Hills, New York. She stepped from the plane wearing a traditional Chinese costume in red, the good luck color, reinforced by a lucky symbol embroidered on the jacket. Shirley, now five, arrived under a quota-free visa issued by the State Department to children under 14 who are to be adopted by United States citizens. Abandoned on the streets of Hong Kong three years ago, she had been cared for in a children's institution until she left to join the Wongs."[22] ISS-Hong Kong marked the event with a special ceremony and the ISS-USA assistant director, Susan Pettiss, greeted Shirley upon her arrival in New York.[23]

The second event—a 1962 special flight of forty-eight Chinese children arriving at the Los Angeles airport for adoption by white American and Chinese American families across the United States—garnered even more publicity. A news article from the *Los Angeles Herald-Examiner*

Figure 2.2. The ISS-USA collected news articles about the Hong Kong Project in its administrative files. This 1962 news story vividly depicted the plight of abandoned children in Hong Kong and the role of the ISS-USA in arranging the international adoptions of these children by American families.

covered this event under the heading "Bamboo Curtain Tots Arrive." Similar arrival stories were published in the local papers of the adoptive families: *Chicago Daily News*; the *News* in Bridgeton, New Jersey; *News-Free Press* (Chattanooga, Tennessee); *Review-Journal* (Las Vegas, Nevada); *Telegraph* (Painesville, Ohio); *Pioneer Press* (St. Paul, Minnesota); *Globe-Times* (Amarillo, Texas); and many others.[24]

In the 1950s, the ISS-USA had primarily coordinated Asian international adoption from Japan and Korea, but by 1962, the largest number of children it brought to the United States came from Hong Kong. During that year, ISS-USA coordinated the adoptions of 95 children from Hong Kong out of a total of 236 ISS-USA–processed international adoptions, making it the highest sending area, followed by 29 children from Korea. The combined number of Asian adoptive children (114) migrating to the United States outnumbered the 89 white European adoptive children, contributing to a broader demographic shift: American families in the United States turned increasingly to Asian nations as sources of international adoption as the supply of European adoptive children continued to decline.[25]

Nineteen sixty-two was an important year for national, and even some international, publicity about adoption from Hong Kong, as a result of that special flight and the large number of adopted children. But it also signaled the eventual decline of international adoption from this area. In 1963, the ISS-USA attributed the decline to multiple reasons: first, increasing economic stability and opportunity within Hong Kong itself, such as a higher rate of employment; second, the expansion of social services to Chinese refugees in Hong Kong, which reduced the rate of child abandonment; and third, the success of the Hong Kong Project, which the ISS-USA believed had helped open up local adoptions in Hong Kong itself.

A recession in Hong Kong in the mid-1960s caused a slight temporary increase in international adoptions.[26] As late as the mid-1970s, adoption from Hong Kong appeared in the ISS-USA archival records.[27] But its levels never reached those of the early 1960s. While the organization actively facilitated Chinese international adoption from Hong Kong, the ISS-USA stayed true to the ISS principle that "an intercountry adoption program meets an immediate need, but it is not a permanent solution for a country or its children. Therefore all ISS branches also work to help overcome conditions that produce homeless children." The ISS-USA referred to the rise and fall of international adoption from Hong Kong as a good example of these principles in action.[28]

The Different, and Not So Different, History of Chinese International Adoption from Hong Kong

Chinese international adoption from Hong Kong differed in specific ways from Asian international adoption from Japan and Korea. Although some adoptive children in Hong Kong were classified as orphans, the majority were "known" children, meaning that adoptive families in the United States (especially Chinese American ones) had previously known of or were related to these children. A 1958–1959 study of Asian international adoption from Japan, Korea, Hong Kong, and Okinawa noted that, in the Hong Kong case, the "application for adoption of 'known' children was approximately double the number of children placed or considered for placement through the matching process."[29]

The Hong Kong Project provides a fascinating lens through which to view the international adoption of Chinese children by Chinese American parents, a practice that has been overshadowed by the attention to Asian transracial adoption by white American families. ISS-USA adoption case files reveal the diverse socioeconomic, religious, and regional backgrounds of Chinese American adoptive families. Although the Chinese American colonel advised the ISS-USA on how to publicize the Hong Kong Project to a highly educated and professional Chinese American community, the occupations of Chinese American adoptive parents ranged from restaurant workers and grocery store owners to physicians, engineers, and university professors. They professed different religious faiths, both Christian and non-Christian. And they hailed from different regions of the United States, from New York to Illinois, Oklahoma, Texas, Arizona, California, and Washington.

The majority of them adopted "known" Chinese children, both related children (especially nephews and nieces) and nonrelated children as in the cases of the Bing and Lee families discussed earlier in the chapter. As a result, some social workers believed that international adoption in the United States was being deliberately used as a strategic form of migration to obtain socioeconomic mobility, especially through perceived greater access to educational opportunities. As an ISS case-worker, Eugenie Hochfeld, observed in 1959: "Since the cultural belief in Hong Kong seems to be that a child cannot help but benefit by immigration to the United States, and since this can only be accomplished by means of an adoption plan, families in Hong Kong are often willing to surrender their children for adoption in the hope that this will provide a more secure future with more educational opportunities."[30]

ISS workers in Hong Kong struggled over how to proceed with specific cases in which they wondered whether a Chinese family's relinquishment of a son was primarily a financial issue that could be ameliorated locally or whether it signified the family's rejection of the boy. On the one hand, the workers tried to adhere to the general ISS principle of not separating children from their families for reasons of poverty alone. One social worker suggested that it was hard to aid and encourage a permanent separation of children from parents or close relatives unless the separation appeared to be in the best interests of the children.[31] On the other hand, socioeconomic opportunity and the "best interest" of the child often overlapped.

Adoption case files reveal that some ISS workers in Hong Kong were highly aware of and, at times, even sympathetic to these strategies. In the case of Mr. and Mrs. Bing's adoption of their goddaughter Belinda's eldest son, Wynne Chan, a caseworker from ISS–Hong Kong, documented that "[the eldest son] stated besides his youngest sister, he was the one whom their mother loved the best as he was the oldest son in the family. He realized that even though he loved his mother very much he must take the opportunity to go to the States." Given the family's dire situation in Hong Kong, Chan recommended international adoption, concluding, "There is no doubt that the prospective adoptive parents . . . can offer much more in the way of a better education and other material matters than the child's present situation."[32]

Another distinctive characteristic of "known" adoption cases was that they led to the development of truly transnational families. Some of the adoptive children maintained ties to their Chinese birth families in addition to creating new ones with their Chinese American adoptive families. They defied formal adoption's legal emphasis on the children's exclusive belonging to their adoptive family: what has been popularly referred to as the "clean break" from their past. After Mr. and Mrs. Bing adopted Belinda's two oldest sons, an adoptions worker named Patricia Seavers conducted a follow-up interview with the boys in 1959. She reported to the ISS-USA that "they were very eager during this interview to show me pictures of the family in Hong Kong. They have assembled an album in which they have their parents' wedding picture and a running account of the growth of this family. They stated that they correspond regularly with their mother and siblings and hope that one day the family can join them here." Mr. and Mrs. Bing continued to send financial support to the boys' birth mother and their remaining siblings in Hong Kong. They conveyed to Seavers that they felt a "heavy responsibility to her and to the remaining children."[33]

In another "known" adoption case, Mr. and Mrs. Tien of Chicago expressed openness regarding continued communication between their ten-year-old adoptive son Samuel and his birth mother in Hong Kong. The regional director and child welfare supervisor of the Illinois Department of Public Welfare corresponded with the ISS-USA: "It appears that [Mr. and Mrs. Tien] have an understanding with [Samuel]'s mother of the finality of adoption, but they would not at all discourage [Samuel] from maintaining contact with his mother through correspondence."[34] According to case file documents, Samuel kept in touch with his birth mother.

Some birth mothers attempted to ensure that communication with their children would continue after adoption. After Mr. and Mrs. Fong from Sacramento, California, tried to adopt Mei-ling, a three-year-old girl from Hong Kong, the birth mother insisted that the potential adoptive parents "write and inform her of [Mei-ling's] life four times yearly." Because the ISS could not guarantee this arrangement, the intermediary in Hong Kong who had initiated the adoption plan asked the Fongs to send the birth mother a letter stating their opinion about this condition. Margaret U, an ISS-Hong Kong caseworker, reported the following to the ISS-USA:

> This letter has been received by the mother and we learn from this letter that the PAPs [potential adoptive parents] regarded the mother's request as a token of omnipotent maternal love and have agreed to observe it after [Mei-ling] becomes their adoptive child. We absolutely made it clear to [Mei-ling's] mother that it was very unlikely that the PAPs will break their promise, but should such [an] unfortunate event arise in

the future, this agency will not assume the responsibility in offering her protection. The mother conveyed her understanding of this matter and prepared to take a risk. She retained the letter in her possession for her future safeguard.[35]

The predominance of "known" adoptive children created other distinctions between the Hong Kong case and other Asian sending nations, especially regarding age and sex. Specifically, Chinese American families adopted "known" Chinese children who were older, and they displayed a preference for males. Despite the high preponderance of female children available in Hong Kong orphanages, this gendered preference had its basis in Chinese cultural patterns regarding the relative importance of males and females in society. Historically, the preference for male adoptive children influenced Chinese global family making as early as the late nineteenth century, when tens of thousands of Chinese men hailing primarily from Taishan County migrated to California after the discovery of gold in 1848. The historian Madeline Hsu writes:

> The absence of Gold Mountain guests from Taishan also made it difficult to produce children, and especially the sons, that were essential to perpetuating the family line and continuing the generational exchange of support. . . . The main strategy for dealing with this problem was adoption. The importance of sons, and the popularity of adoption as a means of acquiring them, is suggested by the actions of four of the thirteen women honored in the 1893 gazetteer as virtuous women. These four women, who had merely been engaged to men who had disappeared or died, decided to adopt sons to carry on their fiancés' legacies as well as provide for themselves in the future. In letters to Gold Mountain guests during the 1930s, the most frequently voiced request, after pleas for more money and return visits, was for permission to adopt sons.[36]

Under the auspices of the Hong Kong Project, Chinese American families also adopted girls, albeit in fewer numbers.[37]

A 1958–1959 study of the ISS's international adoption program in the Far East also observed that of "a total of 66 'known' children placed, none was under 3 years of age, only 5 were under 7, 28 were 7–10 years, and 33 were 11 years or older."[38] The difference in age stemmed from the fact that a high proportion of the Chinese adoptive children were join-ing relatives or close family friends. By contrast, applications for chil-dren unknown to the adoptive parents, like placements from elsewhere in Asia, showed a preference for younger children.

Adoption case files document a spectrum of experiences of older adopted children from Hong Kong. Some of their challenges included learning colloquial English. After Mr. and Mrs. Chang adopted their nine-year-old nephew Benjamin in 1959, he developed an interest in baseball and joined the school's team. During a supervisory visit, the child welfare worker recorded: "An amusing example of his learning to use our language in the 'slang' was given to me in that he once got hit by a ball because they were yelling at him to 'duck' and he was turning around to look for a duck."[39]

Other challenges were more serious. When Mr. and Mrs. Lin relo-cated to a new community in California, their adopted sons (two neph-ews) had to transfer to a new school. The eight-year-old son resented the move as well as his adoptive parents' insistence that he also attend a Chinese school, and he tried to run away from home. During a 1963 supervisory visit, an adoptions worker, Grace C. Beals, learned that "he was gone overnight, was found by police officers and finally returned home. On two or three occasions since then, he has taken the same action but has been found each time on these occasions by Mr. [Lin]."[40]

Older adoptive children's experiences present a more complex pic-ture of adoptee life in the United States, providing a stark contrast to news articles of the time period, which typically featured younger adoptive children's relatively smooth assimilation. For example, in 1958, Mr. and Mrs. Leung, a Chinese American couple in New York, began proceedings to adopt Christopher, an eleven-year-old boy from Hong Kong. The Leungs had an adult son, but Mrs. Leung was lonely. Across the Pacific Ocean, after Chinese communists arrested Christopher's father in 1951, his mother fled to Hong Kong with Christopher and his two sisters. However, their poverty was so great that she placed the chil-dren in an orphanage and relinquished Christopher for adoption.

After the caseworker Crystal Breeding visited the Leungs and Chris-topher in December 1959, she expressed optimism about Christopher's initial adjustment, writing that, although he was quiet, "he seemed happy and relaxed." Christopher loved chewing gum. He was interested in the "cowboys on television" and the Leungs planned to get him a toy gun. They also bought him new clothes such as "blue jeans and T-shirts."[41]

However, four months later, Breeding corresponded with an ISS-USA case consultant, Althea Knickerbocker, to convey concern about the slow development of Christopher's English-language ability: "He is attending a special class in school where very little work is given to him. . . . It seems that the school may have placed him in a class for slow learners rather than in a class for non-English speaking children."[42] The Leungs' own inability to communicate fluently in English and the absence of Christopher's school records from Hong Kong contributed to what the caseworker suspected was a poor grade-level and classroom placement for the boy. When Breeding interviewed Christopher alone, Christopher related that "he has very little to do in school, the arithmetic is too easy."[43] He also said that American boys bullied him in school.

Older children, like Christopher, had established close relationships with their birth families and, at times, conveyed the emotional difficulty of their adoptions. In her correspondence with the ISS-USA, Breeding noted, "He expressed the feeling of being happy here with the [Leungs], but he has a deep hurt over not having heard from his mother. After his arrival he wrote his mother once, with the [Leungs'] permission, but never heard from her. In our discussion, he asked for a report on her and his two younger siblings in Hong Kong. He remembers his mother with deep attachment, and the younger sisters." These sentiments led Breeding to conclude: "We feel that it is important for this little boy's future happiness for him to have some understanding of his mother's situation at present. Perhaps the International Social Service representative in Hong Kong could send a message from, or report on the mother and siblings prior to the completion of legal steps to complete the adoption."

Ho Kam Fai worked on this request over several months. He located Christopher's mother in Hong Kong, who admitted that she had received several letters from Christopher but that she had purposely not responded because she did not want him to remember his family in Hong Kong. The mother told ISS workers that she wanted Christopher to be loyal and obedient to his new parents. After Ho related this news to Althea Knickerbocker, she asked for his help in obtaining a personal letter from Christopher's mother so that they could give it to the boy. Her request was based on her previous experience with older adoptive children:

We have had this sort of experience in other cases where older children came to this country for adoption, leaving behind a mother with whom they had a rather strong relationship. A letter from the mother saying that she is glad that the child is well and happy, and at the same time assuring him that she is getting along well, does much to free the child to enter into his new life and new family without reservation. . . . Let us know what you think of this, and whether you are in agreement with asking the mother to write, and also whether she does actually write this letter to her son.[44]

Ho agreed. ISS-Hong Kong received a letter from Christopher's mother, which they translated so that ISS-USA and the New York local adoption agency would know what the mother had written. The translated letter read as follows:

My son,

I have not sent you any letter for over a year now—since we departed. I have lately heard from the International Social Service that you are getting on well, physically as well as in other respects, in the home of your new parents. I am glad to know that you are very fortunate in being thus brought up. You must always remain faithful and obedient to your new parents.

I am still working for Sixth Uncle and am well. You need not worry about me. Fifth Sister is now on vacation and had come out to live with Sixth Uncle for many weeks before returning to the Institution. Sixth Sister has entered . . . school and one of the elder brothers (previously in Canton) has recently come to Hong Kong to complete his driving course soon and to find work.

You need not worry about the family affairs here. You must, first, be obedient to your new parents; secondly, be diligent in your studies, and never talk of low school grades and thus become inattentive in your school work. You have to start from low grades and advance gradually before you are able to enter college and become a useful citizen in society. This will make your new parents and myself happy. I hope you are doing well in your school work. With kind regards to your new parents.

Your mama[45]

ISS-USA officials expressed their gratitude to the ISS-Hong Kong caseworkers for their help in this regard. Whether this letter helped "free" Christopher to enter his new life and fit in with his new family in the United States without reservation is unknown. The case file did not have further information about Christopher's reaction or his teen-age and adult life. What it does present, however, is a moving example of the complicated, multifaceted adjustment of Chinese older adoptive children and of the ISS social workers' diligent, transnational collabora-tion to respond to these children's needs with sensitivity.

In other specific ways, Chinese international adoption from Hong Kong during this time resembled adoption from Japan and Korea. War was a contributing factor in all cases: the Cold War in China, the post–World War II American occupation of Japan, and the Korean War. Thus, throughout the 1950s and 1960s, connections were drawn between adoption and refugee resettlement. U.S. refugee legislation, especially Section 5 of the Refugee Relief Act, facilitated the immigration of Chi-nese adoptive children, as it did for Japanese and Korean adoptive chil-dren, given the absence of a permanent provision in U.S. immigration policy to enable the entry of internationally adoptive children.

In 1957, Susan T. Pettiss requested reimbursement of $292.74 from the Refugee Relief Program for the travel expenses of one orphan from Hong Kong. Pettiss explained the reason for this:

> The [American] sponsors are willing but unable to pay the transpor-tation and specified costs because it was necessary for them to pay for both the child and the escort. There were no other orphans to be brought from Hong Kong under the RRA [Refugee Relief Act] program so that it was impossible for the child to come in a group of children and for the services of the escort to be shared among several adoptive families.[46]

Similar to the Japanese and Korean cases, narratives of the rescue and liberation of Chinese children through international adoption infused news media and charitable solicitations, presenting interna-tional adoption as the sole opportunity for the children's survival. As one flyer, titled "Chinese Orphans Need Adoptive Homes in the U.S.A.," proclaimed:

The abandoned children—mostly little girls—crowd the orphanages which are "bursting at the seams" and are unable to deal adequately with ever increasing demands. Many of the children—from one to ten years old—in the institutions are free for adoption and *their adoption outside Hong Kong is their only chance for a normal life and a secure future.*[47]

A February 1959 ISS newsletter featured a photograph of seven Chinese babies with a caption that placed the burden of global family making on American families: "WAITING—Thousands of children like these are growing up in orphanages in Hong Kong because *not enough American families will make homes for them.*"[48]

As part of an ISS delegation to Asia, the ISS director, William T. Kirk, visited Hong Kong and described the situation there as "especially pitiful." "The situation in Hong Kong is unbelievable," he said. "Institutions are crowded with thousands of orphans, most of them abandoned by their parents."[49] He urged the United States to hasten the passage of permanent legislation that would guarantee the admission of orphan children to the United States for adoption above and beyond the small quotas for Asian immigration then in effect. He also recommended the gradual easing of quotas and other restrictions on Asian immigration in general. Kirk then linked Chinese international adoption from Hong Kong, U.S. immigration policy, and U.S. involvement in the Cold War, commenting that "if we are to keep these people as our friends and allies, we must humanize our approach to the refugee problem before all of Southeast Asia succumbs to the false lure of Communism."[50] Permanent orphan legislation would help convince "people of the world that the heart of America is truly a big heart."[51]

An issue of the ISS newsletter from the summer of 1959 reemphasized the importance of Chinese international adoption by American families by including a photograph of two girls from Hong Kong en route to the United States for adoption. Its caption stated that "1,000 Chinese children . . . face bleak and uncertain futures unless adopted. Unless new adoption legislation is passed by Congress, thousands of children like these in all parts of the world will be deprived of the opportunity to live a normal, happy life with American couples."[52]

Finally, although social customs and language barriers sometimes differentiated Chinese Americans from other American adoptive parents, they shared similar motivations and experiences. For example, humanitarian reasons led some Chinese American adoptive parents to adopt internationally. In 1959, Mr. and Mrs. Hong of Houston, Texas, chose to adopt a Chinese girl from Hong Kong even though they had the unusual opportunity to adopt a Chinese baby in the United States. The adoption supervisor explained: "Their strong feeling that they want to take a baby who would have no chance for a good life in Hong Kong motivated their decision to select this baby."[53]

Like many other adoptive parents, Chinese American adoptive parents experienced anxiety about the length of time it took to process international adoptions. In 1958, Mr. and Mrs. Cheng wrote to the ISS-USA caseworker Margaret A. Valk to express their concern:

> Since we have not heard from either you or Mrs. Miller of Welcome House for several weeks, we wonder whether there is anything that we can do to help in speeding up the adoption procedures. We would greatly appreciate it, if you could give us some idea of the current progress of our case. We are of course anxious to know that reason or reasons for such a delay in completing the investigation of the two children. If you can give us a rough idea of the length of time still required to complete the final procedures, we shall be most grateful.[54]

Their adoptive children from Hong Kong arrived in the United States one year later.

Other Chinese American adoptive parents were highly critical of social agencies' investigations and the extensive bureaucracy of international adoption organizations. After Mr. and Mrs. Feng approached California's Department of Social Welfare in December 1957 to begin the process of adopting internationally, the California legislature discontinued funding for the state's international adoption program. Thus, the Department of Social Welfare was unable to provide service to the Fengs until 1959 when funding was renewed. In her correspondence to the ISS-USA, Patricia Seavers reported:

> As you know, [Mr. Feng] has had many disappointments in the two years he has been working to bring [his adoptive son, Philip,] to this country. While he places much of the blame for this on his attorney

he quite naturally feels some hostility toward our agency. . . . He rebels strenuously against the payment of fees, feeling that the orphanage in Hong Kong should be glad to have one less mouth to feed. His idea of a welfare agency is to give and not to ask for money. When this point was cleared, to his apparent satisfaction, he questioned the need for supervisory visits following placement. He feels that social agencies are involved only in criticism, and it was difficult to convince him that we might be of some help.[55]

In the 1950s, Harry Holt, the founder of the Holt Adoption Program (now known as Holt International), popularized these critiques of social agencies' authority and their time-consuming bureaucracy in the case of Korean international adoption, which I discuss in chapter 3.

Yet, after detailing Mr. Feng's many complaints against her social agency, Seavers concluded that "for all our frequent clashes and differences of opinion, [Mr. Feng] emerged in my opinion as a deep-thinking, sensitive man who took a great deal of interest in the process and philosophy of the home study."[56] And, after the Fengs formally adopted Philip in 1961, Mr. Feng contributed regularly to the ISS-USA's annual appeal, donating $20 each year until 1965.

Race in Chinese International Adoption

In chapter 1, I argued that race is fundamental to understanding the demographics, discourses, and institutions of Japanese and Korean international adoption in the 1950s and 1960s. The distinctive racial features of mixed Japanese American and Korean American children exacerbated their social ostracism by making them a visible target for discrimination and abuse in their home countries. Media representations, scholarly studies, and social welfare casework racialized the Far East as a stagnant, homogeneous place of backward-thinking people in contrast to a progressive and dynamic United States. ISS-USA workers, however, recognized that racial, ethnic, and national differences mattered both in the initial stages of the adoptive placement and throughout the mixed-race Japanese American or Korean American child's development.

The growing number of white Americans expressing interest in international and transracial adoption of Chinese children from Hong Kong in the late 1950s presented social workers with new problems related to race in Asian international adoption. They had to begin assessing racial tolerance among the potential white American adoptive parents and their communities now with regard to the adoption of full-blooded Chinese children. A fascinating 1959 symposium on the "adoption of Oriental children by white American families" emerged from a group of questions posed by ISS workers who surmised that adoption of "pure-blood Chinese children might present different and more complex considerations than adoption of children of mixed Oriental-American parentage."[57]

The breadth and depth of these questions were striking. The questions and the ensuing discussions deserve more attention now because they provide a model of open, direct, complex, and multilayered examination of the significance of race and cultural heritage, an issue that continues to be hotly debated in the context of international and transracial adoption in the United States today. Among the questions posed by ISS workers in 1959 were the following: "How important is it for a Chinese child adopted by a Caucasian family to retain an awareness of, and pride in his Chinese heritage? Or, should he be encouraged to ignore such difference? . . . To what extent can families identify with a child markedly different in appearance when this difference is 'racial'? . . . How can a family's ability really to accept a Chinese child be assessed? . . . How can a community's attitudes, trends, and degree of tolerance be evaluated? . . . What conflicts should be expected in a Chinese child adopted by a Caucasian family? How can the family be prepared to be helped to deal with them?"

Margaret Valk pointed out that, similar to the previous waves of mixed-race Japanese American and Korean American adoptees, the international, transracial adoption of Chinese children from Hong Kong involved "many special factors which are not involved in placement of local American-born children, and which do not arise in this particular form when we place European children in [the United States]." However, she noted an important distinction between the Asian and American mixed-race children and the Chinese children:

Because of a certain family and community identification with these children as half-American, some of the problems in placing them have been less acute than those we now face in placing Chinese children. For instance, agencies will report that a family would like to be considered for an Oriental-American child, but could not accept a *purely* Oriental child. The family themselves might accept the latter but doubt that the community would. What does this mean? . . . We need help in clarifying or verifying such attitudes.[58]

ISS workers posed these complex questions to five panelists: the geneticist Richard Osborne, the psychologist Robert Chin, the anthropologist Thomas Maretzki, the anthropologist Rhoda Métraux, and the psychiatrist Mottram Torre. Overall, their insights highlighted the ability of the Chinese adoptive child to adapt in white American society. For example, Osborne concluded that "the only problems which might result from the genetic background of an Oriental in a Caucasian environment would be imposed by [the] social or psychological environment and would not be the consequences of inherited differences."[59] Métraux emphasized that "a Chinese child could become a member of the new culture."[60]

The panelists believed that American communities, too, had the ability to change. Although Maretzki tempered his optimism by noting that "there are yet a great number of obstacles to the successful placement of Chinese children in American communities," he also pointed out that "in Chicago, for instance, the Japanese have found a surprising amount of acceptance since the end of World War II. California's attitudes seem to be changing rapidly in a favorable direction. . . . There is a great deal of favorable change going on in many communities. Within a broader historical perspective it is a rapid change, and hopeful. So children from the Orient will, on the whole, face a much brighter future within the community."[61]

Torre critiqued what she considered to be an overemphasis on matching specific American adoptive parents with specific Chinese children. She mused, "It seems to me that we could think much more broadly about almost any parents adopting almost any child. . . . There is a tremendously wide variety of children who could be adopted, and a tremendously wide variety of couples who can become adoptive parents."[62]

Chin cautioned, however, that international, transracial adoption did involve a physical visibility that introduced extra complications. Nevertheless, he believed that these were manageable.[63] Thus, despite the numerous problems encountered, the reports from this period of Chinese international adoption often concluded that these challenges could be overcome.

Conclusion: How Adoption Works

In the years immediately following the 1959 symposium, U.S. news media echoed the participants' optimism regarding the formation and integration of international and transracial adoptive families. In a 1962 news article entitled "Orphans from Hong Kong Look to U.S. for a Home," Susan Pettiss is quoted as saying that "love and understanding are just as important as [a] cultural background." She reminisced about a Chinese boy who had worn a satin coat and cap but who now donned blue jeans and cowboy regalia, commenting that "except for the Oriental slant to his eyes, he was as American as any little boy in any American backyard."[64]

However, these news stories typically presented a seamless picture of successful adjustment without the complications raised by social workers and other professionals. They erased the tremendous amount of political, intellectual, emotional, and physical work that transformed the United States into an international adoption nation. This work is represented by the voluminous amounts of written correspondence in the ISS-USA archives by social workers seeking to match an adoptive child with an adoptive family; to arrange international travel; to meet the complex and continually changing international, national, and state immigration requirements, as well as adoption laws; and to create, execute, and enforce the principles of an approach to international adoption that would serve the best interests of the children.

Much of this work has not been publicized because the detail is staggering and overwhelming. It lacks the allure and excitement of heroic deeds, the moral persuasion of humanitarian rescue, and the deep satisfaction of happy endings. Take, for example, the 1958 letter below in which Margaret Valk tries to "succinctly" explain to Mr. and Mrs.

Cheng the steps that potential adoptive parents needed to take in order to adopt from Hong Kong:

> The social information about you and your home made available to us through Welcome House has been forwarded to the Department of Social Welfare in Hong Kong who are closely in touch with [St. Theresa's Home]. [St. Theresa's Home] has been asked to make available social, developmental, and medical information about the little boy and girl who have been selected for placement with you. When this information has been received as well as the documentation for the children (this usually includes certificates of birth and official Consents to the placement for adoption), we shall forward it to Welcome House. Welcome House is your local Child Welfare Agency who will be able to keep in touch with you after the children's arrival until they are legally adopted in this country and who will be able to provide information about the children's progress though our agency to [St. Theresa's Home] and the interested Child Welfare authority in Hong Kong.
>
> After we receive from Hong Kong the information and documentation about the children, we and Welcome House will be able to help you prepare the I-600 petition form, which, together with the substantiating documentation about yourselves will be submitted to the United States Immigration and Naturalization Service. By agreement with the Immigration and Naturalization Service we submit with the I-600 form and documentation, an abstract of the social information approving you as prospective adoptive parents. The Immigration and Naturalization Service, upon receipt of the I-600 form, make their own inquiries of you and approve your petition for the children. The Immigration and Naturalization Service then so inform the American Consulate General in Hong Kong. In Hong Kong the American Consul gets in touch with the children and their guardian and processes them at that end. The processing includes a medical examination, according to standards set by the United States Public Health Service (following which the children are issued their visas). Then, transportation arrangements can be worked out for the children to fly to the United States. In the past we have been able to make adequate arrangements for children to be accompanied to New York City unless prospective adoptive parents prefer to meet them at the Port of Entry on the West Coast.[65]

Anticipating the potential adoptive parents' anxiety, Valk empa-thized, "You may think that the above description of the steps which remain to be taken sounds very complicated." She tried to allay their concerns:

> We do not believe that it will take very long to process the case through the United States Immigration and Naturalization Service. The latter are anxious to process orphan cases as quickly as possible. In Hong Kong we now have our own office and staff with a view to helping the Hong Kong agencies placing their children, who are available for adoption, with all possible speed—as is sound.[66]

During my last visit to the Social Welfare History Archives at the University of Minnesota, Twin Cities (where the ISS-USA archival records are housed), an archivist and I talked about the incredible historical significance of, but lack of public knowledge about, the work of the ISS-USA in international adoption. She made this insightful point: "It wasn't sexy work."

While there is truth in that statement, it is also true that the work of international adoption required tremendous passion as well as patience. The ISS-USA archival records give voice to the cacophony of emotions—frustration as well as gratification—that the process of global family making aroused in social workers. The dissonance is due in large part to the fact that they were among the pioneers of international and transracial adoption, wading through yet uncharted territory.

3

A World Vision

The Labor of Asian International Adoption

From the 1950s to the 1970s, Asian international adoption in the United States grew increasingly popular, despite remaining controversial. In order to understand this transformation, we must place the work of agencies, organizations, and individuals at center stage. Their labor is currently overshadowed by the focus on the triadic female relationships among the birth mother, the child, and adoptive mother, which have been made famous in Hollywood and independent films such as *Losing Isaiah* (1995), *Casa de los Babys* (2003), and *Mother and Child* (2010) and in documentary films such as *First Person Plural* (1999) and *Daughter from Danang* (2002). But global family making has involved a wider range of political, emotional, and physical work. The United States became an international adoption nation as a result of the labor of social service agencies, independent adoption organizations, humanitarian organizations, and individuals who put the idea of international adoption into practice.

Recent studies importantly acknowledge the efforts of charismatic individuals who popularized international and transracial adoption in the United States in the mid-twentieth century. The most famous example of international adoption during this time period was the adoption of eight Korean children by Harry and Bertha Holt in 1955. The Holts went on to organize mass adoptions of Korean War orphans by American born-again Christian families, and the Holt Adoption Program was officially incorporated in 1956. Holt International, as it is known today, continues to be a major force in the placement of internationally adopted children.

Other notable individuals include the Nobel Prize–winning writer Pearl S. Buck. Best known for her best-selling and Pulitzer Prize–winning novel *The Good Earth*, which was developed into an Academy

Award–winning film in 1937, Buck also made adoption history as a pioneer in publicizing the plight of mixed-race children born to U.S. servicemen and Asian women. She is credited for coining the word "Amerasian." In 1949, Buck founded Welcome House, an international and transracial adoption agency in the United States, which continues to place children in adoptive families today.

The archival records of the International Social Service-United States of America (ISS-USA) branch show that, in addition to the Holts and Pearl S. Buck, other key individuals were involved in Asian international adoption during this time period. Before there was Angelina Jolie, there was Jane Russell. Russell catapulted to fame as a screen siren after starring in Howard Hughes's 1943 film *The Outlaw*. Hughes's publicity of Russell's voluptuous figure garnered notoriety, and Russell became a favorite pinup for World War II GIs. Russell passed away

Figure 3.1. Pearl Buck sits outdoors with Chinese American children who had been placed with families through her Welcome House adoption agency. (*New York World-Telegram* and the Sun Newspaper Photograph Collection, Library of Congress)

in March 2011 at the age of eighty-nine, and her obituaries universally mention the highly controversial publicity stills that featured her stunning sex appeal (and cleavage) and that would set the standard for the marketing of Hollywood films. Less well known, however, was Russell's own global family—she and her first husband adopted three children, including a boy from Great Britain—and her leadership and dedication to the nonprofit organization WAIF (World Adoption International Fund) during the 1950s.

ISS-USA archival records show that many more social service agencies and independent adoption organizations were involved in Asian international adoption from the 1950s through the 1970s. These social service agencies included, for example, the Child Placement Service in Korea and various U.S. state departments of public welfare, in addition to the ISS-USA itself. In the United States, each of the states regulates adoption law, so ISS-USA officials not only had to coordinate social service efforts between the United States and Asian nations but also had to work within the legalities of the adoption practices for each state. Independent organizations were also subject to state regulations. Many of the other independent organizations involved in facilitating Asian international adoption in the United States were, like the Holt Adoption Program, evangelical Christian organizations. These include World Vision, Christ Is the Answer Foundation, and Everett Swanson Evangelistic Association.

A focus on the broad, complex range of organizations and individuals involved in Asian international adoption in the United States shows on the one hand how diverse individuals, communities, and nations came together through the work of adoption. On the other hand, it illuminates the many tensions stemming from the massive, multilevel government bureaucracy associated with the process of international adoption and from the conflicting ideas among social service agencies, independent adoption organizations, and individuals about how the process should function.

Although collaboration between rival organizations would eventually prevail, the legacy left by the rescue efforts undertaken by certain individuals and independent organizations is complicated. The power of the individual to rescue and save children across national and racial borders continues to appeal to the general American public, but as one

observer of Korean international adoption in the 1960s warned: "Altru-
ism is not enough, however. We are told that the road to Hell is paved
with good intentions."[1] The vast majority of individual and independent
organizational efforts was stymied by professional inexperience that
good intentions could not overcome.

A World Vision

Studies that mention the historical origins of international adoption
typically locate them in the context of postwar political and humanitarian efforts (especially related to World War II, the Korean War,
and the Vietnam War). Relatively few studies have emphasized the
role that international adoptive children play as immigrants.[2] Situating
Asian international adoption in the historical context of U.S. immigration is useful for understanding the radical nature of this phenomenon. For the first half of the twentieth century, exclusion was the
dominant theme in the history of Asian immigration to the United
States. From the mid-nineteenth century through the mid-twentieth
century, U.S. legislation marked various Asian peoples—Chinese, Japanese, Koreans, South Asians, and Filipinos—as strange, dangerous,
and unassimilable. These differences were codified in U.S. immigration laws, which by 1924 had virtually banned Asian immigration to
the United States; in naturalization and citizenship laws that deemed
Asians ineligible for U.S. citizenship; and in antimiscegenation laws in
fourteen states that banned sex and marriage between Asian men and
white women.

   By contrast, the practice of Asian international adoption created a
vision of the world in which national, cultural, and political borders
could and should be crossed. Organizations utilized section five of the
Refugee Relief Act of 1953 to facilitate the immigration of Asian adoptees. Section five of the act allocated four thousand special nonquota
immigrant visas to eligible orphans under the age of ten. It defined an
eligible orphan as a child who "lost both parents through death, disappearance, abandonment, desertion, or separation, or who has only one
parent who is incapable of providing care for such orphan and has in
writing irrevocably released the child for emigration and adoption" and
"who has been lawfully adopted abroad by a U.S. citizen and spouse or

received commitment by a U.S. citizen and spouse to adopt the child and care for the child properly if the child is admitted."

Immigration laws alone could not sustain a vision of the world that legitimized a global sense of family, however. Favorable attitudes and beliefs about U.S. involvement in Asia had to be cultivated to put new legal provisions in use. In 1950, a Christian minister named Dr. Bob Pierce founded an organization in Portland, Oregon, appropriately named World Vision that facilitated international adoption from Asia. He described World Vision broadly as an "interdenominational missionary service organization seeking to help meet emergency needs in crisis areas through existing evangelical agencies."[3] By the late 1950s, World Vision provided aid to children in nineteen countries. Korea was the key crisis area (specifically regarding the emergency needs of Korean War orphans) in the founding of this organization. One of World Vision's five major areas of activity was Christian social welfare service, which involved the administration of a sponsorship program that solicited monetary assistance to Asian orphans and destitute children. According to a 1950s World Vision newsletter, "North American friends who provide $10 each month ($11 in Canada) as 'parents' for 'their' child—a precious little one in some distant part of the world" participated in the sponsorship program, which built "Christian hospitals, clinics, milk bars and schools throughout the Orient."[4]

World Vision's sponsorship program in Asia was not a new idea; rather, it was part of a broader cultural movement in the United States that forged bonds between Asia and America in familial, and more specifically parental, terms by inviting American "parents" to sponsor "their" poor and helpless Asian "children." In 1938, Dr. J. Calvitt Clarke, a Presbyterian minister, founded the Children's Christian Fund (originally called the China's Children Fund) to raise money for homeless and orphaned Chinese children of the Sino-Japanese War. According to the scholar Christina Klein, appealing to prospective American donors by representing their relationship with the children they sponsored as "adoption" was the fund-raising innovation of Dr. Clarke.[5] Thus, by 1954, when Erwin Raetz, World Vision's overseas director, collected pictures and case histories of 1,200 Korean orphans for sponsorship, at least some of their potential American donors were already aware of the possibility of taking on parental obligations to Asian children.[6] Klein argues that these sponsorship programs complemented the U.S. government's agenda in Asia during the Cold War by cultivating a sense of obligation to Asia among Americans who might not initially support U.S. political and military intervention in that region. These organizations and their sponsorship programs also set in motion another phenomenon: the legal adoption of Asian children by families in the United States.

The following example illustrates that although sponsorship and legal adoption were distinct, the initial sponsorship of a child could result in desires for legal adoption. In 1955, Mr. and Mrs. Carter of Oregon initated proceedings to adopt Rebecca, a mixed-race Korean female infant. Mrs. Carter worked for World Vision's "adoption unit," a

Figure 3.2. A tired but happy Cresswell, Oregon farmer, Harry Holt, introduces two of 12 Korean orphans arriving here for adoption to customs officials. The children of Korean women and United Nations soldiers will be adopted by families in various sections of the U.S. Holt brought 12 other orphans to the States last fall at his own expense and has adopted eight. He plans to aid in finding homes for the children of mixed blood who have been abandoned. This photograph was taken on April 7, 1956. (© Bettmann / CORBIS)

unit that filed pictures of orphans and distributed literature that solicited donations from the United States. While looking through these
pictures, Mrs. Carter had found a picture of Rebecca, and she and Mr.
Carter "sponsored" her by sending her money and clothing. After several months of sponsorship, they contacted their county's public welfare commission to discuss the possibility of bringing her to the United
States for legal adoption.[7]

World Vision also played an instrumental role in helping to secure
homes for the twelve Korean adoptive children that Harry Holt brought
to the United States in October 1955. Three American families (including Mr. and Mrs. Carter) adopted four of the children. Because section
five of the Refugee Relief Act limited each U.S. citizen and spouse to
two nonquota immigrant visas for eligible orphans, special legislation
was needed to enable Harry and Bertha Holt to adopt the other eight
children. In June 1955, Erwin Raetz wrote a letter to Senator Richard
Neuberger of Oregon to urge Congress to pass the special legislation.
According to Raetz, Holt was at that time residing in a World Vision
missionary's home in Seoul while waiting for the processing of the children. On behalf of World Vision, Raetz communicated to Senator Neuberger that "we all appreciate your interest in this splendid effort of his,
and wish you every success in having the enabling act passed before
Congress adjourns for the summer." Raetz's tone was filled with urgency
as he characterized the conditions under which the children were being
processed as "deplorable." He described Holt's visit to Korea as a "most
worthy and humanitarian" mission.[8] In his address to the U.S. Senate,
Senator Neuberger echoed that sentiment with great rhetorical drama:
"What nobler and more unselfish deed could there be than to bring to
the security and comfort of America, eight small children from the ravages and tormented country of Korea? If the brotherhood of man still
has meaning in this troubled world, then that sentiment is exemplified
by Harry Holt and his family."[9]

The mainstream news media publicized Harry Holt's rescue of twelve
Korean children in October 1955 with much celebration and fanfare.
A *Washington Post* article described Harry Holt as a "pied piper" who
"shepherded 12 Korean-American babies through [the] crowded Tokyo
International Airport . . . to a plane taking them to new homes in the
United States."[10] Such publicity created the mistaken impression that this

historical moment was the product of a sole individual's efforts. In addition to World Vision's participation, the ISS-USA played a fundamental role by endorsing the immigration papers of nine of the twelve children. Nevertheless, while a news story in the *Oregonian* acknowledged World Vision's help in the matter, it concluded, "But the spark of initiative and the flame of determination were Mr. Holt's. . . . He has virtually given life to hundreds of children. Given his example, can anyone doubt the power of the individual?"[11] With politicians and the press on his side, Holt's efforts did not end there. With the provisions of the 1953 Refugee Act about to expire in December 1956, he started to organize mass international adoptions of several hundred children from Korea by appealing to thousands of American families through written correspondence. His fervor stirred major controversies about who should oversee the process of international adoption and how it should be done.

From Rescue to Rivalry

The favorable publicity given to Holt's story generated outright confusion and critical concerns about the role of non–social service agencies in international adoption practice. ISS-USA archival records reveal that the 1955 adoption activities of World Vision and Holt sparked numerous inquiries between World Vision and individual U.S. state welfare departments and also between these departments and the ISS-USA. For example, in August 1955, World Vision's Erwin Raetz—clearly aware of individual states' regulations of adoption practice—wrote to governors' offices in Wisconsin and Nevada requesting detailed information on state laws and state welfare department requirements and procedures related to adoption.[12] Unfamiliar with World Vision and its interest in international adoption, individual state departments contacted the ISS-USA about how to proceed.

The ISS-USA was unprepared for the volume of these inquiries. Assistant Director Susan Pettiss wrote to the state public welfare commission of Oregon, where World Vision was incorporated, claiming that the ISS-USA office was "being swamped with requests for advice from many of the Departments and [was] at somewhat of a loss as this organization has only recently come to our attention."[13] In November 1955, Pettiss communicated with Bob Pierce, the founding president of World Vision, and inquired if there was a way to work together given their mutual inter-est in alleviating the plight of orphaned, mixed-race Korean and Ameri-can children.[14] Pettiss explained that although the ISS had developed an "effective machinery" to deal with social service problems that cut across national boundaries—including the international adoption of children by American families since the end of World War II—the ISS did not have a branch in Korea. Instead the ISS-USA was working closely with the American-Korean Foundation, the Church World Service, the Child Placement Service in Seoul, and Korean governmental bodies. An ISS unit in Korea was established soon after in April 1957. In her account of the history of ISS-Korea, Florence Boester, an ISS headquarters field rep-resentative in Asia-Oceania, noted that, "as in Japan, the motivating fac-tor for ISS service in Korea was the plight of fatherless children for whom there was a possibility of a future through inter-country adoption."[15]

The mutual interest in the plight of Asian and American mixed-race children and war orphans could not overcome the political and personal differences over minimum standards in adoption practice, however. Social service agencies, such as the ISS-USA and individual U.S. state welfare departments, insisted that the well-being of adoptive children necessitated minimum standards of investigation, placement, and supervision. Individuals and independent adoption organizations flouted these minimum standards by practicing and promoting proxy adoptions in Japan and Korea. In proxy adoptions, U.S. citizens des-ignated a proxy agent to act in their place in order to adopt a child in a foreign court. In other words, they adopted a child "sight unseen" through a third party abroad.

The proxy method had initially been used to facilitate post–World War II international adoptions from Germany and Greece, but it became more widespread in Japan and Korea, especially after the pas-sage of the 1953 Refugee Relief Act, which enabled the immigration of eligible orphans from war-torn countries, and given the tireless efforts of Harry Holt to organize mass international adoptions from Korea. As Susan Pettiss reported to ISS headquarters and branches in 1958:

> The initial emigration of children from Japan to American families for adoption was heavily weighted with a number adopted by proxy through the efforts of Mrs. Sawada who operated an institution in Tokyo for the

mixed-blood children. . . . The most flagrant use of this proxy method of
adoption as a basis for immigration is in Korea. Following the hostilities
in Korea, a religiously motivated individual, Mr. Harry Holt of Oregon,
became interested in the plight of mixed-blood children and himself
adopted 8 of these children by special legislation. Since that time he has
spent endless energy and money in building an organization operating
out of Korea and has placed almost 1,000 mixed-blood children, both
Negro and Caucasian, with families throughout the United States.[16]

In the 1950s, families from different Western nations, and not solely
the United States, adopted children by proxy. One of the most famous
cases involved the adoption of two boys from Japan by the dancer/
singer/actress Josephine Baker and her fourth husband, Jo Bouillon. All
together, Baker adopted twelve children, whom she called her "Rainbow Tribe," from Colombia, Venezuela, Algeria, Finland, and Côte
d'Ivoire in addition to Japan between 1953 and 1963. According to the
historian Matthew Pratt Guterl:

> The children were sometimes collected by Baker and sometimes by
> a friend. There was little attention paid to procedure. The first two
> children—Akio and Janot—were brought back from Miki Sawada's
> famous compound for "Amerasian" and "mixed" children in Japan,
> "order[ed] . . . as you would a take out dinner" with a special request for
> a racially "pure" child. At almost every step, these retrievals were out-
> side of the law and came well ahead of the international legal agreements
> emerging to make sense of adoption as a worldwide issue.[17]

In the United States, children adopted by proxy immigrated to the
country as the legal children of adoptive parents without any endorsement from a social service agency. Social service agencies, however, believed their endorsements to be integral to the welfare of the
adopted child. In a 1954 letter to the U.S. Refugee Relief Program,
ISS Executive Director William Kirk emphasized the importance of
professional social workers in the international adoption of mixed-
race Japanese and Korean children: "It is necessary that competent
professional service be available in Japan and Korea to locate, prepare
histories, do the casework, and other things necessary . . . if we are to

Figure 3.3. Josephine Baker with her husband Jo Bouillon and their children in her property of Milandes. (Photo by Maurice Zalewski/Gamma-Rapho via Getty Images)

find suitable placements for children of mixed Japanese or Korean and American background."[18]

Harry Holt's operations further challenged the expertise and autonomy of social work professionals by employing a private company to conduct the investigations that determined whether or not prospective adoptive families' homes were suitable. Holt's primary concern was that the adoptive families be "saved" and "born again" Christians. As he explained to prospective adoptive families in a 1955 letter, "If we help to place a child in a home, we are responsible before the Lord." Holt concluded the letter with a "personal word": "It is our desire that these children go into the homes of born again believers."[19]

These differences developed into a rivalry between the Holts and U.S. social service workers. In one of his letters to prospective American adoptive families, Harry Holt claimed that "we are not in competition with the [social] welfare [agencies]." He insisted that his sole motivation was the knowledge that "little boys and girls are dying in Korea for want of homes, and we know that many people have their hearts and homes open to these little ones." Yet, in his letters to prospective adoptive families, his comparison of the methods of adoption "through welfare and international social service" and those of adoption "by proxy" characterized adoption by proxy as more efficient and advantageous. His letters functioned in effect as advertisements for proxy adoptions. Under the heading of "Adoption by Proxy," Holt touted:

> People who are financially able and can spend two or three months in a foreign country can adopt war orphans; however, most people who have big hearts are not able to do this. The only answer that we know is for them to have someone be their proxy and adopt the child or children in the foreign country under the laws of that country. . . . Then the child or children enter the country as the sons and daughters of the adoptive parents. They do not have to be adopted in the states.[20]

By contrast to the seemingly easy method of adoption by proxy, Holt represented the method of adoption though welfare and international social service agencies as time-consuming and unrealistic. Holt sarcastically critiqued social service workers' methods with the following description:

> First, one has to contact the local welfare and ask them to make an inspection of the home. This may involve months of questioning. In time the home may be approved. If so, then the local welfare sends its report to the International Social Service at New York, and after due process the International Social Service contacts its agencies in the foreign country to find a child to fit the home. It is very hard to pass on the physiological background of some little child that was found abandoned in a ditch, but they always try. This takes time. If they find a child which they think is suitable, the couple in the States are allowed to sponsor the child's entry into the country, and it may be placed in their home, where it is kept under the watchful eyes of the local welfare for six months or a year. If after this trial period the child is all right and the welfare are satisfied, the child may be placed in an American orphanage for re-adoption.[21]

Social service workers in various states criticized Holt's methods, such as his bulk mailing of letters like the one above. Sibyl Thompson, the supervisor of the adoption unit of Minnesota's Department of Public Welfare, had brought the letter to the attention of the director of the ISS-USA in April 1956. She characterized Holt's procedures as "unsound" and the Holt operation as a "problem" and wanted to know what the ISS-USA thought about the matter before her unit gave any response. Thompson concluded her letter by writing that "it will be most helpful if we knew what steps are being taken to prevent further importation of children for purposes of adoption in this manner carried out by this fervent but misguided group."[22] Lucile Kennedy, the chief of California's Divison of Child Welfare, also wrote to the ISS-USA during the same period about the "activities of Mr. Holt and World Vision," which she similarly characterized as a "very serious problem" that would attract and enable unfit families to adopt. Kennedy gave the example of a Mr. and Mrs. L who wrote repeatedly to their agency expressing interest in international adoption. The agency expressed doubts about the writers' suitability as adoptive parents of mixed-race foreign children after they made comments while residing in Texas such as "[We] love the southern people and we know their [*sic*] wouldn't be any mixed blood as here in California." Later, the Ls wrote to say that they had heard from "some cotton pickers that it would be possible to go to Morro Bay, California, and adopt a child immediately as two boats full of children came in."[23]

Despite social welfare workers' disapproval of his methods, Holt continued to send similar bulk letters to prospective American adoptive families the following year. Aware of social service workers' opposition to his methods, Holt strongly criticized them for what he believed to be action in their own self-interest: "Welfare groups [are] building up strong opposition against adoption by proxy, as social workers have no authority over and do not get any income from children adopted by proxy. This irritates them and they are going all out to influence congress to turn it down early this session." Holt urged readers to engage in the political battle over international adoptions: "Explain that if adoption by proxy is stopped you will not be able to get a child. . . . it is very important that you write these letters today to all your congressmen. If they receive a flood of letters they will do something about it."[24]

As before, these letters were brought to the attention of individual state departments of public welfare, often by local citizens who were interested in international adoption from Korea. Heber Robertson, a child welfare worker in Utah's Department of Public Welfare, then forwarded one such Holt letter to the ISS-USA. Robertson relayed, "We were quite alarmed to see that he is encouraging people to continue with the proxy adoption program and also interested in a statement he makes regarding social workers."[25] The ISS-USA did not take Holt's criticisms lightly. Pettiss characterized his zeal as a troubling "Messiah complex" and, with great prescience, she sadly remarked,"We are all aware of the serious damage being done to the future of these kids being brought in by proxy adoption or the potential danger to them."[26]

Such harsh criticisms and name-calling might best be understood in the context of the chaotic situation in postwar Korea, a situation that created trauma for mixed-race children and war orphans as well

Figure 3.4. Susan Pettiss visiting the Caritas school in Vietnam, August 1967. (Aslanian, Guettler, and Montgomery, "Finding Home: Fifty Years of International Adoption")

as frustrating desperation for those who sincerely wanted to help. Pettiss acknowledged the sincerity of Holt's desire to give opportunities to Korean mixed-race children and she praised his "generosity in making available his financial resources to help bringing these children to the United States."[27] Yet, because of their disagreements over international adoption methods, Holt and the ISS-USA staff members accused one another of being noncooperative and detrimental to the welfare of Korean orphans. In an April 1956 letter, Susan Pettiss aired the ISS-USA's frustrations: "Things are happening so fast here in regard to Korea that we find it hard to keep up with them. . . . Sometimes I feel as if I am punching a pillow in attacking each of the major problems in handling these Korean cases. You have no idea of the repercussions which are resounding all over the U.S. about Mr. Holt's activities. I was in Washington two days last week and met in several places his accusations against the ISS as obstructing his plans."[28]

Pettiss's revelation of her own exasperation was uncharacteristic of her typically poised and diplomatic demeanor during her tenure as ISS-USA's assistant director from the mid-1950s through the early 1960s. Pettiss's experience in refugee relief work as well as international adoption was pioneering and remarkable. Born and raised in Alabama, she graduated from the University of Alabama amid the Great Depression and then left an unhappy marriage to pursue what would become a singular career in social work.

In 1945, Pettiss joined the United Nations Relief and Rehabilitation Administration and traveled to Berlin soon after Germany's surrender in World War II to provide care and assistance for all United Nations displaced persons. Shifting territorial borders after the war created a critical situation in which one million displaced persons could no longer be repatriated. Compounding this crisis were increasing numbers of Jewish refugees in the western occupation zones of Germany, who were fleeing persecution and demanding admission to Palestine.[29] Much of Pettiss's work focused on the needs of children. In addition to serving on a search committee to reunite children—especially those who had been brought to Germany from other countries in order to be "indoctrinated into German policy"—with their parents, Pettiss also worked with Jewish children who were being organized into groups to go to kibbutzim in Palestine. Pettiss reminisced, "We fed them, clothed them and then closed our eyes when we let them go illegally."³⁰ Upon her return to the United States, she located sponsors for refugees from Latvia, Poland, and Lithuania. Pettiss then worked in Shanghai to assist Russian and Jewish refugees after the Communist Revolution. Given her extensive social service work during some of the most challenging historical moments of the twentieth century, Pettiss's frustration regarding the situation in Korea spoke volumes about how difficult the proxy debate and the clash with Harry Holt had become in the mid-1950s.

Florence Boester, the ISS headquarters field representative in Asia-Oceania, observed the dramatic contrast between postwar Japan and Korea regarding their populations of mixed-race Asian and American children, and the international and domestic social services available to them and their families. In 1952, an American coalition comprised of representatives from civil, social, educational, and religious organizations had formed the American Joint Committee for Assisting Japanese-American Orphans. The committee organized social and medical services for mothers and their mixed-race children. Soon after the passage of the 1953 Refugee Relief Act, it voted itself out of existence in favor of establishing a Japan delegation of the ISS that could offer a wider range of international social services, including, but not limited to, international adoption. Boester described the staff of the ISS-Japan delegation as "competent" with an "unusually large and active group of well qualified volunteers of several nationalities" who enjoyed cordial relationships with Japanese ministries and family courts. She characterized the appointment of the delegation's first director, Kimi Tamura, as "an insurance of quality for the new agency."³¹

Tracing the subsequent establishment of ISS-Korea, Boester observed that "the situations in these two countries, however, were far from identical." She described the Korean situation as "abnormal," the result of an uneasy truce following a bitter civil war. She pointed out that the wives of the peace-keeping forces under United Nations command were not allowed to live in Korea, a circumstance that "tended to increase the resultant social problems." Imploding domestic social services and Korean government directives to send mixed-race Korean and American children overseas created even more chaos in the war-torn nation. Boester continued:

The adoption and emigration of "mixed blood orphans" . . . was strongly urged by the Korean government, as the woefully inadequate orphanages were already overflowing with some 50,000 children of Korean parentage, due to the ravages of the recent war and the flight of refugees from one part of the country to another. In the few minutes allowed for this summary account, I cannot begin to describe the deplorable conditions under which I saw children living—and dying. To facilitate the departure of large numbers of children, several agencies in Korea, local and foreign, were arranging American adoptions "by proxy," shipping planeloads of children to adoptive parents who had been hastily chosen and given little or no advance information about the children for whom they had already accepted legal responsibility.[32]

Despite the unpleasant aspects of the rivalry, both sides of the international adoption methods controversy importantly raised awareness about salient issues in international adoption practice. Holt's methods brought to light the frustrating ways in which the multilevel bureaucracy associated with domestic adoption practice could prove unrealistic and overly time-consuming in the context of international adoption practice, especially in the immediate postwar period. Even the American-Korean Foundation, which sympathized with Susan Pettiss regarding the "serious questions about Mr. Holt's plan to complete adoptions by proxy" and the "dubious aspects of employing a business firm to make home studies" urged the ISS-USA to find another plan through which home studies or investigations of prospective American adoptive families could be conducted more expeditiously. In a 1956 letter to Pettiss, Lucile Chamberlin, the chief of the welfare division of the American-Korean Foundation, emphasized that Korean President Rhee and the Korean Ministry of Health and Social Affairs' "number one welfare project" was the sending of as many Korean war orphans as possible to adoptive homes in the United States. Chamberlin noted that many of the Korean war orphans were "really badly abused" and that "this fact together with the great pressure of the government to get them out of Korea makes this program very important from the standpoint of the welfare of the children and also from a public relations aspect."[33]

Across the Pacific Ocean, some American adoptive parents organized to advocate for proxy adoptions and to protest a U.S. state welfare bureaucracy that inadequately addressed international adoption. In the early 1960s, parents who had encountered frustrating bureaucratic situations with various U.S. state welfare departments formed the group Parents for Overseas Adoption, which advocated for proxy adoptions. In a 1963 letter, John Braxton documented his and his wife's ordeal as they tried to adopt a second Korean child while they were living in Minnesota. Their story illuminates the inadequacy of state adoption legislation and resources to deal with international adoption during that time and the ways that U.S. state and national bureaucracy combined to make the process more confusing and frustrating. Braxton related:

> Federal law required that we meet the adoption requirements of the State. To our amazement, the State of Minnesota had a requirement that the adoptive child must be a resident of the state for a six month period. It was immediately obvious that a child in Korea could not meet such a requirement. They gave me encouragement and indicated that they would assist us in getting the child to this country if I met all other state requirements. I proceeded to do this, to include a home study by the County Welfare office even though we had already been carefully examined and studied by the Naturalization and Immigration Service. The Welfare office would not consider their report at all. I had continued to maintain contact with the State Welfare during November, December, and January. I discovered that little or nothing was being done for my case in late December.

Such experiences led Braxton to conclude that "delaying tactics were being employed by the State Welfare" and that their ordeal was "uncalled for and unnecessary simply because we wished to become parents of these children who might have otherwise died in their poverty and unwanted condition."[34]

Even some local social service agencies avoided working with the ISS-USA because of its bureaucratic complexities. As Lillian M. Lewis, the supervisor of the Inter-Country Adoption Program of the Boston Children's Service Association, relayed to the ISS in 1963:

> I have had two recent experiences with local agencies which has sharpened my negative feelings about any unnecessary "paperwork." As you know, I have been trying to stimulate other agencies to handle some applications

for overseas children because we can do so few with our limited staff and budget. The response had been disheartening and always because it seems so complicated to work through International Social Service. In the past two months I have received two approved home studies, one from an agency in Salem, the other from Fall River, of applicants asking for foreign children. The agencies were willing to do the studies but I just could not persuade them to forward the summaries directly to International Social Service. They refused to get involved with the complexities.[35]

Yet, for the ISS-USA, the best interests of the children, and by extension the children's biological and adoptive families, complicated quick and easy adoptive placements. The ISS-USA maintained that the need for sound and ethical international adoption principles outweighed the popular demand for fast and simple adoptions. It opposed the practice of proxy adoption, charging that it failed to protect the child by sidestepping professional standards of investigation of the child's and adoptive parents' backgrounds, and of supervision of the adoptive placement. Its critique illuminated how proxy adoption ran the risk of moving mixed-race children from one abusive situation to another.

A 1958 study conducted by Laurin Hyde and Virginia Hyde and sponsored by the Child Welfare League of America and the ISS-USA detailed the risks that accompanied proxy adoptions. The study featured one case of " a nine-year-old boy of Japanese and American parentage who had run away from the home of his adoptive parents after being beaten by the mother. . . . In her [court] testimony, the mother described how 'half-breeds' like the boy . . . 'couldn't intermingle' in Japan, whereupon the boy was sent out of the courtroom." In another case, "a seven-year-old boy of Asian and American parentage came to the attention of a voluntary child-caring agency after he had been severely beaten by his adoptive parents, who had had great difficulty in disciplining him."[36]

Social service workers' bureaucratic methods tried to address an important issue regarding the welfare of internationally adopted children: accountability upon their arrival in the United States. In the summer of 1957, a Douglas County grand jury in Roseberg, Oregon, indicted Edith Ott for second-degree murder in the death of her adopted Korean daughter. According to the indictment, twenty-two-month-old Korean adoptee Wendy Kay Ott died after being struck in the head. Edith Ott had adopted the girl through Holt's program in October 1956. Rather than accept any responsibility for or raise critical questions about what had transpired, Bertha Holt lashed out at social service workers who, in her mind, had promoted negative publicity about the Otts whom she referred to as "this wonderful Christian family."[37] In the 1950s and early 1960s, the Holts' and some adoptive parents' assumptions about the inherent goodness of Christian adoptive families blinded them to the very real possibilities of brutality in the United States.

Finally, ISS-USA social workers acknowledged the existence of American racial prejudices against Asian Americans and African Americans, and they criticized the racial ignorance that sometimes accompanied proxy adoption methods. They emphasized the importance of local community support in their placement of Asian international and transracial adoptees. In the 1955 case of a white American couple from Ohio adopting a four-year-old mixed-race Korean and American boy, Margaret Valk, the ISS-USA senior case consultant, stressed:

> In this connection we have found that local workers also found it useful to test out the feeling in the community by finding out how local people who do not know the family concerned react to the idea of bringing a child of different racial background into the community. For instance, what do the men at the drug store and the grocery store think? It has seemed important too, of course, to sound out the local school teachers.[38]

After the Holt Adoption Program placed a mixed-race Korean and African American child in an all-white neighborhood, the ISS-USA learned that "the family was selling their home and moving away because the people of that section would not accept the little girl." Pettiss characterized this case as "an example of the dangers of the Holt proxy adoption plan."[39]

A 1956 study on the "adjustment of foreign children in their adoptive homes" showed that professional social workers took seriously issues of race and national origin in international adoption, not solely for the sake of racial matching, but in order to protect the adoptive child in the United States from potential immediate and future prejudice. As a Boston Children's Service Association caseworker named Letitia Di Virgilio wrote:

There has been no attempt to "match" the coloring of the child to parents, except in special instances when similarity of coloring seemed particularly important. There have been a few of the perennial requests for the blonde blue-eyed child which one gets in any adoption program. In addition to seeking to learn whether behind this request there is, for example, an immature mother whose needs call for a doll-like creature whom she can display for her own satisfaction, or whether it is a normal wish to have a child who somewhat resembles prospective parents or other children in the family, it has seemed advisable to evaluate the relationship between the limitations put on coloring of the child and the attitude toward the child's nationality. . . . There are also such statements as: "Of course, we would love a Korean child, but how would the neighbors treat him—we live in a small town—it may be all right when he is small but no one would ever marry him." We do not believe that parents can be helped to want a child of mixed origin . . . But as the child becomes older, and in the stress of personal difficulties, basic prejudices and doubts of parents can be reactivated to create havoc in the child's growing up years.[40]

Professional social workers recognized that racial, ethnic, and national differences mattered both in the initial stages of the adoptive placement and throughout the child's development.

Independent Adoption Schemes: An Uneven Legacy

New independent adoption programs continued to form in the early 1960s. Individuals such as V. A. Kelley, Lillie Reed Smith, and Everett Swanson engaged in work very similar to that of Bob Pierce and Harry Holt. Like their predecessors, Kelley, Smith, and Swanson were Christian evangelists whose adoption methods directly or inadvertently flouted social service workers' minimum standards.

Kelley operated a private adoption agency named Christ Is the Answer Foundation in Vandalia, Illinois. With the help of Oak Soon Hong of Korea's Child Placement Service, he himself had adopted two Korean children in 1956. Social welfare workers criticized Kelley's "unorthodox" adoption methods, which included conducting home studies of prospective adoptive parents himself while using forms that emphasized the importance of "church attendance, and family prayer" and "no smoking or drinking" in addition to work record, income, and insurance.[41] ISS representatives in Korea also suspected that Kelley benefited from child placement referrals from the Child Placement Service in Korea after giving the service enough money monthly to employ a driver, typist, and social worker.[42]

In Denton, Texas, Lillie Reed Smith, a retired Methodist missionary, embarked on finding adoptive homes for Korean children after a 1958 visit to Seoul, where she visited several orphanages. Smith claimed that the directors of the orphanages urged her to find adoptive homes for the children under fourteen years of age. According to Smith, these directors told her that the ISS would "handle the investigation and take full responsibility of securing the adoption papers, and expense incurred therein and also arrange transportation." In a 1960 letter addressed to the ISS in Korea, she claimed:

> I spent all of 1959 contacting couples who wanted to adopt a Korean orphan. Through our church papers, I received more than 150 letters of inquiry as to how and where they could apply for a child in one of these three orphanages. I sent them 2 application blanks and full information together with a personal letter. When they stated the age and sex of child desired, I referred them to the orphanage having those ages and sex.

Smith expressed frustration toward the ISS, who she assumed had been processing these adoption applications all along. She continued:

> Now, I have no way of knowing where and what were the results of their applications to these 3 Directors. Seldom do they write me the second time unless they have grown tired in not being able to hear whether your agency is processing their application or not. . . . I have had letters from many fine Christian couples, most of them childless and young and in good circumstances who crave to have a child to love and rear and many of them will be disappointed and censure me unless the directors and you live up to your obligations and the children are missing a most wonderful opportunity to be loved and reared in some of the best Christian homes in Texas.[43]

In later correspondence, Pettiss wrote to Smith, claiming that only one orphanage in Korea, the Holy King Orphanage, had been in touch with the ISS representative in Korea and had corresponded with them about only four prospective adoptive families. The ISS had contacted the four families and suggested that they get in touch with their state department of public welfare to locate an authorized child welfare agency near them to help them meet the multiple requirements for international adoption. The ISS representative had not heard anything from the other two orphanages in question, Green Meadows and Mapo.⁴⁴ In a separate letter to Commissioner John Winters of the Texas State Department of Public Welfare, Pettiss urged him to contact Smith "in order to explain the complexities of any inter-country child placement program and why it is not such a simple matter to undertake the transplanting of children from one country to another."⁴⁵

In Chicago, Illinois, the Everett Swanson Evangelistic Association, headed by the former Presbyterian minister Everett Swanson, operated a "sponsorship plan" to help Korean orphans. American individuals who participated in the Swanson plan paid eight dollars monthly to assist a child they selected. Similar to the sponsorship plan of World Vision, the relationship between the American sponsor and Korean child was represented in parental and other familial terms. As one advertisement for the Everett Swanson Evangelistic Association beckoned: "Be a 'Daddy and Mommie' or 'Big Brother or Sister' to a Korean orphan who will know you as sponsor."⁴⁶ Although Swanson's association did not operate a legal adoption program, its sponsorship plan led some "parents" and "big siblings" to want to legally adopt their sponsored children. Swanson advocated adoption only by born-again Christians and not surprisingly referred prospective adoptive families to the Holt Adoption Program.⁴⁷

Harry Holt was not the only prominent critic of professional social workers' approach to international adoption. According to the historian Ellen Herman in her study of modern American adoption, Pearl Buck charged that social workers held children hostage to their own vested interests. Although Buck objected to the Holts' fundamentalism, she "admired their determination to solve the problem that social workers failed to address. Why couldn't all the children who needed parents simply be transferred, quickly and easily, to adults who were seeking children, proxy or no proxy?"[48]

In 1964, Buck founded the Pearl S. Buck Foundation to address poverty and discrimination faced by children in Asian countries. Its establishment reflected Buck's personal as well as humanitarian interest in Asia, which stemmed from having been raised by Presbyterian missionaries in China, an upbringing that also inspired her focus on East-West relations in her prolific writing career. In 1965, the foundation established the Opportunity Center and Orphanage in South Korea to serve mixed-race Korean and American children. Several Korean news reports harshly criticized the presence of the Pearl S. Buck Foundation, alleging that it offered direct cash grants to the mothers of mixed-race children, thereby raising the specter of paying mothers for the relinquishment of their children as well as encouraging mothers' dependency on monetary handouts. The Pearl S. Buck Foundation, the reports charged, demonstrated a "total lack of concern" for existing social welfare programs in Korea, such as ECLAIR (Eurasian Child Living as Indigenous Residents), exaggerated the numbers of mixed-race children in Korea, and claimed the foundation to be the only agency that was concerned about the children's welfare.

In a 1965 letter to the Korean Ministry of Health and Social Affairs, Pearl S. Buck herself and the Pearl S. Buck Foundation president, Theodore Harris, condemned these allegations, characterizing them as "misrepresentations and actual falsehoods."[49] However, in the United States, the ISS also felt the sting of Buck's claim that only her foundation cared for the well-being of mixed-race Asian and American children. In a 1965 letter to the *Milwaukee Journal*, Carol W. Johnson, a member of the National Advisory Council of the ISS, attempted to correct that false representation:

> To The Journal: Pearl Buck, whose efforts on behalf of Oriental-American children are well known is quoted in the Oct. 5 Journal as saying: "We don't have adoptive agencies able and willing to do the processing necessary to bring the children (of mixed parentage) into the United States." There is one nonsectarian case work agency in the United States, the American branch of an international organization operating in the non-Communist world, which is both able—to the extent of its

resources—and willing to carry on international adoptions. This is the American branch of the International Social Service, with headquarters in New York City. . . . The adoptions handled through ISS are financed by voluntary money raised by WAIF/ISS started for this purpose through efforts of movie actress Jane Russell Waterfield, with chapters in several cities. . . . Between Jan. 1 and Sept. 30, 1964, ISS placed 684 foreign children in adoption with American families. . . . Eighty-eight of them were of oriental racial background and 40 were Eurasian.[50]

In his letter to Carol Johnson, ISS General Director Paul Cherney revealed the tense emotions and animosity created by Buck's public attempt to take all of the credit for alleviating the plight of mixed-race Asian and American children:

She travels about this country promoting her Pearl Buck Foundation by ignoring and derogating the excellent work that is being done by ISS and other agencies to alleviate the plight of these children. She should know better, because she has had many contacts with ISS people, some very recently, and we are on excellent terms with her adoption agency, Welcome House, cooperating on cases, flights from Korea, etc. It is hard to explain why she is acting in this competitive way. She has upset and angered our WAIF people in several cities. At the WAIF National Conference last spring there was divided feeling whether or not to do battle with her. We decided that our best strategy was not to strike out at her but to tell our own story as objectively and clearly as possible, to answer with facts as you did in your letter to the *Milwaukee Journal*.[51]

Conclusion: Before Angelina Jolie, There Was Jane Russell

The facts do matter, but they do not necessarily make for a memorable story. The history of the ISS-USA and other social service agencies' participation in Asian international adoption in the 1950s and 1960s is relatively unknown, lost to historical amnesia. Despite the agencies' best efforts, the stories that remain tell about their work not in facilitating adoptions, but rather in preventing them. Meanwhile Harry Holt's role in the history of Asian international adoption has reached the level of

Figure 3.5. Hollywood, Los Angeles, California. Actress Jane Russell and her husband, former professional football star Bob Waterfield, pose with their adopted son, Tommy, 5, who received his U.S. citizenship. Miss Russell brought the youngster back from Great Britain three years ago. Date Photographed: March 29, 1955. (© Bettmann / CORBIS)

what the anthropologist Eleana Kim has called "mythology." These narratives are, at best, only partial truths that suggest that there are many other stories worth telling.

Because the stories of valiant and pioneering individuals continue to capture our imaginations, the life story of the movie actress and adoption advocate Jane Russell seems a fitting conclusion to this chapter. After she and her first husband, the football player Robert Waterfield, were unable to conceive children biologically, they adopted three children, two domestically and one internationally. In her 1985 autobiography, *My Paths and My Detours*, Russell described having been married for almost eight years and without children as "unthinkable."[52] She decided

Figure 3.6. Actress Jane Russell during a charity event with W.A.I.F. , the World Adoption International Fund, that she founded in 1955. (Photo by NBC/NBC Universal Collection/ NBC Universal via Getty Images)

that they would adopt, but there was a waiting list of no less than two years at any agency and, being close to thirty years old, Russell didn't want to wait. They adopted their first child, a baby girl, after a woman heard about Russell's desire to adopt children in the news and contacted Russell about the possibility of adopting her daughter's baby. Wanting next to adopt a boy about one or two years old, Russell inquired about international adoption during a 1951 visit to Paris and Genoa, where she visited orphanages, and in London, where she performed for King George and the royal family. After the British press publicized her interest in adoption with photos of Russell and a newly reelected Winston Churchill with the caption "Miss Russell in London to Adopt Baby Boy," an Irish woman contacted Russell to relinquish her baby boy. Although Russell was able to obtain the paperwork for his adoption, an international controversy over the adoption emerged because the boy had been born in London and only British subjects were allowed to adopt British subjects at that time. Russell wrote that "it wasn't long before a member of Parliament stood up and demanded that American movie stars stop stealing British children."[53] After a protracted legal battle waged against the boy's birth parents had cleared them of breaking British law, Russell and Waterfield were able to complete the boy's adoption.

After this experience, Russell reflected, "I had my own children, yes, but I couldn't forget the children I had seen in the orphanages. There were too many people waiting, longing for children here. It just wasn't right; the laws were made to help people, not hinder justice. . . . I didn't know what or how, but I wanted to do something to help these kids and the parents-to-be waiting for them."[54] Russell went on to advocate for 1953 U.S. immigration legislation that would enable international adoptive children to enter the United States on a nonquota basis. In her autobiography, she documented meeting with Eleanor Roosevelt to discuss the idea of an international organization that would help facilitate international adoptions in the United States. After a friend referred her to the Ford Foundation, she learned about the International Social Service and contacted its director, William Kirk.

A devout Christian throughout her life, Russell held deeply religious beliefs as the Holts did. However, under her leadership, the organization WAIF (World Adoption International Fund) affiliated with the nonsectarian ISS-USA as the fund-raising arm of its adoption division. As a result, ISS-USA newsletters in the 1950s prominently featured Russell's activism for the organization's international adoption work. Russell's autobiography moves seamlessly from praising the ISS as an organization with "an excellent reputation" to praising "the Lord" for unexpected opportunities throughout her life, providing an example of how religiously motivated individuals could work successfully with nonsectarian organizations. It is refreshing reading for its laid-back, colloquial language and for its human portrayal of ISS social workers in the context of 1950s Hollywood glamour.

Russell described "Bill Kirk" as a father figure and a "warm, calm, gray-haired Aries" whom she liked immediately.[55] She wrote of the first

WAIF fund-raising ball: "Every name you can think of was there—Robert Mitchum, Fred MacMurray, Clark Gable, John Wayne, David Niven, Red Skelton, James Franciscus, Gregory Peck, Jimmy Stewart, David Brian. . . . It looked like an evening at the Academy Awards."[56] WAIF consisted of many different local chapters in places such as Los Angeles, Chicago, and New York. Russell documented how WAIF, working together with the ISS (including, according to Russell, "one gal, Susan Pettiss" who had contacted agencies in every state to process adoptive parents), "had brought thousands of children from Europe and the Far East for adoption to American couples. International Social Service hired extra social workers for their offices overseas to process children. . . . The plan worked beautifully."

Russell described "living a split-level existence" as a "wife-mother" with a movie career and an adoption program. Among the indelible memories of this time of her life were seeing a planeload of adoptive children arriving from Greece and entertaining U.S. military troops while also visiting the Choong Hyun Orphanage in Seoul. In her autobiography, she reflected:

> I've often been asked if I'm not proud of what I've done in WAIF. The answer is no—grateful and amazed is more like it. The Lord gave me the idea and asked me to obey. I simply put one foot in front of the other and started knocking on doors. That's really all I did. Other people did the rest. I feel humble about WAIF. It is as though I am watching a wonderful parade pass by and my only part in it is that I've told it where to line up. Each chapter has decorated its own float in this parade. Each chapter president has been behind the wheel. The agencies did a wonderful job and learned a lot in the process about our own "hard to place" children. But it's the Lord's parade, not any one individual's, and nobody knows that better than I.[57]

We continue to be drawn to stories about the power of individuals. But it is also important to remember their humanity or, quite simply, their fallibility. The history of Asian international adoption in the United States must move beyond mythology. The transformation of the United States into an international adoption nation is rooted in a collective past involving many different individuals, independent organizations, and social service agencies.

4

Global Family Making

Narratives by and about Adoptive Families

Attention to celebrity adoptions has hardly waned, but Americans' fascination with international adoption has also been cultivated by the stories of ordinary American families who adopted children overseas. Their stories became increasingly familiar in the 1950s and 1960s through national and local news media reportage. Tucked within a variety of ISS-USA folders are numerous magazine and newspaper articles from that period about Americans adopting Asian children. They are the best-known stories about Asian international adoption because of their publication and distribution to the American masses.

A 1958 *Parade* magazine article by Karl Kohrs entitled "An Orphan Boy Comes 'Home' to America," featuring the transformation of a four-and-a-half-year-old Korean war orphan named Kwang Jin Chun into Timothy David Daines, is typical of news stories about Asian international adoption in the United States during the 1950s and 1960s. It shares five characteristics with other stories of its type.[1] First, it presents the Daines family as an all-American family: white, Protestant, and upwardly mobile. Bill Daines and his wife, Marvel, are "an attractive, young-looking couple," with three "pretty" daughters.[2] Bill is a lawyer, the president of the local board of education, and an elder in the Palmer Park Presbyterian Church.

Second, the article characterizes Kwang Jin as a model child with a propensity for becoming American. Describing him as having "a good knowledge of 'Americanese,' " Kohrs continues that the boy "kept saying to anybody who would listen: 'Pretty soon I go America where the Hellos [GIs] are. I get plenty of chocolate, plenty bubble gum.' "[3]

Third, the story contrasts a bleak picture of Asian society with the joyful arrival of the Asian adopted child in a U.S. airport, popularizing the idea that happiness begins in the United States. Kohrs writes that the Daines knew about "the plight of Korean children from friends in that country."[4] U.S. military involvement in the Korean War serves as the unfortunate backdrop, but the main setting of the story is the United States. As Kohrs reports:

> All five [Daineses] were there when little Kwang Jin finally arrived at the Willow Run airport in Detroit. As they waited for him, the Dainses paced and fidgeted in an almost unbearable excitement. When the big Northwest-Orient airliner finally taxied up, the girls pointed to the face of the youngster pressed against the window of the plane and shrieked: "There he is!" . . . Mrs. Daines swept him into her arms as the rest of the family clustered around to greet him. As Bill carried him to the family car for the trip home, Mrs. Daines and the girls kept murmuring: "Oh, he's wonderful . . . just wonderful!"[5]

This intimate, often exuberant, encounter is linked to a fourth prominent theme: destiny. Destiny is typically represented in the form of a familial bond created in the moment when the adoptive parents first view a photograph of the child. As Kohrs explains: "It was in the fall of 1956 that the Dainses heard of Kwang Jin. When they received a snapshot of him with two six-shooters in holsters slung about his waist, they knew he was the boy they wanted. . . . 'From that moment on,' said Mrs. Daines, 'we were won over irrevocably.' "[6] Christian religious references reinforce the notion that the Daines family and Kwang Jin Chun were meant to be together. Mrs. Daines continues: "We spent days discussing a name for him, and we finally agreed on Timothy David. Both are Biblical names, and we felt he was really a child sent to us from God. Besides, 'Timmy' seemed like a good American nickname."[7]

Finally, in addition to the renaming of Kwang Jin, his consumption of American food and his use of American material items like toys and clothes signify his transformation into the American child Timmy Daines:

> From then on nothing else mattered to Timmy Daines. Getting him to take time out for lunch was a problem. Coaxed to the table, he pushed away a bowl of rice, then turned to look longingly at the toys. A slice of layer cake, baked by Mrs. Daines that morning, persuaded him to pick

up his fork and devour it to the last crumb. Then he went back to his toys. That night, with their parents looking on, the girls tucked their new brother into Bonnie's bed—which she insisted was to be his. And there, at the end of his first day in America, safe, snug, and loved, Timothy David Daines looked up with shining eyes at a family all his own. Says Bill Daines, speaking for his whole household: "I'd like to see anyone take him away from us!"[8]

Although no two news stories were exactly alike, recurring places (the U.S. airport and middle-class suburban home) and symbolic objects (food, clothing, furniture, toys) created an increasingly familiar narrative. International adoption in the United States unfolded in a neat and linear way, devoid of the messiness of family life. Above all, the dominant theme was the successful Americanization of the Asian adopted child, a theme that reflected the politics of the specific historical time period in which the news stories were written. These stories soothed anxieties about American racism and U.S. military involvement in Asia during the Cold War.[9] At the same time, they complemented the war's conformist agendas by emphasizing tales of American upward mobility and assimilation. In other words, these stories did not simply report the news. They performed ideological work by rationalizing U.S. Cold War aims and validating the American dream.

This chapter critiques the notion that the adopted child experienced a smooth and joyful transition upon arrival in the United States by featuring less well-known stories. These stories are archived by the ISS-USA, but most of them were not distributed to the general public. They reveal breakdowns in adoptive family placements and the need for family replacements; the stress created by the financial costs of international adoption; and one family's story about the mundane, but also highly emotional, challenges of adopting a Chinese child in the early 1960s. The outcomes of these adoptions are unknown, but the available archival records suggest that they would become successful placements. The significance of these stories is not simply their portrayal of rough spots in global family making; when read together, they present a more nuanced and honest portrayal of the emotional work undertaken by American families who adopted Asian children.

Mainstream journalism played a role in stereotyping international adoption through the focus on its simple joys, but it occasionally challenged this depiction with the publication of different stories. The chapter's final story features the former New York Yankees' pitcher Jim Bouton's adoption of a Korean boy in the late 1960s. Although Bouton is best known for his controversial exposé of baseball in his book *Ball Four*, his family's experience with international adoption has been for the most part forgotten. Leonard Shecter's magazine article featuring Bouton's frank revelations about the difficult and complicated decision to adopt an Asian child and of his family's struggles to raise their Korean son is a fine example of complex reportage about international adoption within the mainstream media.

The Emotional and Financial Costs of Creating Global Families

In contrast to the more familiar story of quick, simple, and smooth transitions, the following social workers' case summary highlights the complicated process of attempting to successfully place a child in an adoptive home. Issues such as adoptive family neglect, financial difficulties, marital conflicts, school adjustment problems, and social workers' doubts about placements reveal the many layers of emotional work involved in making a family through international adoption.

In the late 1940s, a private arrangement resulted in the placement of a six-month-old mixed-race Japanese and American child (born of a married American serviceman and a married Japanese woman) with an American couple stationed in Japan. That couple sadly neglected him. In the mid-1950s, the ISS-USA, with the help of a local agency, matched the boy (then nine years old) with a couple in California who had been married since 1940 and had no children of their own. The husband was fifty-three and the wife was thirty-nine. An ISS-USA worker wondered whether the husband was too old to adopt a nine-year-old. Another concern was whether the boy—who was described as "having blue eyes, black wavy hair, an average build and an I.Q. of 125"—should be matched with a father who did not have an education beyond grade school. But, at the time of their application, the adoptive parents had a good income and lived in a community where many Japanese families had settled and among whom they had close friends. Local social workers had received good references for the couple and felt that the age difference would not be an issue when taking into account the father's personality.[10]

The couple dramatically changed their livelihoods to prepare for the boy's arrival in August 1956. The wife stopped working outside of the home, while the husband changed jobs in order to earn a higher income. Two subsequent supervisory reports (one received at the end of August, the other in October of the same year) reveal the ups and downs of their adjustment. The first report was optimistic. It described the adoptive parents as "warm, affectionate, and imaginative in trying to meet the child's needs."[11] A Japanese friend helped as an interpreter, and a Japanese man whom the boy met on the plane ride to the United States became a family friend who visited the household. The child expressed a sense of belonging in the United States by calling himself by his American name. However, the report also hinted at some important challenges. While the parents maintained that they wished to adopt the boy, they expressed concerns about their financial stability and wanted to wait for their finances to improve before formal adoption. Another troubling factor was that while the child developed a favorable relationship with the father "whom he liked to imitate and eagerly awaited his return from work," his relationship with the mother developed much more slowly.[12] The fact that the boy knew his birth mother in Japan and had developed a relationship with her undoubtedly influenced his initial interactions with his adoptive parents in the United States. The acknowledgment of her presence in the case summary is important, though it is unfortunately brief and matter of fact.

The second supervisory report revealed new as well as continuing problems. The boy encountered a teacher who was impatient with his lack of fluency in English and who had called him "stupid" and "dumb." A transfer to a different grade and help with language interpretation from a Japanese American classmate changed the teacher's assessment of the boy, who was now called "brilliant."[13] Some problems were resolved, but the family's financial situation had, unfortunately, deteriorated. The mother resumed work as a bookkeeper while the father sold cemetery lots, but business was slow. After the father fractured his arm, he was unemployed for a long period. By April of the following year, the couple contemplated divorce.

A local agency placed the boy in a new home in June 1957. The child asked social service workers if this family was "happy" and he was particularly glad to learn that they had another adopted son, so that he would have the company of a child close to his age.[14] According to the case summary, the boy did very well in this home. He developed an outgoing personality and musical and artistic ability. He also performed well in school.

Had the case summary been written in the genre of the mainstream news stories of the time period, it might have ended on that happy note, but instead it concludes with an interesting question. One social worker wondered whether the possibility of keeping the boy with the former adoptive mother, even after the couple divorced, should have been explored more fully. The conclusion of the case summary reminds us that there is no given ending. Rather, the formation of adoptive families is an ongoing process composed of conflict and resolution, of knowledge and uncertainty.

While this case summary relates only one adoptive family's story, other reports documented the strain resulting from the financial costs related to creating and maintaining an adoptive family. In 1956 and 1957, the ISS-USA advocated for financial assistance from the U.S. Department of State's Refugee Relief Program on behalf of thirty-five American adoptive families. The organization specifically requested reimbursement for the international transportation of orphans who migrated under the auspices of the Refugee Relief Act on the grounds that many American adoptive families came from stable but modest socioeconomic backgrounds. They needed support, given their many different financial obligations including, but not limited to, processing fees, escort services, clothing, and medical care.

The ISS-USA submitted invoices for the American families who were adopting children from Japan, Korea, and Hong Kong.[15] These families resided in various states across the country: Ohio, Oklahoma, Massachusetts, New York, North Dakota, Oregon, Missouri, Illinois, Arizona, California, Pennsylvania, Tennessee, Florida, North Carolina, Louisiana, Iowa, and Michigan. They engaged in a range of livelihoods. Their occupations included a farmer, U.S. naval officer, school bus driver, minister, foreman, army sergeant, janitor, carpenter, and teacher. And their racial backgrounds included African American as well as white. One adoptive mother was a Japanese woman who was married to a U.S. army sergeant.

Figure 4.1. "New York: War Orphans Find Homes In New Land." Shown at Idlewild Airport shortly after their arrival are the Korean War orphans and their new parents who were on hand to greet the children as they completed one of the last legs of their journey from Korea to their new homes in America. From left are: Mr. and Mrs. Manuel Santos and their adopted girl, Kyung Ja Kwon, 2 1/2 years old; Mrs. Lung F. Chong, with Kyong Sik Kim, 7; Mr. and Mrs. Stanley McFarlane and Chang Il Kim, 3; and Mr. and Mrs. George Hill with their adopted children Anna Choi, and Yoman Choi, 3. The children were adopted through the efforts of Harry Holt, an Oregon farmer, who made a second career of finding American homes for war-orphaned Korean children. Date Photographed: April 8, 1956. (© Bettmann / CORBIS)

In her correspondence with officials from the Refugee Relief Program, ISS-USA Assistant Director Susan T. Pettiss wrote that "in each of these cases the payment of the cost of ocean transportation would have been a hardship to the adoptive family."[16] The ISS-USA argued that the assistance was necessary when one took into consideration the larger financial picture of each of the families. Most of the families had children they were already supporting. For example, the ISS-USA submitted a request for financial assistance for a family in Ohio who were adopting Betty, a girl from Korea. The family had three children ranging from eighteen months to ten years of age. The ISS-USA further explained that the family had "been supporting [Betty] in the orphanage and have contributed $60 towards processing costs in Korea as well as the $49.50 for her inland transportation from the West Coast to Ohio."[17]

Other families were adopting two children at once or were planning to adopt a second child soon thereafter. An African American couple in Ohio, who had already adopted a mixed-race Japanese and African American girl, was in the process of adopting a boy from Korea. The ISS-USA noted:

> The sponsors are willing but unable to pay the transportation and specific costs, because they are a Negro couple of modest means, [Mr. Stanley] being employed as a teacher at approximately $4200 a year. This family have also adopted a Negro-Japanese orphan from Japan last year paying the full cost of her transportation and processing in Japan. They have paid processing costs for [Jeffrey] in Korea and the inland transportation of $41.80. They, themselves, went to Chicago to bring the little boy home. They need to budget for the child's entire wardrobe and for medical supervision during the first few months.[18]

The ISS-USA pointed out that current large expenditures, such as the family's purchase of a new home and furnishings, also needed to be taken into account. One adoptive family from New York had bought a new home "with better accommodation to house the little boy from Korea. . . . They are budgeting for his wardrobe and medical expenses and school incidentals."[19] Similarly, an African American family of "very modest circumstances" in Chicago was adopting a girl from Japan and also buying a new home. They had already provided funds for the girl's care in Japan and had also paid documentation fees.[20]

Escort fees and medical expenses also strained the finances of adoptive households. A couple from New York was willing but unable to pay the transportation costs for their Chinese girl from Hong Kong because they had to pay for an escort's transportation in addition to the child's. The ISS-USA explained:

> There were no other orphans to be brought from Hong Kong under the [Refugee Relief Act] program so that it was impossible for the child to come in a group of children and for the services of the escort to be shared among several adoptive families. Their income is a very moderate

one. . . . They are affording this little orphan a very splendid opportunity, and are having to budget for her medical care and full wardrobe. Medical care will be very carefully attended to as she had been very ill last year. As the child's visa was about to expire it was necessary to incur the expenses indicated above for cables, telegrams, etc. in order to clarify the child's immigration status at the last minute.[21]

The ISS-USA's advocacy for adoptive families of modest means continued through the 1960s. Archival records from 1970 indicated that the organization had instituted a sliding scale of adoption fees: $350 for families with annual incomes below $15,000; $400 for those with incomes between $15,000 and $20,000, and $500 for a family with an income over $20,000.[22] By that time, increased interest in adoption from Vietnam resulted in a $100 fee for supplemental adoptive services in that country. ISS-USA officials explained that the fees helped to recover increasing costs for international adoption, but they also attempted to ensure that they did not create "undue hardship on the adopting parents."[23]

The excerpts from the invoices and other documents indicate that government and social welfare support enabled American families to adopt Asian children. This form of support contrasts dramatically with the minimal institutional support offered in Asian countries during this same time period to help Asian mothers and other family members raise their children and to prevent their relinquishment. The ISS-USA's efforts to increase social services in Asian countries *as well as* their advocacy for financial support for American adoptive families demonstrated that love alone cannot make and sustain families. Structural support from international, national, and local governmental and nongovernmental organizations makes a profound difference in the ability of families to thrive.

The Not-So-Easy Adventure of Becoming Part of a Family

Organizational records offer rich perspectives on some of the concerns of families who adopted children from Asia. The families' experiences, however, are filtered through the voices of social service workers, who not only recorded the information but also echoed the views of ISS-USA officials and staff. The voices of adoptive families are marginal.

Few published narratives by adoptive parents in the 1950s and 1960s exist. Of those that do, their main objective was to encourage international adoption. Bertha Holt's 1956 account, as told to David Wisner, entitled *The Seed from the East*, is one well-known example.[24] Holt describes the efforts of her husband, Harry Holt, an Oregon farmer and Christian evangelical, to carry out their family's divine mission to rescue war-torn Korean children as well as recounts their own adoption of eight mixed-race Korean and American children. The majority of the book is devoted to Harry's trials and tribulations in Korea in 1955 and 1956 as he learns about the plight of Korean children in the aftermath of war, attempts to rescue and care for them in various orphanages, and arranges for their adoption of eight children, while Bertha and their six children—Stewart, Wanda, Molly, Barbara, Suzanne, and Linda—dutifully manage the Oregon farm, excitedly prepare for the arrival of the eight children, and support Harry's efforts through individual and collective prayer.

The book concludes with the much-publicized and heralded arrival of Harry and the Korean children in the United States, but it does not delve into the family's life after this event. Rather, it emphasizes the continued need for the adoption of Korean children by American Christian families as a matter of life and death. In her conversation with Paul, a close family friend, Bertha relates, "Harry keeps remembering the hundreds of children he was forced to leave behind. Just recently he learned that little Jeanie (the starved girl he hospitalized so long) died. Paul II is once again in the hospital, seriously ill. Harry can't help but wonder how many more of them have died."[25] She refers to the hundreds of letters they continue to receive from American families willing to adopt Korean children. Setting the stage for the creation of the Holt Adoption Program, Paul foreshadows, "I feel that God *wants* Harry to assume the responsibility of getting the rest of those children into these homes that so obviously are open to adopting them."[26]

The Dutch American playwright and novelist Jan de Hartog's 1969 book *The Children* is another example of published writing by and about an adoptive parent.[27] De Hartog is known for his fiction and nonfiction about various subjects: the sea, World War II, hospital care, marriage and domestic life, and the Quakers. His personal history and commitment to social justice united these diverse topics. Similarly, Jan and his wife's adoption of two Korean children while they were involved in the Friends Meeting for the Sufferings of Vietnamese Children (founded in 1966 to bring injured and orphaned Vietnamese and Amerasian children to the United States for medical treatment) influenced the writing of *The Children*. De Hartog explicitly advocated for the international adoption of Korean and Vietnamese war orphans in the preface:

> For my hope is that this book may encourage couples who are thinking of adoption to consider adopting a child from Asia and, should they decide to do so, to take an older one. Any child over the age of three is officially considered "hard to place"; large numbers of them, here as well as abroad, have little hope of ever realizing their full potential unless they find parents who will encourage and stimulate them with interest and affection.[28]

The book is subtitled *A Personal Record for the Use of Adoptive Parents*, but its contents seldom focus on the de Hartogs' personal experience as an adoptive family. Rather, it educates the reader about how to raise Asian adopted children in the United States. Divided into three parts (the beginning, settling down, and family life), the book covers a wide range of mundane topics such as clinging, bed-wetting, pets, and whining as well as how to answer deep, provocative questions and comments such as "They Call Me Chinese," "Who Were My Parents?" and "Will I Ever Go Back?" De Hartog administers detailed but succinctly written advice, peppered with personal anecdotes and humor. As a result, *The Children* reads more like a how-to guide and does not explore the de Hartogs' personal experience of raising their children in depth.

A set of thank you letters written by American adoptive parents to Child Welfare Service workers at the Illinois State Department of Social Welfare in 1961, now preserved in the ISS-USA archives, allows readers to view the adoption experience through the parents' eyes. The majority of the letters, however, are brief and unrevealing. For example, there is a thank you note from a Japanese American couple, Mr. and Mrs. Nomura, who adopted Richard, a boy from Tokyo, Japan. They write, "We are really grateful to you and all the others that have made it possible for us to become a happy family."[29] In the middle of this group of letters is a more substantial story about the adoption of a Chinese girl,

Theresa, written by her American father, Mr. Thayer.[30] Like the other letters, it expresses gratitude to the ISS-USA. But its extensive narrative regarding the ups and downs of developing family stability and intimacy over the period of one year complicates the usual short and sweet synopsis about global family making presented in the majority of newspaper articles as well as the other thank you letters.

The letter begins with a hopeful description of Theresa's arrival at Chicago's O'Hare airport:

> On June 11, 1960, after months of procedure and arrangement, [Theresa] arrived at O'Hare airport at approximately 8:30 p.m. [My wife, Evelyn], [son Albert], [son Matthew], Grandma and Grandpa and myself were waiting with open arms to receive our little Chinese orphan. With a doll in one arm and a spring coat in the other we were just about to embark on one of the greatest experiences of our lives. After a few words with [Theresa's] escort we left for home. . . . [Theresa] accepted the doll as a matter of fact, as she did many things in the next few days. We had a very uneventful trip home. [Theresa] seemed to do just exactly as we wished. Just to lead her by the hand.[31]

This encounter at the U.S. airport echoes the news stories of the time in its expression of the emotional excitement felt by the adoptive parents and other family members, as well as their willingness to embrace the Asian child as a member of their family. The only slight difference is that Theresa's behavior is so compliant that becoming a new member of an American family seems automatic. Mr. Thayer even predicts, "After the first 24 hours [Evelyn] and I thought this would be a very easy adventure and began to relax as far as [Theresa's] becoming part of our family."[32]

What seems too good to be true, however, is. Mr. Thayer continues: "However two days later [Theresa] had now become actually belligerent and objected to almost everything we attempted to do for her. We tried to wash her hair and she all but tore the house down, screaming, kicking and crying, but we accomplished our mission. When we put her to bed she would cry herself to sleep, which took hours."[33]

Similar to the case summary about the Japanese adoptee featured earlier in this chapter, Theresa took to certain family members, but not others, including the family dog, Pal. According to Mr. Thayer,

Our dog, Pal took a pushing around for months. She found out if she opened the door, Pal would go out—then all she had to do was to close it to keep him out. [Evelyn] and our boy, [Matthew], she wanted no part of. [Albert], who was older, and myself she seemed to get along with better than anyone else. Why, I cannot explain. She would not even walk with [Evelyn] and very often scream if [Evelyn] would try to help her with anything at all. Grandma and Grandpa were not accepted until months later.[34]

The language barrier greatly contributed to the frustration. Mr. Thayer related that Theresa "could not even as much as say yes or no in English, so our conversation was a matter of sign language."[35] The ISS-USA published simple Asian-language guides to help prepare American adoptive parents for the new additions to their families.[36] But Mr. Thayer felt that "the little Chinese I had learned was of little or no advantage."[37]

Mr. and Mrs. Thayer had scheduled a family vacation in Wisconsin two weeks after her arrival and were determined to go, despite Theresa's antagonistic behavior. There, they began to notice a change in their interactions:

In the two weeks we were at the lake, [Theresa] had become not easy to get along with, but at least we could live with her without it being a constant battle. After we arrived home [Theresa] seemed to realize this was to be her home—no one hated her but loved her and it began to reflect in her habits. She had learned about 25 or 30 American words and used them intelligently—home life was slowly coming back to normal.[38]

Challenges emerged throughout their first year of living together, but they were resolved or, at the very least, made manageable. Theresa learned to enjoy many different kinds of food that she had initially rejected. She continued to dislike milk, but eventually—after several months of coaxing—drank one glass per day. And, after "a very poor start," Theresa slowly developed a closer relationship with her American mother and her brother Matthew. Theresa enjoyed helping her mother with everyday chores like cleaning the dishes though she did not understand why her older brothers received a bigger allowance than she did. After multiple discussions about this issue, Mr. Thayer reflected, "But as we found out in the past a little time and understanding and a great deal of patience will win out."³⁹

School played a major role in Theresa's adjustment. In first grade, she was an eager learner who earned excellent grades in everything but classroom behavior. Mr. Thayer related, "After considerable talks with her I think we finally convinced her what behavior meant and this began to improve."⁴⁰ By the second semester, Theresa was on the honor roll. Her family also credited her attendance at Sunday school with helping Theresa become more sociable and more fluent in English.

At the time the letter was written, Theresa's legal adoption and naturalization were in progress. Mr. Thayer expressed frustration with the requirements for her naturalization. After a courtroom visit for her legal adoption, he explained that Theresa thought she was becoming a U.S. citizen and was "wholly disappointed when she found out different." Mr. Thayer lamented, "We cannot begin to understand why it takes two years to become a citizen of the United States."⁴¹ (It was not until 2000, with the passage of the Child Citizenship Act, that internationally adopted children could acquire U.S. citizenship automatically if they met certain requirements.⁴²)

It is because of (and not in spite of) these trials and tribulations that the letter concludes with an expression of love:

> After almost a year with [Theresa], our Chinese orphan, we feel that much has been accomplished, both for [Theresa] and our family, for she has become so entwined within our home that I feel if she were to leave us anytime now or anytime in the future, it would be detrimental to [Theresa's] health and our well being. In the past she has said she *likes* us, but has changed the word like to *love* now, and shows it in her many ways.
>
> [Evelyn and Adam Thayer]

Conclusion: Before *Ball Four*, "Kyong Jo—for Boutons"

If mainstream journalism perpetuated stereotypes of international adoption as totally joyful, it also had the power to debunk them. Unfortunately, the latter has been rare. The sportswriter Leonard Shecter's

1968–1969 feature article about the New York Yankees pitcher Jim Bouton's adoption of a Korean boy is one of these rarities.[43]

As a major league ballplayer and a well-known author, Jim Bouton is no ordinary American. But at the time of Shecter's interview for the article, Bouton's baseball career was almost finished. In 1963, he had won twenty-one games for the New York Yankees and made the all-star team. He won eighteen more games the following year and beat the Cardinals twice in the 1964 World Series. An arm injury in 1965 marked the beginning of the decline in his Major League career. As Shecter writes, "His skills deserted him. Arm trouble, difficulty with Manager Ralph Houk, a slide down to the minor leagues . . . all the indignities heaped on the professional athlete on his way down descended upon Bouton."[44]

Furthermore, Bouton's now-famous writing career was only in its infancy in 1968. Shecter, who had befriended Bouton at the time Bouton had played for the Yankees, encouraged him to write a season-long diary for publication. The result, completed a little more than a year later, was *Ball Four: My Life and Hard Times Throwing the Knuckleball in the Big Leagues.* First published in 1970, Bouton's controversial, no-holds-barred account of his decline as a Major League pitcher, the antics of professional baseball players, and his rocky relations with management was a massive success. In 1995, the New York Public Library selected it as one of the "Books of the Century." And, in 1996, Bouton was featured in *The Sports 100: The 100 Most Important People in American Sports History*, published by Macmillan.[45]

During the low point of his baseball career, Bouton and his wife, Bobbie, adopted a three-year-old boy from Korea. Following the pattern of news articles about international adoption in the United States, Shecter's article began with the initial encounter between Kyong Jo and the Boutons at the airport:

> He was not yet four years old and he was a forlorn figure as he scuffed off the immense jet airplane at the Seattle airport. He wore a red shirt and baggy red trousers, a tiny blue hat on his head and broken-backed loafers on his feet. In one hand he clutched a sweater, in the other a passport. A handprinted tag pinned on his chest read, "Kyong Jo—for Boutons." That was all of it, all he had in the world. There was not even a paper sack to hold his sweater.[46]

The pathetic portrayal of the Asian child prior to and upon arrival was familiar. What was distinct about Shecter's writing about the airport encounter, however, was his depiction of Kyong Jo's fear about this new stage of his life alongside his American family's joy:

> His eyes, big and round and black, were tearless, but brimming with terror. When the lady from Travelers Aid tried to pick him up, he wrestled free and squatted on the ground, his elbows between his knees and his hands shielding his head. He was a despairing figure, a wounded animal, cringing, unmoving, apparently unhearing. Finally Jim Bouton, a large, pleasant-looking man of 29 with blond hair, deeply set blue eyes and a cheerful, gravelly voice, crouched down beside him and started speaking in heavily accented Korean. "Kyong Jo," he said, "do not be afraid. We will not hurt you. We will take good care of you."[47]

Jim and Bobbie Bouton had prepared themselves and their children, five-year-old Michael and three-year-old Laurie, for Kyong Jo's arrival. They had studied the Korean language. They planned to eat Asian food so that Kyong Jo would feel more at home. This well-intentioned preparation could not overcome the traumatic realities of the child's origins, however. In a stunning departure from the news stories about the smooth assimilation of the adopted child into the American family, Shecter contrasted the "heart-warming adventure" that the Boutons had hoped for with the "heartbreak" of Kyong Jo's personal history. The Boutons' welcoming gestures of language study and consumption of Asian food "meant nothing to a child given up by his mother and wrenched across the Pacific to a place where all the faces were pale and all the words were incomprehensible. Kyong just cried."[48]

The inclusion of the adoptee's painful perception of the experience is strikingly different from most accounts of the time, which represented the adopted child as a blank slate or as an American-already-in-progress after his or her first day in the United States. After several days passed and the Boutons were still unable to console Kyong Jo, they invited the Korean woman who had given them language lessons for a visit. She translated her forty-five-minute conversation with Kyong Jo to the Boutons. Shecter characterized Kyong Jo's story as a "long tale of woe." The sadness derived not solely from his plight in Korea but also from the confusion and anger experienced by a perceptive but very young adopted child separated from his mother and transplanted to the United States:

> Speaking rapidly and with a vocabulary and sentence structure that the teacher said were years beyond his chronological age, Kyong Jo said that he was very unhappy. He said he was angry at his mother for sending him away and that while he knew the Boutons were nice people who were trying to be good to him, they were simply not very bright. Every time he said anything to them, their only answer was that they didn't understand. Besides, they spoke funny and too rapidly and he wished they wouldn't talk so much, always gabble, gabble, gabble. Also, he couldn't understand why he was not living in America. Everybody told him that in America there were thousands of toys for everyone and each child had his own television set. The Boutons had only one. They had visited America briefly the other day, he admitted, where there were many toys and enough television sets for everyone (it was a department store), and perhaps he would be taken there for another visit soon. But by and large, he did not like living here and if he couldn't go back to Korea, he would at least like somebody to sleep with him as his mother did. No, not Bobbie. He preferred Jim.[49]

Another stunning element of Shecter's article is the discussion of Kyong Jo's Korean birth mother. Shecter explained that the mother who was "deserted by her American soldier, could barely afford to feed herself and her child. So she put him up for adoption, hoping that someone, somewhere, would do for him what she could not."[50] Kyong Jo, like an untold number of children in Asian orphanages, was not a true orphan. Not only did he have living birth parents, but he had lived a hybrid existence in Korea, split between institutional and parental care. Shecter wrote that, "in a way, this made it especially difficult for Kyong Jo, for while he spent his days in an orphanage, his evenings were still spent with his mother. Leaving her was a great wrench."[51] Although Shecter did not go into any more detail about the boy's past, he highlighted the existence of this relationship, while many other news stories of the time excluded mention of the birth mother and other relatives altogether. The erasure of the child's origins would become part of an increasing legal trend in international adoption in the second half of the twentieth century: emphasis on the adoptive families' and receiving nations' exclusive entitlement to the children.[52] Shecter may not have anticipated the increasing interest in the adoptive child's birth family and especially the birth mother in the late twentieth century, but his writing revealed an understanding of the emotional significance of her presence in Kyong Jo's life.[53]

As Jim had to return to the ballpark, Bobbie had to handle the brunt of Kyong Jo's emotional distress. Their first evening together was especially difficult. Bobbie sadly reminisced:

> *Oma* is the Korean word for mommy. . . . That's all he would say. "*Oma, oma, oma,*" over and over. I tried to get him to take a bath with the children. He wouldn't. I tried to get him into pajamas. He wouldn't let me. I laid him down in bed and told him everything I could say in Korean, that he was a good boy and we loved and would take good care of him. And he settled down for a while. Then I heard him get up and I came out and he was on the davenport, crying.[54]

According to Jim, "It tore you up to hear it. When I came home, I tried to comfort him and every once in a while he'd drop off to sleep. But then he'd wake up and sort of look around. As soon as he decided he hadn't been dreaming, he started crying again."[55]

Kyong Jo's physical pain contributed to his incessant crying. His vitamin-poor diet had rotted his teeth so that most of them were black, with many rotted down to the gum line. The attempt to feed Kyong Jo Asian food—really, an Americanized version of Asian food—was a "disaster." He did not eat more than a spoonful of the rice with bean sprouts and vegetables for lunch or the chow mein for dinner. A change in his appetite came after a few days when the Boutons brought him to a hamburger place. Jim recalled, "He must've thought he was in heaven. He didn't stop eating until we dragged him away."[56]

Had the Boutons' story followed the pattern of most narratives, this promising turn would have marked the start of the swift and happy Americanization of Kyong Jo, with the rejection of Asian food and the ravenous consumption of the all-American hamburger serving as the undeniable metaphor for Kyong Jo's assimilation. But in this narrative,

Figure 4.2. Jim Bouton and his wife Bobbie take their children, David [also known as Kyong Jo], 6, Michael, 7, and Laurie, 4, (l. to r.) out for a walk along Wyckoff street in New Jersey. Date Created: 30 Aug 1970. (New York Daily News Archive / New York Daily News / NY Daily News via Getty Images)

the eating gave him energy for even more crying. In his interview with Shecter about this time period, Jim revealed his serious self-doubt and lack of confidence:

> I began to think that I had wrecked the family. . . . For the first time in my life, I had trouble sleeping. I thought that I'd made a move which was a foolish one and that we'd done something we shouldn't have. There was so much tension, and we couldn't devote any attention to the other kids. Just that crying and sobbing. You couldn't get away from it. And while I agonized with him, I was afraid I had done a terrible thing.[57]

Jim Bouton's highly critical and desperate self-reflection is a dramatic departure from his and his wife's very thoughtful and well-planned decision to adopt an Asian child. Shecter's in-depth writing about their decision, which was steeped in the Boutons' personal as well as political views about their immediate family, population growth, and American racial politics, is the third major contribution of the article. On a personal level, the Boutons wanted a child who was healthy enough to endure their intense travel schedule and who was in between the ages of their other two children, Laurie and Michael, so that the younger Laurie would continue to be the baby of the family.

Their decision to adopt was also rooted in their political and ethical beliefs in zero population growth and Americans' moral responsibility to children fathered by Americans abroad. As Bobbie explained, "We wanted to give a home to someone who couldn't have it any other way. We'd sort of satisfied our desire for creating our own children. One of each. What more can you have?"[58] Jim continued, "We figured there are so many kids in the world who have no place to live and no family, that it's silly to just go on and have hordes of kids. Once your wife has had the pleasure of having her own child and you've satisfied your own ego, there are enough kids that don't have homes."[59] As a result of his deep concern about the overpopulation crisis, Jim openly advocated for men to have vasectomies and proposed a tax structure that would reward men who did so with a tax deduction. His proposal would also give tax deductions to families who adopted children, with larger deductions for families who adopted nonwhite and handicapped children. His proposal provided no tax deduction for "natural children," although he criticized the use of this term: "We had two of our children naturally (though what's unnatural about adoption?)"[60] Jim himself underwent a vasectomy in 1969 and wrote about this decision for a book titled *The Vasectomy Information Manual.*

Furthermore, by the late 1960s, the issues of race and racism continued to play central roles in shaping the practice of international adoption in the United States. Reflecting on his decision-making process, Bouton discussed these issues with a candor and complexity that is difficult to find in mainstream narratives about international adoption in the 1950s and early 1960s. His openness was, on one level, a reflection of his political engagement with the social protest movements of the times. Jim was a vocal opponent of apartheid in South Africa, and he had traveled to the 1968 Summer Olympics in Mexico City with a contingent of antiapartheid activists from Jackie Robinson's American Committee on Africa to protest the participation of South Africa's white-only teams.[61] On another level, the significance of racial issues in his decision to adopt an Asian child reflected increasingly controversial attitudes in the United States about transracial adoption, specifically the adoption of African American and Native American children by white American families.

In the 1960s, some advocates of international adoption tried to make positive connections between international and domestic adoption. They were aware of the irony of "rescuing" children abroad when there were children already in the United States in need of families. Arguing against an "us versus them" mentality, they emphasized that international adoption contributed to the general American public's awareness of "hard-to-place" children (children of color, older children, and/or handicapped children) in the United States and increased their willingness to adopt them. In 1965, the ISS-USA and Child Welfare League of America held joint discussions in order to develop a national project to expand local agencies' service for the adoption of foreign children *and* "hard-to-place" children in the United States.[62] During the same year, WAIF leadership advocated for the recruitment of homes in the United States for the placement of "special needs" children: "Just as ISS has taught people to adopt in other countries, we would like to see this program expanded from State to State and County to County."[63]

News stories featured American families who adopted both internationally and domestically in a positive light. For example, a 1961 news article featured the Newhall family of Vermont, a white American couple who had adopted Kim, an eight-year-old Korean boy. Not surprisingly, Kim's warm welcome and his assimilation into American life were highlighted in the article: "Kim was a frightened, weak war-sick boy of eight when he stepped out of the airplane and into the bosom of the Newhall family. At the age of thirteen, he is a burgeoning Vermonter, even to the accent."[64] Over the next five years, the Newhalls adopted three more children: an African American girl and two Native American children. They did not intend to adopt children from different racial backgrounds, but, after the death of their only birth child, Mrs. Newhall explained, "We were told [by recognized agencies] we were too old to adopt a child, and that we didn't have enough money. When we heard we could adopt Korean orphans, we jumped at the chance."[65]

By the late 1960s, however, social protest movements, decolonization, and increasing race consciousness and pride created a social and political climate that placed transracial adoption, especially the adoption of African American and Native American children by white parents, under fire. These tensions would culminate in the National Association of Black Social Workers' 1972 "Position Statement on Trans-Racial Adoption" in which the association took a "vehement stand against the placement of black children in white homes for any reason." Members argued that black children belonged "physically, psychologically and culturally" within black families in order to achieve "the total sense of themselves and develop a sound projection of their future." They linked transracial adoptions of African American children by white Americans to the systemic racism that discouraged if not prevented African American families from adopting children and that catered to the interests of white middle-class Americans. Similar tensions over the long history of displacement of Native American children through their placement in boarding schools and through the Indian Adoption Project of the 1950s and 1960s would result in the passage of the 1978 Indian Child Welfare Act, which erected barriers to the adoption of Native American children by people without tribal affiliation. Many tribes had likened the transracial adoption of Native American children by white Americans to a form of cultural imperialism, an impingement on the sovereignty of Native American nations, and even tantamount to a genocidal policy.[66]

These passionate critiques of U.S. domestic transracial adoption would influence American potential adoptive parents to adopt internationally. Such was the case with the Boutons' decision to adopt a child from Korea. Pearl Buck's Welcome House suggested that they adopt a Korean child. The racial discrimination against mixed-race Asian and American children in Korea and increasingly Vietnam continued to move the American public. As Shecter wrote, "Prejudice is not an American invention."[67] The Boutons seriously considered adopting an African American child, but Jim reflected on how past and present-day racisms and racial anxieties shaped their decision to look overseas:

I suppose in the end we just didn't have the courage. . . . Suppose we adopted a little Negro boy. I'm concerned about how he would look at us, how the Negro community would look at us for taking one of their kids and raising a black Anglo-Saxon Protestant. And he might say, "Why did you take me into your home? I'd have been better off growing up in the ghetto. Now my own people won't take me." Certainly he wouldn't be 100 per cent accepted by all our friends, white people. Our close friends, yes, but certainly not everybody in whatever neighborhood we moved into. We saw all kinds of problems—reaction against him by white people, reaction against him by black people, reaction against us by black people, and worst, reaction against us by him. I mean how do you raise a black kid in a suburban home and still have him grow up with some feeling of identity? He may always be angry at you for having made an Uncle Tom out of him. And even if you raised a little militant, his own community might not accept him. He could really be lost.[68]

Given that Asian immigrants and Americans of Asian descent had experienced racial discrimination in the United States in the forms of immigration exclusion, job discrimination, and mob violence through-out the first half of the twentieth century, one wonders why the Boutons would not have considered the same critical questions when adopting an Asian child. In the late 1950s, as discussed in chapter 2, the ISS-USA and local social service workers debated how to assess the tolerance of an Asian child in predominantly white American communities. That a politically active and astute American like Jim Bouton did not consider the implications of American racial politics for Asian international adoption is striking, but it reflects a pervasive historical amnesia about Asian American history in the United States.

In the late 1960s, the histories and social concerns of Asians in the United States were not well known to the general American public. This ignorance can partly be attributed to the erasure of a longer Asian American historical presence in the United States, a product of the mob violence that destroyed Chinese American temples, villages, and ethnic enclaves through looting and fire and that expelled Chinese Americans from the Pacific Northwest and Rocky Mountain region in the second half of the nineteenth century and the early twentieth century.[69] Dis-placement and expulsion through repatriation campaigns, alien land laws, racial segregation in housing, education, and employment, and internment as well as outright violence would also obscure the histori-cal presence of Japanese, Filipino, Korean, and Asian Indian American experiences in the first half of the twentieth century.[70] The American general public's ignorance about Asian American history is also the result of the racist attitudes as well as benign neglect of the majority of American academics until the growth of ethnic studies programs and the emergence of the field of Asian American history in the late twentieth century.[71] In 1968 when Shecter interviewed the Boutons for his magazine article, Third World Strikes at San Francisco State University and the University of California, Berkeley, which demanded ethnic studies programs on these campuses, were just beginning.

Furthermore, the assumption of Asian racial flexibility—what some scholars have described as an "honorary whiteness" and what the sociologist Sara Dorow has argued has contributed to the desirability of Chinese baby girls for adoption in the 1990s until the present day—had begun to take hold during the late 1960s.[72] In 1966, two news articles in well-known, mainstream national magazines, *New York Times Magazine* and *U.S. News and World Report*, publicized what Asian American Studies scholars have called the myth of the Asian American as the model minority.[73] What made the myth so pernicious was that it was based on a false dichotomy that contrasted the social and economic "success" of Asian Americans against the "failure" of African Americans, with some journalists and academics heralding the hardworking "American" spirit exhibited by Japanese and Chinese American small business owners and their families.

Shecter's article did not pit African Americans against Asian Americans, but its conclusion reinforced the notion that the Americanization of Asian adopted children was possible and described that process in familiar ways, for example, through Kyong Jo's increasing fluency in English language and his love for American food and popular culture. Although Bobbie had mentioned that various family members had tried to get him to repeat English words, "he wouldn't. Not for a long time."[74] The oldest son Michael learned to speak several Korean phrases, like "come with us," and translated for Kyong Jo in nursery school when Kyong Jo said he had to go to the bathroom. All of the Boutons learned the Korean phrase for "I am hungry," because Kyong seemed to be famished most of the time. Jim reminisced about Kyong Jo's growing tolerance for his very basic Korean-language skills with a sense of humor: "I made a lot of mistakes . . . and he'd just sort of smile. I found out, for example, that I was always using the wrong tone. I'd say in a loud voice, 'I love you.' In Korean that's always said in a very low voice. So I was like the Wizard of Oz, saying, 'I LOVE YOU!' "[75] By the article's conclusion, however, Shecter described Kyong Jo's transformation into an American as follows:

> And suddenly he was making a great effort to learn English. Dr. Seuss's books were put aside at bedtime and children's dictionaries were picked up. . . . Kyong Jo is becoming an American boy. You can tell because peanut butter is his favorite food. You can tell, because he wanders around with a children's book in his hands singing "Rudolph the Red-Nosed Reindeer" to himself.[76]

Kyong Jo's outward expression of love for his American family was further proof of his metamorphosis from an Asian child into an American child. Shecter wrote that "he even started to tolerate Laurie. She is a blond, pretty, most affectionate child and would often embrace Kyong Jo. . . . At first, with Oriental stoicism, he would push her away. And then, one day, he walked up to Jim Bouton . . . threw his arms around him and hugged. It was a sure sign that he was at last becoming a part of the family."[77] Jim related that "Michael" had been his first English word, then "Laurie," then "Daddy." He added that Kyong Jo calls Bobbie "Mommy," though she qualified that statement with "once in a while."[78]

Thus, while Shecter's article importantly contributes to our understanding of the emotional work of global family making, it inadvertently reinforced the end goal of the Americanization of the Asian adopted child. It presented assimilation as a linear and benign process enabled by the speaking of English and by engaging with American popular culture. This representation of Americanization, however, elided the centrality of race in what constitutes the typical American, and specifically how Asians—even second-, third-, and fourth-generation Americans of Asian descent—have been perceived as antithetical to or have been excluded from that very definition. Similarly, Jim Bouton's frank discussion about the centrality of race when considering the best interest of the African American adopted child is commendable, but it did not acknowledge the significance of race in the life of the Asian adopted child.

Thankfully, later work would address these crucial omissions. Beginning in the 1990s, the coming of age of Asian adopted children and the increase in outlets—on the Internet, in the mainstream and alternative press, and in visual art, creative writing, and documentary film—for adult adoptees to share their experiences enabled them to tell different stories to a broader audience. Given the absence of their perspectives in organizational records, these works make up an alternative and invaluable archive for the history of Asian international adoption. One of the major contributors to this collection of work, the filmmaker Deann Borshay Liem, is a Korean American adoptee whose adoption had been facilitated by the ISS-USA.

5

To Make Historical Their Own Stories

Adoptee Narratives as Asian American History

Some sociologists have characterized international adoption as a "quiet migration."[1] And some Asian adoptees have referred to themselves as "seeds from a silent tree."[2] By the late twentieth century, however, those seeds had taken root and had produced a collective critique of Asian international and transracial adoption through memoirs and creative nonfiction.[3] In order to fully comprehend the history of Asian international and transracial adoption, we must engage with this body of work because it shows that adoptees are not solely the "precious objects" of rescue and affection that they have often been imagined to be in media news reports. Rather, like international social service workers, independent adoption agencies, and adoptive parents, they, too, are historical actors in the making of international adoption history. And, as adult adoptees, they narrate this history differently.

The documentation of Asian adoptee experience through film is a major part of this emergent collective expression.[4] Perhaps the most well known of these documentary films is Deann Borshay Liem's *First Person Plural* (1999). Its distribution through the Center for Asian American Media has made it accessible to many university and college classes, and its PBS broadcast through the P.O.V. program (which airs documentaries with a point of view) has garnered a broader general audience.[5] Eleven years later, Borshay Liem wrote and directed *In the Matter of Cha Jung Hee*, a film that further investigated one of the story lines documented in *First Person Plural*.[6] *In the Matter of Cha Jung Hee* was also broadcast on PBS's P.O.V. program in September 2010.

While Borshay Liem's films are part of a larger body of cultural production by and about Korean adult adoptees, this chapter focuses on her two films because the ISS-USA arranged for Borshay Liem's adoption and because Borshay Liem's films analyze the prominent role that organizational records played in her life history as a Korean adoptee in the United States. As a result, *First Person Plural* and *In the Matter of Cha Jung Hee* offer a direct and provocative link between ISS-USA organizational records and one of its adoptees speaking back as an adult. *First Person Plural* continues the discussion of the ISS-USA's earlier concerns about the role of race and racism in the upbringing of the Asian adoptee in the United States. *In the Matter of Cha Jung Hee* highlights the power of organizational records to shape an Asian adoptee's unique history, while simultaneously creating a template for the model Asian adoptive child.

Like many of the new works by Asian adult adoptees, *First Person Plural* and *In the Matter of Cha Jung Hee* challenge the celebratory portrayal of international and transracial adoption as a privileged form of re-birth in a progressive and prosperous United States. Rather, they present a more ambivalent picture of the phenomenon. A major contribution of *First Person Plural* is that it makes visible the racial hierarchies and social costs associated with U.S. assimilation. Racial difference continues to haunt the lives of Americans of Asian descent, even in an era of what some observers have called our "postracial society," in which racial hierarchies have been overcome and no longer matter. *In the Matter of Cha Jung Hee* importantly examines the loss of adoptees' histories and memories in the context of the transformation of Korean international adoption into a global industry. The significance of these critiques is magnified when one considers that current media representations of international and transracial adoption—for example, the public admiration of Angelina Jolie and Brad Pitt's family—have been used as evidence of our increasingly progressive, multicultural sensibilities.

Furthermore, *First Person Plural* and *In the Matter of Cha Jung Hee* are important works for Asian American history and not solely for adoption studies. When these two films are read critically with other Asian American documentary films, such as Marlon Fuentes's *Bontoc Eulogy* and Rea Tajiri's *History and Memory*, these films convey a powerful message about loss—in the stories of a Korean birth mother and siblings, an Igorot grandfather's whereabouts, and the lived experience of Japanese American internment, respectively—on multiple levels. Loss is an intensely personal experience, but it is also a collective one shared by other Korean adoptees, indigenous Filipinos, and Japanese American internees and their descendants.

Finally, these films illuminate that loss goes beyond the specific spatial and temporal experience of the death, disappearance, or relocation of persons. It also signifies the *loss of knowledge* of this collective experience. The films are a poignant meditation on how the histories of Korean international and transracial adoption, of the display of Bontoc Igorots at the 1904 St. Louis World's Fair, and of Japanese American internment during World War II are suppressed by the dominant narratives of U.S. humanitarianism and benevolent assimilation in Asia and America. Viewers learn through these filmmakers' attempts to recover history that the past cannot be completely recuperated through the traditional historical method of archival research because archival documents, photographs, and film footage privilege some perspectives and exclude others. In these films, the narrators' memories present viewers with a different lens to imagine and to examine the Asian American experience.

Re-Envisioning the Global Family in *First Person Plural*

While many of us juggle multiple roles and identities, the unique premise of *First Person Plural* is that, by the time of her adoption at age nine, Deann Borshay Liem had three distinct identities and histories. She is Kang Ok Jin, born on June 14, 1957, and placed in a South Korean orphanage by her birth mother for international adoption. But she is also Cha Jung Hee, born on November 5, 1956, because the orphanage gave her Jung Hee's identification papers before being sent abroad. Finally, she is also Deann Borshay, born upon her arrival at the San Francisco International Airport on March 3, 1966, and her subsequent adoption by the Borshay family.

Arnold and Alveen Borshay's Christian ethic as well as economic success in real estate motivated them to help others. Like other potential American adoptive parents of Asian children during that time, the Borshays became knowledgeable of international adoption through news reports. An NBC television announcement about helping children abroad through the Foster Parents Plan for only $15 a month influenced Alveen to sponsor a Korean child, Cha Jung Hee, at the Sun Duk

Orphanage. Alveen became emotionally attached to Jung Hee over their two and a half years of correspondence under the auspices of the sponsorship program. This attachment fueled her desire for formal adoption, and the ISS-USA facilitated the adoption.

ISS-USA archival records contain documents that present the perspectives of some American adoptive parents, but they do not preserve the critical insights of the Asian adoptive children nor do they account for the children when they become adults. Thus, *First Person Plural* is a historically significant work that presents the point of

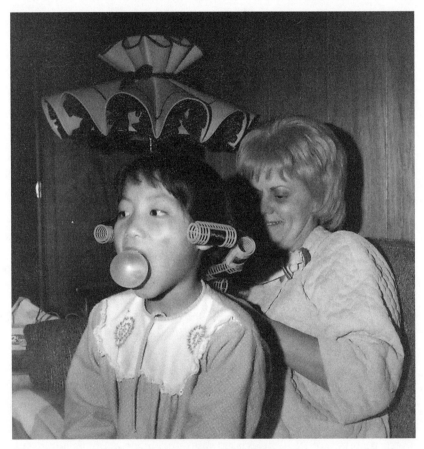

Figure 5.1. Deann with her American mother, Alveen Borshay. As a nine-year-old girl, Deann was desperate to fit in with her new American family and community. (Courtesy of Deann Borshay Liem)

view of a Korean international and transracial adoptee. The Borshays believed that they were adopting Cha Jung Hee in 1966. Deann did not tell the Borshays the truth about her identity at first because the director of the Sun Duk Orphanage warned her not to tell them who she really was until she was old enough to take care of herself. And, as a nine-year-old girl, fluent only in Korean language, and fearful of never seeing her birth family again, she was desperate to fit in with her new American family and community.

The Borshay family—brother Duncan and sister Denise as well as parents Alveen and Arnold—enthusiastically embraced Deann as a full member of their family. In the film, this acceptance is expressed verbally. Denise explains, "From the moment you came here, you were my sister and we were your family. And that was it." Their acceptance of Deann is also expressed visually through the many excerpts of Arnold's home movies, which feature a smiling and playful Deann during Halloween and Christmas holidays and family vacations that are interspersed throughout this first part of the film's narrative. These moments might be interpreted as "color-blind" love and as evidence of America's increasingly postracial society. As Denise states matter-of-factly, "Even though we look different, and different nationality or whatever, we're your family." And Duncan acknowledges Deann as a sister "as much as Denise is."

The acceptance of Deann into the all-American Borshay family is on one important level a radical and progressive departure from the vehement anti-Asian sentiment of the late nineteenth and early twentieth-centuries. Yet *First Person Plural* also illuminates how the specter of anti-Asian racism haunts Deann's integration into her new American family and community. Although Duncan tells Deann, "You didn't have the family eyes, but I don't care. You got the family smile," the film points out that physical appearances—specifically the contrast between Asian and white American faces and bodies—do matter. A panoramic shot of Deann's second- and third-grade classes from her elementary school yearbook presents Deann as one of no more than a handful of Asian American students in a sea of white American faces. Her attempt to "fit in" is about becoming emotionally part of the Borshay family, but it is also about assimilating to the prevailing standards of white American physical beauty.

Figure 5.2. Deann with her American siblings, Duncan and Denise. A major part of
Deann's American childhood was spent trying to "look like everyone else." (Courtesy of
Deann Borshay Liem)

While Denise reminisces, "People would see us and ask, 'Is that
your sister?' You guys look just alike," the film exposes the fallacy in
this statement by illustrating the difficulty and hard work invested by
Deann to look like her white American sister and peers. A major part
of Deann's American childhood was spent trying to "look like everyone else" by perming her naturally straight hair, wearing makeup to
make her eyes look bigger, and even having cosmetic surgery done
on her ears. Alveen relates that after a young Deann had complained
that her ears stuck out too much, she told Deann, "Honey, that can
be fixed if you want." Arnold recalls, however, that after they took off
her bandages following the cosmetic procedure, Deann cried. As an
adult, Deann reflects on this time period of her life wistfully: "Somehow I had created a collage of things and made myself over to fit all
the things I had seen." Thus, the slow-motion family film footage of a
smiling Deann cheering for a college football team, which accompanies
these words belies the strain of physically as well as culturally trying to
become an all-American girl.[7]

Deann's physical transformation to look and act American did not signify a complete break with her Korean past, however. Deann's memories of Korea, her effort to "picture the road from the orphanage to the house," formed a silent strategy of resistance to the identities and histories given to her by the Sun Duk Orphanage and the Borshay family. She promised herself to never forget Korea though it was becoming increasingly difficult to "remember how to get home." When she became fluent enough in English, she broke her silence by telling Alveen that she was not Jung Hee and that she had a mother and a brother and sisters in Korea. Official documents erased her personal history, however. Alveen, referring to Deann's (switched and falsified) adoption papers, insisted that Deann's memories were "just bad dreams" and "a natural part of getting used to living in a new country." As time went by, Deann's memories of Korea—her birth family, the Korean language, her real name—were "beginning to fade." And, in their place, Arnold's home movies began to constitute Deann's memories. Her Korean memories become relegated to dreams.

As a young adult living away from her American home for the first time, those memories come back later to haunt her, and Deann experienced a downward spiral of depression. Her devastation led her to search for her Korean family in 1981 and she was able to locate them in part because her birth family had been searching for her, too. Six weeks after contacting the Sun Duk Orphanage, Deann received a letter from her Korean brother Ho Jin. "My dear sister, Ok Jin, you don't know how happy I am to be writing a letter to you now. I'm your second brother and my name is Ho Jin. Your mother who used to think of you day and night is so happy to read the letter you wrote." He explained to her that she is from a family of five brothers and sisters and that she is Kang Ok Jin, the fourth child in the family.

This intensely personal moment of the film is also the point at which Deann connects her unique individual histories and identities to the broader, post–Korean War history of international and transracial adoption. She narrates that the phenomenon began as a short-term humanitarian effort, popularized initially by the efforts of Harry Holt, an Oregon farmer, to rescue Korean War orphans vis-à-vis international adoption by American families. However, Deann continues that without a South Korean plan to deal with postwar poverty and Korean families in need, Korean international adoption, transformed into a global market, was steeped in unequal relations between nations. "The more children orphanages had, the more money they received from abroad. . . . South Korea became the largest supplier of children to developed countries in the world, causing some to argue that the country's economic miracle was due in part to its export of its most precious natural resource, its children."

In the presentation of this larger history, the title *First Person Plural* speaks to the highly individual but also collective experience of international and transracial adoptees. It refers to the multiple identities of Kang Ok Jin/Cha Jung Hee/Deann Borshay, but it also insists that viewers pay attention to the significant diaspora of Korean adoptees in the Western world in the second half of the twentieth century. Since the end of the Korean War, approximately two hundred thousand Korean children have been sent to the United States for adoption. An additional fifty thousand children have been sent to Europe, where, according to the historian Ji-Yeon Yuh, they make up the largest ethnic Korean community in that region.[8]

In *First Person Plural*, the visual and narrative juxtaposition of this broader history of Korean adoption with Deann's depression signals an important critique of the highly positive portrayal of Korean international adoption's history as humanitarian rescue and as love in American popular culture. These positive representations have become well known through Hollywood films such as Universal Studios' *Battle Hymn* (1957); television episodes such as *Armstrong Circle Theatre*'s "Have Jacket, Will Travel" (1957), and numerous news media reports and photographs from the 1950s through the 1970s.[9] In *First Person Plural*, viewers see how a 1966 news article featuring Deann's adoption by the Borshay family proclaimed that in this new American world for a Korean orphan, her adoptive parents have assured her that "her world was now safe."

Viewers also see images of love *and* of commodification of Korean children—images that are often discussed separately—placed alongside one another. For example, the archival film footage of a white military serviceman embracing a young Korean girl with fondness follows images of the growing number of children in South Korean orphanages. Meanwhile, Deann narrates the inextricable link between the

Cold War origins of Korean international adoption and its transformation into a global industry.

After establishing this broader historical context, *First Person Plural* reveals more details about the falsification of Kang Ok Jin's identity. One month before Cha Jung Hee was scheduled to go to the United States for adoption by the Borshay family, her father found her at the Sun Duk Orphanage and brought her home. The booming business of Korean international adoption led the adoption agency to assume that no one would notice if it falsified Ok Jin's paperwork and sent her in Jung Hee's place. The interchangeability of Korean children in the international adoption industry contrasts sharply with the highly personal story of Jung Hee's father removing her from the orphanage at the last moment. That story speaks to the strength of the emotional attachment between the birth parent and child, an intimacy rarely revealed in organizational records and news media reports.

The erasure of Deann's birth family makes the subsequent interaction between Deann, Alveen, and Denise in *First Person Plural* awkward and uncomfortable. As Deann grapples with her multiple identities created by the global industry of Korean international adoption, Alveen and Denise approach the falsification of Ok Jin's identity primarily through their insistence of their love of Deann. Their approach comes at the expense of disavowing Deann's personal history, however. Alveen insists, "Well, I didn't care that they had switched a child on us. You couldn't be loved more. And just because suddenly you weren't Cha Jung Hee, you were Ok Chin Kang . . . Kong . . . whatever, it didn't matter to me. You were Deann and you were mine." And Denise ponders, "What was your other name, your real name?" When Deann tells her that it is Kang Ok Jin, Denise responds, "See, that doesn't mean nothing to me. You're still Cha Jung Hee."

Although viewers see that the Borshays' emotional attachment to Deann is on one level an expression of love, it is based on the condition or assumption that Deann belongs to only her adoptive family. In his psychoanalytical reading of the film, the scholar David Eng highlights Deann's inability to have two mothers.[10] This inability partly stems from U.S. laws regarding international adoption: Legal ties to the adoptive family are predicated on the dissolution of ties to the birth family.[11] These legal codes also have social ramifications. Deann characterizes the absent presence of her birth family as "an unspoken contract" between her and her adoptive family: "I belonged only to my American parents. It meant that I didn't have a Korean history or a Korean identity." She recollects that she could not talk to her American parents about her Korean family for a long time because she felt that she was somehow being disloyal to them. Since they had provided her with opportunities and loved her, to talk to them about her Korean mother "was like putting dirt" in her mouth.

First Person Plural calls attention to the existing hierarchies in international adoption between sending and receiving nations and between birth and adoptive families. But it also helps viewers reimagine what an international adoptive family looks like beyond a simplistic binary. Unlike other documentary films about international adoption in which the reunion with the birth family is the climax of the narrative, *First Person Plural* features a different gathering: the coming together of Deann's adoptive parents and her birth mother and siblings in Korea after Deann has already reunited with her birth family. The birth family's perspectives of Deann's international adoption together with Deann's and her adoptive parents' understanding of their family history create a fuller and more complex understanding of international and transracial adoption.

In *First Person Plural*, Deann reflects on seeing her Korean family twice in the last thirty years, relating that these return visits are a mixture of familiarity and strangeness for her. On the one hand, the difficulty of fitting in physically in the United States starkly contrasts with her experience in Korea and with her Korean family:

> What struck me when I was with my Korean family was the physical similarity, the amazing feeling of looking at somebody's face that one resembles because for so many years I had looked into blue eyes, blonde hair, and all of a sudden there were these people in the room who, when I looked at them, I could see parts of myself in them. There is sort of a physical closeness as if my body remembers something but my mind is resistant.

On the other hand, her loss of fluency in the Korean language creates a painful emotional and cultural distance between her and her Korean family. In one scene, Deann's Korean mother speaks to her in Korean while

Deann is hunched over a thick book, most probably a Korean-English language dictionary. "I don't understand a word that you're saying, but I get the gist of it . . . I guess," Deann says tearfully. Later she reflects, "I know that language is a barrier between me and my Korean family. There is something about Korean that I cannot get access to. I've tried to learn it since I was in college. It's not just words and it's not just sounds or letters. I think learning the Korean language is about emotion, and about memory."

Deann also acknowledges the existence of an emotional distance between her and her American parents, a distance stemming from racial differences and her vulnerability when she was a child. As I discussed in chapters 1 and 2, ISS workers expressed critical concerns about these differences and their potential impact on the welfare of the adoptive children. Deann's self-reflections affirm that those concerns continue to be valid:

> There's a way in which I see my parents as my parents. But sometimes I look at them and I see two white American people that are so different from me that I can't fathom how we are related to each other, and how it could be possible that these two people could be my parents. When they adopted me they really accepted me as their child and I really became a part of their family. Even though I wasn't related to them by blood it was as if I had been born to them somehow. As a child, I accepted them as my parents because I depended on them for survival but as an adult I think that I haven't accepted them as my parents and I think that's part of the distance I've been feeling with them for a lot of years.

Although the buildup to the encounter between Deann's Korean and American families is emotionally tense, their reunion is cordial and the families interact with one another graciously and respectfully. *First Person Plural* presents viewers with the possibility of dialogue between family members about the difficult issues of relinquishment and estrangement. But it also compels viewers to confront and to think more deeply about the unequal political economy of international adoption. The memories of Deann's older Korean brother, Ho Jin, and her Korean mother, Chun Kil-Soon, provide a social, economic, and political context for the family's relinquishment of Deann to an orphanage for adoption. Ho Jin emphasizes the significance of economic hardship in Korea as well as the powerful allure of opportunities abroad: "At the time she may have wondered why she was sent away when the rest of our family stayed together. Families should stay together, but we were hard-pressed financially. By sending her away we thought she might have better opportunities than us. . . . We thought it would be better than living with us." He connects their family's story to the broader phenomenon of Korea's adopted children overseas: "All of the adopted children suffered equally in some way. It's not that they were abandoned. The children were sent for a better life."

Chun Kil-Soon elaborates this larger history while importantly placing a human face on the story of abandonment:

> For five years after her father died, I made just enough to feed my children but not enough to send them to school. Next door there was this man who worked at an orphanage. And he said to me you can barely feed these five children. Why don't you put the three youngest into the orphanage where I work? I had no idea about such things. So I just followed his suggestion and sent them to the orphanage. After a while the orphanage asked me to give up Ok Jin for adoption. They asked me on three separate occasions, and each time I refused. At the time I was going to church and the deacon at the church said since I already have three daughters I should send one to the U.S. to get a better life.

After the adoption agency sent Deann abroad for adoption sooner than scheduled, she lamented, "I have no words to describe the agonizing years after that." Through her words, tears, and facial expressions, film viewers learn that Deann's emotional devastation was not singular. Rather it was deeply felt on both sides of the Pacific Ocean.

Although the film focuses on an individual story—even Deann describes it as a "personal story of my experiences being adopted and growing up in America"—the birth mother's memory of the institutional pressure to relinquish her daughter for adoption harkens back to the earlier narrative part of *First Person Plural* on the history of international and transracial adoption in the post–Korean War period, specifically its transformation from humanitarian rescue efforts into a global industry marked by South Korean families' and orphanages' increasing dependency on international adoption to alleviate poverty.

Thus, while Deann professes a closer connection to her adoptive parents at the conclusion of *First Person Plural*, she also leaves viewers with ambivalent feelings about international adoption. She reflects that while adoption brought her and her American family much happiness, it also engendered a lot of sadness that "we couldn't deal with as a family." That sadness had to do with loss. Her family connection to the Borshays in the "new world" of the United States was inextricably linked to her separation from her Korean birth family. And it was a grief that was exacerbated because it could not be articulated or acknowledged. As Deann puts it, "I was never able to mourn what I had lost with my American parents." *First Person Plural* reclaims that inability. It is a profound visual and narrative expression of mourning the loss of family in the process of creating a new one through international and transracial adoption.

In the Matter of Cha Jung Hee: Meditations on the Loss of History

What would happen if you had lived someone else's life, literally had walked in someone else's shoes? Deann Borshay Liem confronts the conundrum she has lived in the 2010 documentary film *In the Matter of Cha Jung Hee*: "When I came to the United States, I arrived as Cha Jung Hee. My papers indicated that I was an orphan with no living family. But there was one problem. I wasn't really Cha Jung Hee." Eleven years after the release of *First Person Plural*, the documentary film *In the Matter of Cha Jung Hee* delves into the whereabouts of the girl whose identity Deann had been given by the Sun Duk Orphanage and whom the Borshays believed they had adopted. After visiting her Korean family multiple times since their initial reunion in the 1980s, Deann decides to go back to Korea this time to look for her "orphan" double whom she had never met but whose identity would become inextricably linked to her own. As a result, the film might be described as a sequel to *First Person Plural*.

One of the film's major contributions that should not be overlooked, however, is its meditation on loss, not solely the loss of the "real" Cha Jung Hee but also the loss of adoptees' histories. At the opening of the film's narration, Deann's melancholic longing for knowledge of her own past challenges the traditional notion of history as the simple and linear progression of change over time that we come to know through memory, material

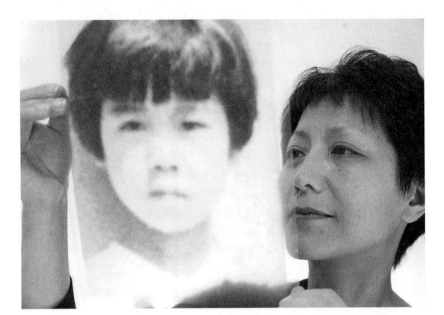

Figure 5.3. In her documentary film *In the Matter of Cha Jung Hee*, Deann Borshay Liem searches for the mysterious girl whose place she took in America. (Courtesy of Deann Borshay Liem)

evidence, reading, and research. Over the dreamlike pastiche of images—girls jumping rope, a child having her feet traced onto tissue paper in pencil, someone's hands carefully cutting out this tracing—Deann narrates: "I wish I could call this memory, my memory of my sisters and friends playing together. I wish I had a picture for all the lost moments of the past so that I could string them together into one unbroken history. Instead I invent stories of what might have been, inserting myself into spaces I never occupy."

The piece of tissue paper with the cut-out tracing of a young girl's feet is a precious object found in Deann's personal collection of her adoption documents. It is a reminder of her dual identity. Deann explains, "When I asked my mother about this she said that when Cha Jung Hee was still at the orphanage she wanted to send her a new pair of shoes. So she asked the social worker to make an outline of her foot and send it to her. The new shoes arrived and plans were made for Cha Jung Hee to go to America." After Jung Hee suddenly left the orphanage, the social worker sent Deann (also known as Kang Ok Jin) in her place. Deann arrived at the airport literally walking in Jung Hee's shoes.

Once she had learned enough English, Deann tried to tell her American mother about her true identity. She explained that her Korean mother was still alive and that they lived in a house on top of a hill. But her American mother dismissed the veracity of these claims, insisting that Deann was a war orphan. Deann relates, "When I asked my mother about my childhood, she always told me the same story: 'Your real mother died while giving birth to you. And your father was killed during the Korean War. That's why we adopted you.'" Later in the film, viewers learn that her American parents' unwillingness to discuss her past and their insistence that her father was killed during the Korean War were influenced by the false tragic stories about Deann's Korean family history. The first letter they had received about Jung Hee explained that her birth mother had died during childbirth and that her grieving father had then committed suicide. Her American parents kept Jung Hee's Korean family history a secret, Deann realizes, to protect her.

In our bureaucratic society, documents have the power to simultaneously erase our personal histories and identities and create new ones, especially when they are stacked against a child's memories. Thus, as her memories of Korea faded, Deann inhabited the world according to her adoption paperwork: "In elementary school, my best friend asked me what my Korean name was. I told her it was Cha Jung Hee and that my parents had died. There was no proof that I had ever been anyone else."

Documents perpetuate falsehoods, but they also have the potential to uncover them. Deann's critical analysis of the adoption-related mementos in her possession led to her arduous quest for self-discovery:

> I would have gone on to live my life happily as Cha Jung Hee, but years later I discovered two photos of two different girls each labeled with the same name. I recognized one of them as myself and knew instantly that the other girl was Cha Jung Hee and that I wasn't. But if I wasn't Cha Jung Hee, who was I? My world began falling apart. All of a sudden, I saw myself in a completely different light. I wondered, "Had I lived my entire life as an impostor?" I know in reality I am not her. But my sense of who I am has been held captive to her name and her identity. Even today her birth date is the one that appears on my driver's license and legal documents.

The search for the "real" Cha Jung Hee creates a detectivelike ambiance. Deann looks for clues at the Sun Duk Orphanage, the place where their lives had intersected. There the mystery of Cha Jung Hee is heightened when Deann finds a photo of a third girl, also with the name Cha Jung Hee. Using a magnifying glass to study the two photos, the orphanage director suggests that there are facial similarities between the two girls, although it is obvious that they look quite different.

Deann's interview with a Korean social worker named Hyo-Sun Park confirms the falsification of Jung Hee's and by extension Deann's identities. Park handled Jung Hee's case in the mid-1960s and was the only person who knew of Deann's true identity for many years. After learning about the plight of Korean war orphans from the news, the Borshays decided to sponsor a Korean child, Jung Hee, under the auspices of the Foster Parents Plan. Park was the social worker who had written letters to the Borshays on Jung Hee's behalf. In her letters, she described Jung Hee as a true orphan and a happy child who wanted to live with the Borshays. According to Park, the orphanage did not know that Cha Jung Hee had living parents until her father showed up suddenly and took her away. By then, the Borshays wanted to formally adopt Jung Hee, so the Foster Parents Plan (also known as Plan Korea) asked the orphanage staff to substitute a similar girl. Park continued to send letters to the Borshays on Jung Hee's behalf for another year *after* the girl had already left the orphanage. In her interview with Deann, Park laments, "The switch was done out of a belief that you would be happy. I'm sorry it's still haunting you."

Thus, the search for Cha Jung Hee continues. A Korean friend, Jong-suk Lee, helps Deann, who can no longer speak Korean, call the 101 Cha Jung Hees listed in the Korean phonebook. They explain that they are looking for a Cha Jung Hee who lived in Kunsan or Jeon Ju and who would be around fifty years old. But their effort is unsuccessful. Deann visits the Jeon Ju police station and city hall, but they, too, have no relevant information. Deann then goes to the media, publicizing her search in a daily newspaper and even making an appeal on national television in a program that includes an "I Miss This Person" segment. Still no leads emerge.

The hunt for clues relating to Cha Jung Hee's existence is both exciting and frustrating. As in any good detective story, viewers want to locate the clue that will solve the mystery and reveal the truth. Yet one of the most important lessons gleaned from *In the Matter of Cha Jung Hee* is that even the most promising clues—in this case Deann's adoption case file—contain radical possibilities as well as limitations.

During this visit to South Korea, Deann decides to visit the Social Welfare Society, Korea's oldest adoption agency, to learn about the current state of Korean international adoption. Although South Korea is no longer the top sending nation of adoptive children in the world, it continues to send approximately 1,500 children abroad annually for adoption. Most of these children are born to unwed mothers. Deann's investigation of the present state of Korean international adoption leads to an unexpected, emotional discovery about her past. The agency informs her that they have old adoption records from the ISS. Deann speaks with Hye Kyoung Sun, the society's Director of Intercountry Adoption: "That's amazing. So you have all the records. I had heard that since the ISS is no longer around [in Korea] that I could never find any documentation. But maybe I can find it through your office?" The director amicably offers to look for Deann's records and, to Deann's amazement, finds her adoption case file. In it, she finds a photo of herself in Jung Hee's shoes. "I'm getting goosebumps," Deann cries. "I just never thought I would see this file. . . . Oh my goodness, I cannot believe this." The file also contains the negative of her passport photo, a document of relinquishment, and a certificate of orphanhood.

As Deann examines the documents, she pinpoints their fabrications. For example, Deann's Korean family informed her that June 14 was her birthday. The birth date in the file—November 5, 1956—is Jung Hee's. Furthermore, a document entitled "Report of the Child" claims that both of her parents were deceased, her mother in 1962 and her father in 1963. Deann asks the director if there is ever a situation in which a child's files are altered in order to get him or her abroad. Despite the blatant inconsistencies in Deann's file, the director insists that the files are accurate. Deann asks her to confirm this problematic point: "Generally the adoption files are accurate, 100 percent?" The director responds with "100 percent," emphasizing that they give the "real" information to the adoptive parents, "not the fake one."

Deann's investigation illuminates a jarring point about the history of Korean international adoption. The falsification of documents makes the recovery of an "unbroken history" impossible. Deann reflects: "It scared me to think how easy it was to replace one girl for another. The first step was to take my picture and simply write Cha Jung Hee's name on the back. Then I was given a guardian who certified that I was an orphan. He, rather than my birth mother, gave his consent to my emigration and adoption. The shoes completed the deception." Toward the conclusion of the film, Deann enlists the help of Sergeant Keon-Su Lee of the Namyangju Police Station. He specializes in reuniting families and agrees to help her search for Jung Hee. He is able to locate a Cha Jung Hee who remembers spending time in an orphanage at Jeon Ju when she was a young girl. This Jung Hee tells Deann that as a young girl, she went on an outing with her uncle and got lost. She fell asleep on the train and when she woke up she was in an orphanage where she stayed for three to four months. Her father finally located her at the orphanage, and he told her that he found her just in time because she was going to be sent to America.

This Jung Hee bears a strong resemblance to the photograph of Cha Jung Hee from the orphanage. When Deann shows her the pair of shoes that the Borshays sent to the Korean orphanage, Jung Hee says that the shoes bring back memories. However, she cannot recall receiving any communication or gifts from the Borshays and she associates the shoes as a gift from her grandfather when he visited the United States. Although Deann believes in her heart that this is *the* Cha Jung Hee whose place she had taken in America, there is no neat and simple resolution in this matter. Deann cannot confirm her strong hunch with evidence, and she admits that there are multiple inconsistencies between the life history of this Jung Hee and the one she has been searching for. Instead, she can only imagine to the best of her ability what transpired at the orphanage. Deann believes that this Jung Hee was the original Cha Jung Hee sponsored by the Borshays. After the girl went home with her father, Deann surmises that another girl was put in her place. A photo of this second "Cha Jung Hee" was sent to the Borshays, but Deann hypothesizes that something happened to this second girl and then she became the third Cha Jung Hee.

In her search for the "real" Cha Jung Hee, Deann confronts a discomfiting truth behind the girl's creation and function. She realizes that Cha Jung Hee was also "a template for the perfect orphan. Once the template existed, any girl could step into it." This "perfect orphan" may have been a product of fiction and fabrication, but its impact on the lived experiences of adoptees was very real. Deann confesses, "Because I wasn't the child my parents had originally fallen in love with, there was a part of me that always questioned whether I belonged and whether I had a right to accept my family's love and to love them." She also tells Jung Hee that she always felt guilty about taking someone's place in America.

Initially wanting an identity distinct from that of Cha Jung Hee, Deann reclaims the complexity of her past, a personal history in which fictional narratives played a prominent role:

> I originally thought if I gave back Cha Jung Hee's shoes, I would be free of the identity they symbolized. But I realize they don't belong to her, they belong to me. Although I arrived in America walking in Cha Jung Hee's shoes, I can see now the path I've taken has always been my own. And if I look closely I can see a glimpse of the girl I used to be and I can picture her stepping out of the past and into the present.

First Person Plural and In the Matter of Cha Jung Hee as Asian American History and Memory

The history of Korean international adoption, especially white American families' embrace of Korean adoptive children in the United States, contrasts dramatically with current Asian American historiography about the Cold War period in which threats of immigration expulsion and family dissolution are prominent themes. In the 1950s and 1960s, Filipino American labor organizers were threatened with deportation by anticommunist propagandists. The Chinese Confession Program attempted to compel illegal Chinese immigrants to declare their illegal status and to name those persons—often family members—who had helped them in the process.

However, when Borshay Liem's films are analyzed closely alongside the documentary films *Bontoc Eulogy* and *History and Memory*, they illuminate discrete themes in the Asian American experience: the "absent presence" of specific persons in history; the suppression of their histories through American popular culture; and the loss of their histories through the lack of traditional historical evidence. The four films criticize these absences in two major ways: first, by creating images that make visible the violence of loss and, second, by presenting a different way of documenting and understanding the past. The filmmakers point out in their work that one of the main impacts of loss (loss of persons, knowledge, traditional historical evidence) is their (as well as our) inability to recover history in its entirety. Only partial stories can be told. Yet, in doing so, their documentation of Asian American history is both an act of mourning and of defiance. By highlighting the misconceptions of popular narratives of American history and by offering alternative stories, they are expressions of historical agency.

In Marlon Fuentes's experimental film, *Bontoc Eulogy*, the celebration of U.S. global power at the 1904 St. Louis World's Fair is the historical gateway into a family history featuring two personal narratives: the narrator, a Filipino immigrant (portrayed by Marlon Fuentes) who is searching for the whereabouts of his grandfather, and the grandfather Markod, a Bontoc Igorot who was among the approximately 1,100 Filipinos brought to the United States to be displayed at the fair's "Philippine Reservation."[12] Markod's fate after the fair is unknown because he never returned to his home in the Philippine mountains.

The narrator poses the following questions: "Why did we leave our home? Why did we come to America? Why have we chosen to stay?" In addition to the narrator and his grandfather, the "we" refers to the sizeable presence of Filipinos in America in the late twentieth century. The narrator is one of more than one million Filipino immigrants in the United States who, along with the displayed Bontoc Igorots, constitute an "absent presence" in the landscape of U.S. history and contemporary society, the result of the lack of scholarly attention devoted to this group as well as the coercive power of U.S. assimilation: "We Filipinos wear this cloak of silence to render us invisible from one another. . . . To survive in this new land, we have to forget."

The personal narratives featured in *Bontoc Eulogy* are, on one level, fictional. Because there are no known surviving records from the perspective of the indigenous Filipino people on display at this fair, the narrator's questions are partly unanswerable. Furthermore, the material evidence that we do have about their presence is unrecognizable. According to the historian Robert Rydell, the renowned physical anthropologist Aleš Hrdlička performed autopsies on three Igorots who died at the St. Louis World's Fair and he had removed and stored their brains.[13] Thus, in *Bontoc Eulogy*, the narrator attempts to follow Markod's trail by visiting anthropology museums (Hrdlička had worked for the Smithsonian). These searches yield unusable pasts, however, because the remaining traces of bones, brains, and skulls defy individuality and subjectivity.[14] The narrator surmises that his grandfather's brain may lie on a "musty shelf waiting to be discovered," but he astutely concludes that, even if the discovery were made, it would be part of "so many objects, identities unknown, labeled, but nameless, anonymous stories permanently preserved in a language that can never be understood."

Furthermore, popular memories of the 1904 St. Louis World's Fair continue to permeate American national consciousness. For example, the 1994 documentary film *A World on Display* discusses how the St. Louis World's Fair had a profound, educational impact on the fairgoers even many decades later. And, even if most Americans were not physically present at the fair, the popularity of the 1944 movie musical *Meet Me in St. Louis* publicized a nostalgic and romantic vision of the fair from the perspective of a white, affluent American family. Starring Judy Garland, *Meet Me in St. Louis* was nominated for four Oscars. It would become the second most successful MGM film (second only to *Gone with the Wind*) and be remembered as "one of the greatest musicals ever made."[15] In *Bontoc Eulogy*, Fuentes juxtaposes the sweet lyrics and happy melodies from one of the film's popular songs—"Meet me in St. Louis, Louis/Meet me at the fair . . ."—with the troubling stories of the narrator and Markod. In doing so, he compels viewers to grapple with the complexity of history and memory: Americans' popular sugar-coated memories of the fair suppress the fair's hidden truths of racism and the dissolution of Filipino families. As Fuentes says of the making of *Bontoc Eulogy*: "I believe that history is really an art of memory. The gaps and ellipses are just as important as the materials we have in our hands. They are missing for certain reasons, whether by accident or force of omission, but they function as an irregularity or bump in an otherwise smooth surface of history."[16]

Fuentes addresses the gaps of our historical knowledge in the film by using imagination and conjecture to construct Markod's perspective. Viewers learn that after listening to the exciting stories told by American recruiters in the Philippines who were working on behalf of the fair organizers, Markod was intrigued by the opportunity to go to the United States and to show Americans his way of life. He hesitated initially, however, because his wife was expecting and he wanted to be at home for the birth of their child. But he keeps in touch with his family by writing letters about his voyage to America. When the fair finally opens, Markod spends most of his time in his Philippine Reservation village where he and other Bontoc Igorots are required to perform rituals of marriage, birth, and death "endlessly, devoid of any connection to what inspired them." He receives a few dollars each month for his participation, but he eventually longs to return home to the Philippines. Markod laments, "There are few things I have seen that we would want in the mountains." He becomes preoccupied with two Bontoc men who died at the fair because he never saw their bodies again. Fair festivities continue with gawking fairgoers who were ignorant of the grief of the men before them. Markod becomes increasingly fearful of disappearing like the other two men.

Markod is a fictional composite of Bontoc Igorots at the fair based on Fuentes's historical research. However, the incredible "living exhibit" of Filipinos at the 1904 St. Louis World's Fair; the popularity of their scantily dressed bodies and dog-eating rituals among American fairgoers; the death and dismemberment of some Bontoc Igorots during the fair; and at least one American university official's interest in the purchase of their body parts are historical truths. Fuentes rejects their depiction as sideshow savages who confirmed white American racial and national superiority or as colonialism's victims, the unfortunate casualties of U.S. westward expansionism. Rather, in *Bontoc Eulogy*, viewers confront Bontoc Igorot humanity. Markod is a seeker of adventure. He is a member of a family.

The recollection of this imperial history, Fuentes suggests, is foundational knowledge for understanding the rise of the United States as a world power at the beginning of the twentieth century. But it also enables him to come to terms with his ambivalence about being a Filipino immigrant in America in more recent times. In ways similar to Deann Borshay Liem, Fuentes uses his film as a vehicle to explore historical issues of racial, familial, and national hierarchies and how they continue to haunt the formation of Asian immigrant, and specifically Filipino American, identity. The beginning of *Bontoc Eulogy* echoes

First Person Plural's opening narrative in its focus on the narrator's displacement from his Philippine homeland and on the resultant multiplicity of the worlds inhabited by the Filipino immigrant. He recalls, "I left Manila for America more than twenty years ago carrying dreams from a past I now barely recognize. . . . In the beginning I lived in two worlds: the sights and sounds of my new life and then the flickering after-images of the place I once called home." His assimilation in the United States reveals, however, a privileging of the new American world over his Philippine life history because it results in the loss of his ability to inhabit multiple places and to equally acknowledge multiple identities. Like the young Deann Borshay, it becomes harder for the narrator to remember his way home to the Philippines. He muses, "The years pass, the urgency of my youthful dreams muted by the dailiness of life's events. Now my memories of life back home have faded to the point where it is sometimes difficult to know when reality ends and imagination begins." All that remains is "remnant dreams" and "recurring landscapes."

Similar to Deann Borshay Liem's attempt to understand her multiple identities, the narrator's decision to confront what has become relegated to dreams results in a personal search that is inextricably linked to a collective struggle shared by Filipinos in the diaspora. After learning to forget their Philippine past, the narrator claims that "the stream changes course and slowly *our* ghost catches up. Now *we* must remember in order to survive" (emphasis mine). For the narrator, memory is an individual, collective, and generational imperative. He believes that his fading memories cannot be transmitted to the next generation of Filipino Americans, such as his children, who are U.S.-born and for whom the United States is the only home they have known. Thus, a sense of urgency defines his quest for knowledge about his grandfather and about his Philippine American heritage: "One day I will be gone and these memories will be lost. Yet questions will remain. . . . What are the stories that define us as a people? What has made us the way we are?" The narrator explains that, after all, "home is what you try to remember not what you try to forget. . . . In the Philippines there is a saying . . . he who does not look back from whence he came from will never ever reach his destination."

Like *First Person Plural* and *Bontoc Eulogy*, Rea Tajiri's documentary *History and Memory* (1991) seeks to rehabilitate fragmented familial pasts from the forgotten ruins of national tragedy.[17] Tajiri's family was part of the 120,000 Japanese Americans interned during World War II, and though Tajiri herself was born after the camps closed, she is haunted by her family's fading memories of the internment camps, what she refers to as an "absence that is presence." The focal image of the film is intensely personal: an image of her mother's face as she fills her cupped hands with water on a dry, hot day, presumably from a spigot at an internment camp. It is an image Tajiri has internalized, yet of which she has no memory—where it came from, what story might have compelled it, or the reason for its recurrence. She can only vaguely associate it with her family's internment camp experience.

Tajiri begins her rehabilitation with this seemingly innocuous thought: "I wondered how movies influenced our lives." Inchoate memories of her relatives' experiences in camp are juxtaposed against excerpts of popular movies about World War II that stoked American nationalist sentiments. Hollywood movies such as *Yankee Doodle Dandy* (1942), *December 7th* (1943), *From Here to Eternity*, (1953) and *The Teahouse of the August Moon* (1956) bespeak stories of Japanese treachery and American sacrifice that form the basis of the popular imagination about the war. Even those few movies that tried to sensitively depict internment managed either to leave Japanese Americans out of the movie (as in the absent presence of the sympathetic character Komoko in the 1954 movie *Bad Day at Black Rock*) or focused on a sympathetic white protagonist (as in the 1990 movie *Come See the Paradise*). Tajiri reflects, "I had known all along that the stories I had heard weren't true and parts had been left out."

In addition to Hollywood's portrayal of World War II, the stories she refers to include U.S. government–sponsored films about the "happy" Japanese American internees as depicted in the War Relocation Authority archival footage, which justified and softened the forced relocation of 120,000 Japanese Americans (two-thirds of whom were American-born U.S. citizens) without due process to the public eye. The excerpt from *The Way Ahead*, showing smiling Japanese Americans walking toward the camera and into a world of possibility during the period immediately after the closing of the internment camps, belies the harsh resettlement realities that many of them faced upon returning to their old neighborhoods to see banners, some of them hanging from the eaves of the very homes they lived in, admonishing "Japs Keep Moving."

Tajiri must peel away layers of grand narrative fortified by Hollywood movies and government propaganda to get to the memory that underlies the lasting image of her mother in camp. However, stories that Tajiri had heard with "parts left out" also include the vague memories of her relatives who could not or would not recall humiliating aspects of internment. Her mother's memories of camp are for the most part sketchy at best, as if she were attempting to remember for the first time, but also as if those memories were buried beneath the monolithic density of U.S. national memory. Tajiri's challenge, then, as she proclaims in the film, is "creating an image where there are so few" in order to "forgive mother her loss of memory" and to "make the image for her."

As in Borshay Liem's and Fuentes's films, meditations on lost histories of coerced movement, uprootedness, and displacement are major thematics in *History and Memory*. Her mother cannot remember the existence of a canteen store in camp as she looks at a picture of internee children, one of whom might be herself, in the store. She attempts, with difficulty, to direct Rea to the assembly center in Salinas where the family gathered before being sent off to the internment camps. In attempting to redeem her own mother's receding memories of camp, Tajiri collects "images without the story." By accumulating these images, or fragments of memory, Tajiri at times discovers that one fragment provides the backstory to another fragment. For example, the photograph of her grandmother in a bird carving class at camp explains what Tajiri's mother cannot when shown one of the birds her own mother had likely carved there. "I don't know where this came from" is her mother's refrain. As she ages, the quotidian aspects of camp life fade, distanced because of a lack of concrete images.

The lack of images compels the desire to create them, just as the existence of an unfounded memory produces the desire to uncover its source. Tajiri's provision of the images and the questions that prompt remembering begin the processes of challenging the grand narratives about World War II with what can be called countermemory and then counternarrative. The recording of a relative's recollections played simultaneously with the soundtrack from a Hollywood movie is one example of Tajiri's filmic technique that sets counternarrative in collision with U.S. national memory. The result is an intentional confusion, or cacophony, of competing narratives.

One of the central anxieties in the film is that when memory fails her relatives and fragments Tajiri's search further, "official" national memory seeps in—in which Japanese Americans are either absent or misrepresented. To the extent that *History and Memory* is a counternarrative to the history of the necessity of internment, it is also an acknowledgment of the difficulty of displacing the grand narratives of World War II regarding internment, which state that internment was a necessary evil, that Japanese Americans simply could not be trusted, that internment occurred for their own protection, or, simply, that "a Jap's a Jap."

However, Tajiri does not, inasmuch as she cannot, rely on an oppositional exchange of facts to "correct" history. Rather, she focuses on the narratives that have imprinted the ways we romanticize and glorify warfare, and consequently rationalize internment, on a nation's memory. Tajiri wants, first, to call our attention to the seamlessness, fluidity, and unity that undergird U.S. national memory of World War II. Footage from John Ford's *December 7th* conjoin with scenes from *Yankee Doodle Dandy* and *From Here to Eternity* to lay out the foundation that collectively silences Tajiri's family's memories of internment—a necessary consequence of victory.

Similar to the ways in which Borshay Liem and Fuentes use cameras as an ironic tool for restaging constructions of truth, Tajiri also calls attention to the world behind the "documenters" of history:

> There are things which have happened in the world while there were cameras watching, things we have images for. . . . There are other things which have happened while there were no cameras watching which we restage in front of cameras to have images of. There are things which have happened for which the only images that exist are in the minds of the observers present at the time, while there are things which have happened for which there have been no observers except for the spirits of the dead.

Owning cameras in the internment camps so as to document internees' own experiences was prohibited, as opposed to white American photographers such as Ansel Adams whose photographs of internment (sanctioned by the War Relocation Authority) became revered as the highest aesthetic in the documentation of camp life. What exists of the images taken by internees have come from contraband cameras. As a result, similar to Borshay Liem and Fuentes, Tajiri can only imagine those things that have happened "for which there have been no observers except for the spirits of the dead." The film pays heed to these spirits by opening with a scrolling text detailing a scene that takes place on December 7, 1961. It begins with a view from above, then down through treetops to street to street lamp, shining a light focusing on two people, the tops of whose heads (with black hair) move in an animated fashion. The scrolling text explains:

> The spirit of my grandfather witnesses my father and mother as they have an argument about the unexplained nightmares their daughter has been having on the 20th anniversary of the bombing of Pearl Harbor, the day that changed the lives of 110,000 Japanese-Americans who shortly after were forced by the U.S. Government to sell their property, homes, cars, possessions, businesses; leave their communities; and relocate to internment camp.

There is more than one audience for *History and Memory*: the living (viewers) and the watchful eyes of the spirits, presumably to whom Tajiri hopes to give voice. Her parents' inability to explain their daughter's nightmares reflect their own shame about the bombing of Pearl Harbor and the camps. To not speak of the camps became a cultural directive *kodomo no tame* (for the sake of the children) to shield them from the loss of face surrounding the internment experience. Yet their child's nightmares on the twentieth anniversary of the bombing of Pearl Harbor speaks to the internalization of the experience by the children, an effect of the silence about the camps by the previous generation. Later in the film, Tajiri's father acknowledges his children's internalization of the camp experience: "The resentment [on the part of the children] must have been there because it's impossible to accept being placed behind barbed wire for no reason at all."

By the end of *History and Memory*, family mementos of camp such as Tajiri's grandmother's wooden bird are not just flashes of memory, but, rather, ethnographic fragments out of which Tajiri expands their

boundaries "to include more of what was left behind." The more fragments her mother is exposed to, the stronger is her compulsion to
remember, so that toward the end of the film, she recalls the exact
address of her family's barrack among a sea of barracks in the camps.

In the film's resolution, Tajiri's nephew's critical review of Alan
Parker's 1990 film *Come See the Paradise* is less a panning of the movie
itself than an analysis of how it continues a legacy of Hollywood movies
about World War II that silence Japanese American perspectives. Movies, Tajiri suggests, may no longer influence us in the chauvinistic ways
they once did. Inasmuch as *History and Memory* is a push back against
U.S. national memory and Hollywood movies, however, Tajiri makes
us aware that it is a push that forecloses neither the grand narratives of
World War II history nor popular memory about the war, as the film's
ending calls attention to the attempt by Representative Gil Ferguson,
a Republican from Orange County, California, in 1990, to pass a bill
authorizing that schools should teach that Japanese Americans had
never been sent to internment camps.

Conclusion: The Power of Counternarratives

In her seminal essay, "The Power of Culture" (1998), the literary scholar
Lisa Lowe makes the following claim about Asian American culture:

> Asian American culture "re-members" the "past" in and through the
> fragmentation, loss, violences and dispersal that constitutes the "past."
> Asian American culture is the site of more than critical negation of the
> nation—it is a site that shifts and marks alternatives to the national ter-
> rain by occupying other spaces, imagining different narratives and criti-
> cal historiographies, and enacting practices that give rise to new forms of
> subjectivity and new ways of questioning the government of human life
> by the national state.[18]

Borshay Liem's, Fuentes's, and Tajiri's struggles to remember and reclaim
resonate with what Lowe terms the "national memory," which "haunts
the conception of the Asian American, persisting beyond the repeal of
laws prohibiting Asians from citizenship from 1943–1952 and sustained
by wars in Asia, in which the Asian is always seen as an immigrant,

as the 'foreigner-within,' even when born in the United States and the descendant of generations born here before."[19]

Lowe uses Jeannie Barroga's 1989 play *Walls*, about the racialized controversy that arose from Maya Lin's selection in a blind contest to design the Vietnam Veterans' War memorial, as her test text in her essay. According to Lowe, U.S. national memory of the Vietnam War desired representational sentimental images and icons reflective of the way the nation remembers its wars nostalgically. Not only was Lin's memorial a nonrepresentative work of art, but the focus of the controversy soon turned to Lin's own "Americanness"—one that was unrecognizable from her Asian face, though Lin was born and raised in Ohio. As hard as Lin tried to keep her race a nonissue in the memorial controversy, the marking of race on her body was simply too contradictory to the national imagery of Americanness for critics not to call attention to it. Unsurprisingly, now that the memorial has withstood the test of time and become a standard by which other memorials are now measured, the backstory of Maya Lin has receded to a remote corner of the nation's memory. She is not remembered for the racism she suffered but is now simply the designer of the memorial. As Jeannie Barroga's play forges a collective memory of Maya Lin's construction of a national war monument, so, too, do Borshay Liem, Fuentes, and Tajiri document collective pasts, heretofore forgotten, silenced, or mistaken.

The four films analyzed here do not so much offer redemption in the face of past legislation and the continuing cultural pressure to keep Asian American subjects and history separate from U.S. national culture as much as they are expressions of the consequence of the very formation of national culture. According to Lowe, "United States national culture—the collectively forged images, histories, and narratives that place, displace, and replace individuals in relation to the national polity—powerfully shapes who the citizenry is, where they dwell, what they remember, and what they forget."[20] As counternarratives, these films not only offer oppositional stories and historical facts but also ask viewers to pay more critical attention to received venues of knowledge—archival records, case files, ethnographic spectacle, government- sponsored reportage, authoritative talking heads, and history textbooks—that gird national memory. They illuminate how cultural rigidity regarding U.S. national memory is solidified through popular culture—Hollywood movies and other forms of sentimental storytelling, which highlight humanitarian rescue, benevolent assimilation, and government protection.

Against the backdrop of this rigidity, it is not enough, as the writer Gloria Anzaldúa warned, "to stand on the opposite river bank, shouting questions, challenging patriarchal, white conventions."[21] Armed with only a cache of memories, Tajiri's Aunt Helen experiences this futility when, during a visit to the city in which she was interned, she asks of a nonbeliever, "What proof do you want?" The answer, of course, is that no amount of "proof" can by now fill in the "gaps and ellipses" where national memory has seeped in to smoothen them seemingly out of existence. Over and against "official documentation," these three filmmakers subvert received forms of "truth telling" that have served to silence their histories.

"Where the political terrain can neither resolve nor suppress inequality," Lowe writes, "it erupts in culture."[22] The verb "erupts" seems *apropos* to the immediacy of response felt in these four films, not so much in the vein of the romantic, spontaneous overflow of powerful feelings as in the stitching of countermemory—fragmented and repressed—to national memory, and in doing so reclaiming their ability to recuperate, to tell, and to make historical their own stories.

New Geographies, Historical Legacies

Much has changed in international adoption since the 1970s. First, the phenomenon has become a truly global industry. The few thousand international adoptions that took place in the 1950s and 1960s pale in comparison to the tens of thousands in the late twentieth and early twenty-first centuries. As the demographer Peter Selman notes in his study of the movement of children for international adoption between 1998 and 2004, "The number of intercountry adoptions has more than doubled in the last twenty years."[1] Between 1998 and 2004 the total number of children adopted in twenty receiving countries increased from 31,667 to 45,016, or by 42 percent.

Second, the national origins of adoptive children in the United States have become much more diverse, involving different regions of the world. Specific Asian nations continue to supply adoptive children, but Eastern European, Latin American, and African countries have also become important sources. From 1993 to 2005, Russia was the largest or second-largest sending country of adopted children to the United States. It led in the total number of adoptions for the years 1997, 1998, and 1999.

Beginning in the late 1980s, postcommunist social upheaval and economic instability created conditions that resulted in increasing numbers of Russian children in state care. Poverty, family violence, disease (including HIV), and alcohol and drug addiction led to Russian parents' relinquishment of their children voluntarily or by court order. According to the sociologist Heather Jacobson, international adoption became a vehicle through which the growing demands of Russian children in state care were addressed.[2]

In 2006 and 2007, Guatemala was the second leading sending country of adopted children to the United States. The historian Karen Dubinsky features the increasing significance of Guatemalan international adoption in her study on adoption and migration across the Americas:

> After the peace accords of 1996, Guatemala's documented participation in transnational adoption systems almost doubled, from 731 children in 1996 to 1,278 in 1997, and climbed steadily every year thereafter. By 2006, 4,918 children were adopted internationally, making Guatemala the country with the highest per capita transnational adoption rate in the world. One hundred and sixty adoption agencies have ties to Guatemalan adoption programs; in 2005 adoption was the fourth-highest earner of foreign currency.[3]

International adoption from Ethiopia increased by 150 percent between 2002 and 2005. According to the anthropologist Barbara Yngvesson, famine, war, and the HIV/AIDS crisis as well as the international publicity about celebrity adoptions from Africa contributed to these growing numbers. Ethiopia's popularity continued to grow as a result of new restrictions—eligibility requirements, adoption agency regulations, domestic adoption initiatives—implemented in China, Russia, and South Korea.

During the 1998 Olympic Games in Seoul, the South Korean government encountered harsh criticism of its international adoption program and has since actively encouraged domestic adoptions by creating monthly allowances and increasing health benefits for domestically adopted children as well as easing restrictions on the maximum age and marital status of potential adoptive parents.[4] South Korean cultural productions, such as Cho Seihon's "Letter from Angels" project, attempt to raise awareness of domestic adoption through celebrity photography that has been publicized in issues of *Vogue Korea*. Cho's forOne license for this photography promotes "promise and consideration for adopted children" and requests the licensee to promise that she or he:

1. Shall not have prejudice against adopted children.
2. Shall not mock or cajole a child for being adopted.
3. Shall caution children as not to discriminate, cajole or mock an adopted child.
4. Shall be cautious to prevent the adopted child feeling left out.
5. Shall be cautious with your words as not to dispirit an adopted child.[5]

Third, other countries have become important receiving nations of internationally adopted children. Deann Borshay Liem's latest film project, tentatively titled *Geographies of Kinship: The Korean Adoption Story*, expands the geographic focus of the history of Korean international adoption beyond the traditional focus on the U.S.-South Korea relationship.[6] The documentary film-in-progress features personal stories of Korean adoptees in Sweden and France as well as other parts of Western Europe, Australia, and North America.

Peter Selman observes that, in 2004, the receiving states with the highest adoption ratios were Norway and Spain. In Spain, international adoptions doubled between 1998 and 2000 and nearly tripled by 2004, making Spain the second-largest receiving country after the United States in terms of the actual number of international adoptions.[7] Other countries showing an above-average increase were Ireland, Italy, the Netherlands, and the United States.

Finally, new controversies have emerged such as the question of gay and lesbian adoption. Beginning in December 2000, international adoptive parents of Chinese children were required to sign a statement that they were not gay or lesbian. Chinese Center of Adoption Affairs regulations state that "foreign homosexuals are not allowed to adopt children in China."[8] In December 2001, China told U.S. adoption agencies that no more than 5 percent of their applicants could be unmarried. The sociologist Sara Dorow writes that "it is generally understood that the latter regulation is to further contain the placement of Chinese children with not just single but more specifically gay and lesbian parents."[9] In their 2009 anthology on international adoption, the gender and women's studies scholar Laura Briggs and the anthropologist Diana Marre observe, however, that "the ability of gay men and lesbians to adopt seems to be expanding within some countries—a third of the EU countries and South Africa now allow this practice—at the same time that it is contracting elsewhere, as conservative religious groups in the United States struggle to outlaw it."[10]

The devastating impacts of war and political instability create linkages between the contemporary landscape of international adoption and its historical origins in the post–World War II period. However, the new geographies of international adoption merit attention on their own terms. Thankfully, an emergent body of adoption studies scholarship has deepened our understanding of current practices.

While some of this pioneering work features specific Asian countries that send large numbers of adoptive children to the United States, such as Sara Dorow's *Transnational Adoption* on China and Eleana Kim's *Adopted Territory* featuring South Korea, other works chart the rise of other international adoption nations. Barbara Yngvesson's 2010 book *Belonging in an Adopted World* focuses on Sweden, which was the country in the late 1970s and early 1980s with the world's highest adoption rate.[11] In more recent times, Sweden continues to distinguish itself among receiving countries of internationally adopted children as the nation with the highest per capita population of transnational adoptees in the world.

Close friendships between the pioneer generation of Swedish adopters and child welfare advocates in India beginning in the 1960s transformed into the expansion of international adoption agency activity in India between the 1970s and 1980s. South Korea and Ethiopia are other major sending countries of adoptive children to Sweden. Yngvesson attributes the increase of international adoption in Sweden to the formation of the nonprofit organization Adoption Centre in 1972. Its organizational structure and policy for transnational adoption in Sweden—most notably its nonprofit status, procedural transparency, and government oversight—became a model for other nations.

In the late twentieth century, generations of internationally and transracially adopted children in Sweden have come of age. In the 1980s and 1990s, they challenged the widespread belief that racism does not exist in Sweden. Memoirs, performances, and research by Asian-Swedish and African-Swedish adult adoptees emphasized the significance of racial difference and racism in their lives, as well as their connection to immigrant populations in Sweden and other parts of the world. Their work illuminates the complex multiracial reality of contemporary societies in Europe.[12]

In contrast to the United States and Sweden, the history of international adoption in Spain is quite recent. It is a phenomenon that became significant in the mid-1990s. Diana Marre points to the repeated broadcasting of a 1995 British television program, "The Rooms of Death," about orphanages in China, which inspired humanitarian impulses to adopt. Furthermore, major social changes in the post-Franco dictatorship period beginning in 1975—such as the legalization of contraception in 1978, divorce in 1981, voluntary sterilization surgery in 1983, and abortion in 1985—contributed to a shortage of domestic children for adoption. Marre also notes that Spain's strong protection of biological parents' rights has discouraged domestic adoption. In the early twenty-first century, the Spanish Parliament vice president Maria Teresa Fernandez de la Vega observes that "almost everyone knows someone who cares for a child adopted in China, Russia, or Ukraine."[13]

Marre's research highlights how trends of international adoption and international immigration from outside of Europe became numerically and socially significant during the same period of the late 1990s, but she finds that the connections between these two trends are problematic. In addition to the different social and legal regulations for non-European immigrants and international adoptees, there are marked differences regarding the general attitude of the population toward both groups. As one teacher at a Barcelona primary school in an upper-class neighborhood told Marre, "We do not have immigrant children, we have children adopted internationally."[14] The general public perceives "different" children in lower-class neighborhoods as "immigrant children" and those in middle- and upper-class neighborhoods as "children adopted internationally." Marre describes the opinion toward internationally adopted children as "generally positive," while that toward immigrants can "vary widely."[15]

After the exponential growth of international adoption between 1998 and 2004, Peter Selman observed that a decrease in numbers in 2005 and 2006 affected many receiving countries, including Spain.[16] In the United States, this downturn made headlines. In 2007, an Associated Press news story reported:

> The number of foreign children adopted by Americans has dropped for the third year in a row, a consequence of tougher policies in the two countries—China and Russia—that over the past decade have provided the most children to U.S. families. . . . It's a dramatic change. The number of foreign adoptions has more than tripled since the early 1990s, reaching a peak of 22,884 in 2004 before dipping slightly in 2005, then falling to 20,679 in 2006.[17]

A 2008 *USA Today* story also highlighted that foreign adoptions by Americans dropped sharply: "The number of foreign children adopted by Americans fell 12 percent in the past year, reaching the lowest level since 1999 as some countries clamped down on the process and others battled with allegations of adoption fraud."[18]

However, current demographic trends cannot undo the Cold War history and legacy of international adoption in the United States in the second half of the twentieth century and the first few years of the new millennium. International adoption continues to influence the American experience through the presence of multiple social, educational, and entrepreneurial networks that serve global families, networks in which the history of Asian international adoption has played a formative role. For example, small groups founded by American parents of Korean adoptees in the late 1970s inspired the formation of one of the largest social networks, Families with Children from China (FCC).

In 1992, a few of the earliest adoptive parents of Chinese children met in New York's Chinatown to celebrate their new adoptions. Today the FCC is a nondenominational organization comprised of more than one hundred separate organizations across the United States, Canada, and the United Kingdom. The organizations provide a network of support for families who have adopted from China as well as information to prospective parents.[19] The anthropologist Toby Alice Volkman characterizes the FCC as a major force in shaping and sustaining "a sense of kinship and community beyond the family."[20] Another organization with a similar mission is Families with Children from Viet Nam (FCV). Founded in 1997, the FCV consists of local chapters from thirty-one states, the District of Columbia, and Toronto, Canada.[21]

Korean adult adoptees in Europe and the United States have also been a major force in creating a sense of community beyond the family. According to the anthropologist Eleana Kim, they have been organizing regionally since 1986 when eighteen-year-old Mattias Tjeder founded the Adopterade Koreaners Förening (Association of Adopted Koreans, AKF) in Stockholm, Sweden. When asked about the origins of the AKF, Tjeder explained that he had known only one other adoptee while growing up in the suburbs of Stockholm. His desire to learn more about his background led to meetings with a handful of other adoptees. This small network blossomed into an organization *for* Korean adoptees *run by* Korean adoptees that has since served over nine hundred members.[22]

Minnesota Adopted Koreans, founded in 1991, would become the first official Korean adoptee organization in the United States.[23] Since then, Korean adult adoptees have organized in various parts of the country. Four Korean adoptees founded the Association of Korean Adoptees—San Francisco in 1997. It aims to serve as a support group for adult Korean adoptees living in the San Francisco Bay Area.[24] The inaugural meeting of Korean Adoptees of Hawai'i (KAHI) was held in 2006. KAHI offers resources and services for its members who wish to explore their Korean heritage while also striving to raise awareness about their unique identity. It provides opportunities for Korean adoptees in Hawaii to connect with one another locally as well as with other adoptees on the mainland and internationally.[25]

Korean adult adoptees have also been at the forefront of creating organizations that serve the broader adoptee community and a pan-Asian adoptee community. For example, Also-Known-As began in May 1996 when a small group of Korean adoptees and friends in the New York metropolitan area planned a mentorship program for a new generation of international adoptees. Since then the outreach of the organization has expanded to recognize and celebrate "the community of people whose lives, through adoption, bridge nations, cultures and races."[26]

Based in Seattle, Asian Adult Adoptees of Washington (AAAW) provides mentoring and educational opportunities for Asian American and Pacific Islander adoptees. The AAAW began when a group of adult adoptees met informally over dinner in December 1996. At that time, there were resources for adopted children as well as teens, but no existing networks for adult adoptees in Washington. Out of this void, the AAAW formed to acknowledge the unique experiences of Asian adult adoptees as well as youth.[27]

Fueling the creation of international adoption networks is the Internet. Toby Alice Volkman notes that the Internet and adoption from China began to grow at approximately the same time. The collusion of these phenomena has resulted in highly specialized virtual networks for Chinese international adoptive families that geographically and intellectually expand traditional notions of family and community. As Volkman writes:

> By 2002, the two largest China adoption lists had a combined membership of over 13,000 subscribers, and more than 350 other lists were

devoted to more specialized interests, from *chinaboys* and *China Dads at Home* to born-again Christian lists. There are lists for those whose adoption dossier went to China in a particular month, and well over 100 lists for families with children adopted from the same orphanage or region. Members of orphanage lists may come to think of all children in their child's orphanage as siblings.[28]

The Internet has also played a central role in the development of Korean adoptee networks. Kim's ethnographic research revealed that Korean adoptees who were ambivalent about attending a face-to-face meeting with other adoptees used the Internet to search for adoptee stories. Learning about these experiences and available resources for adoptees inspired and prepared them to attend networking meetings.[29] After Minnesota Adopted Koreans dissolved in the late 1990s, its successor organization, AKConnection, utilized the Internet to recruit fellow Korean adoptees.

The Internet also facilitated community building among Filipino adult adoptees. The cofounders of the Filipino Adoptees Network (FAN), Lorial Crowder and Sharon Cuartero, thank the Internet for bringing them together and for inspiring the creation of a FAN website. The website aims to provide an online community that was unavailable to Filipino adoptees when Crowder and Cuartero were growing up. Launched in January 2005, FAN is the first web-based organization to provide support and resources for Filipino adoptees and their families.[30]

Listservs and blogs, however, have not supplanted the role of print media in creating and sustaining Asian international adoption communities. The nonprofit quarterly newspaper *Korean Quarterly* features writing by and about the Korean American community within the Twin Cities and the upper Midwest. The staff, contributors, and advisory board define the Korean American community to include "first and second generation Korean Americans and their families (including non-Korean family members), adopted Koreans and their families, and bi-racial/bi-cultural Korean American people."[31] Its premiere issue, entitled "Who We Are," was published in Fall 1997. The commemoration of "50 Years of Korean Adoption" was the focal point of the Fall 2005 issue. However, every issue has included feature stories, reviews, and/or interviews with Korean adoptees, presenting them as central, as opposed to token, members of the Korean American community.

In 1993, Brian Boyd, the father of two Korean adopted children, founded Yeong & Yeong Book Company, which specializes in publishing books on Asian international adoption. He felt that his Korean-born daughters needed a book about their lives in Korea before coming to their new family. The resulting book, *When You Were Born in Korea: A Memory Book for Children Adopted from Korea*, led to the creation of a similar title, *When You Were Born in China*, followed by *When You Were Born in Vietnam*. The books were published as fund-raisers, and a portion of their proceeds supports adoption agencies in Korea, China, and Vietnam. Since the early 1990s, Yeong & Yeong has published and/or distributed fifteen books related to Asian international adoption. Other books feature collected letters and stories by Korean birth mothers; prose, poetry, photography, and art by Asian adoptees; and essays by adoptive parents. These books also contribute royalties to adoption-related organizations based in Asia and the United States.[32]

The rise of Chinese international adoption in the United States led to the publication of *Mei Magazine*, a quarterly publication in Florida that since 1999 features issues specific to Chinese adoptees between the ages of seven to fourteen. The magazine's website emphasizes the unique identities and broad kinship of Asian adoptees: "Mei girls need to see themselves and each other in print! They deserve a forum where they can share in their special sisterhood."[33]

Although the magazine's main audience stems from the more recent phenomenon of Chinese international adoption since the late 1980s, the personal history of Amanda Baden, an advisor and regular columnist for *Mei Magazine*, connects the magazine with the earlier history of Chinese international adoption from Hong Kong. Baden's transracial adoption from Hong Kong by a couple of mixed faith and ethnic backgrounds was arranged by the ISS-USA in the late 1960s.[34] Baden was a committee member for the first Chinese Adult Adoptee Worldwide Reunion, which was held in Hong Kong in 2010.[35] Today, she is an associate professor in the Counseling Program at Montclair State University, and she has published extensively in the areas of counseling, adoption, race, and culture.

As these personal, virtual, and print networks shape a broader sense of community and kinship, they create an audience and niche market for what the sociologist Heather Jacobson has called "culture keeping." Jacobson defines culture keeping as the process through which adoptive parents attempt to ensure that their internationally adopted children have access to the culture of their national origins.[36] Culture keeping, Jacobson observes, is a standard practice in the adoption world. Both real and virtual encounters inspire, facilitate, and sustain culture-keeping industries. As Jacobson writes:

> International-adoptive parents are often told by the adoption community that their children *should* engage in their native cultures; some are told that they *must*. In adoption agency materials, on electronic mailing lists, and in memoirs, support groups, advice books, educational workshops, and conference presentations, culture keeping is framed as a mechanism for facilitating a solid ethnic identity and sense of self-worth in children who may experience difficulties because of their racial, ethnic, and adoptive statuses.[37]

Culture or heritage camps aimed at international adoptees and their families make up one major culture-keeping industry. Given the longer history of Korean international adoption, camps for Korean adoptees and their adoptive families are the most numerous. The Korean American Adoptee Adoptive Family Network (KAAN) is an organization that aims to build strong connections among adoptees, birth and adoptive families, Koreans, and Korean Americans primarily through a national conference held annually in a different city in the United States. KAAN's website also attempts to facilitate these connections by featuring Korean programs such as culture camps. It lists twenty-eight Korean culture camps in New York, Wisconsin, New Jersey, Indiana, North Carolina, Pennsylvania, Illinois, Washington, D.C., Maryland, Virginia, Michigan, Oregon, Nebraska, Iowa, Utah, Ohio, Oklahoma, Kentucky, and Massachusetts.[38] While some of these camps are open to other children of Korean heritage (such as second-generation Korean Americans), most of them are exclusively for Korean adopted children and their adoptive families.

The nonprofit organization Heritage Camps for Adoptive Families began in Colorado in 1991 with a summer heritage camp for sixty families with children adopted from Korea. It currently offers eleven different camps that reflect the diversity and growth of international adoption in the United States.[39] Ten camps are for families with internationally adopted children from the African Caribbean, Cambodia, China, the Philippines, India, Nepal, Latin America, Eastern Europe, and Vietnam.

In global family making, it is not just the potential of niche markets that we should pay attention to, however. What is just as important is that these personal, virtual, and print networks create politicized individuals and organizations that are critical about the global inequalities and the sociopolitical blind spots that persist in international adoption. These activists have called for attention to the significance of birth families in discussions about international adoption, the social reality of *adult* adoptees, and the ties that bind international adoptees to immigrants.

In a June 12, 2012, letter, Kate Mee-Hee Sands, the president of AdopSource, and Jennifer Kwon Dobbs and Bert Ballard, the codirectors of Adoptee Rights and Equality, together with twenty-two organizations and thirty individuals wrote a passionate plea to President Barack Obama about the deportation of Kairi Shepherd, an Indian adoptee with advanced multiple sclerosis, characterizing the issuance of deportation as a "death sentence."[40] Shepherd had been convicted of check fraud for which she had served her time, but she was also a noncitizen. Although she was adopted in the United States when she was three months old, under the Child Citizenship Act she is ineligible for automatic U.S. citizenship because she turned eighteen before February 27, 2001. Her mother had died of breast cancer before she could submit Kairi's naturalization application.

According to the authors, Kairi's case is not a singular one. They pointed to forty additional cases of deported or detained adult adoptees as reported in the media and to overseas postadoption service nongovernmental organizations with all forty cases involving nonviolent offenses. The authors highlighted the stark contradiction between contemporary U.S. immigration policy and its history of international adoption by emphasizing the role of humanitarian rescue efforts in U.S. adoption history:

> Mr. President, how can America break up families like Kairi's and others on account of the CCA's age limit? Does love have an expiration date? As adoptee community leaders and allies, we write to express our great

concern about the inhumanity of Kairi's situation and to request the immediate withdrawal of her immigration charges and those of other adult adoptees who are detained and facing possible removal. . . .

America leads the world in numbers of orphaned children received who become their adoptive parents' legally recognized children and heirs. The vast majority were transported to the U.S. as infants or toddlers and arrived home through post-1953 agency-sponsored programs or were airlifted out via military humanitarian operations such as Babylift from South Vietnam and Peter Pan from Cuba. America's long-standing recognition of the special plight of orphans has also led to the removal of policies that slowed down or acted as barriers to intercountry adoptions out of the belief that expedient placement in loving homes is in children's best interests. Through no fault of their own, not all of these adopted children became citizens under pre-CCA guidelines, or their adoptions were disrupted and they "fell through the cracks."[41]

In the twenty-first century, the ISS-USA continues to participate in these critical discussions about the best interests of children, adults, and families separated by international borders. It continues to do work in international adoption by conducting intercountry home studies and postplacement reports for the purposes of placing children in homes overseas and certifying intercountry home studies for the purpose of international adoption. However, international adoption is no longer its main focus. Other key service areas include providing repatriation assistance to U.S. citizens in times of personal or global crises; locating and reuniting families across international borders; and carrying out document searches.

The ISS-USA continues to publish newsletters and annual reports, but like many other organizations, it also has used the Internet to publicize its positions on recent controversial issues. For example, an ISS-USA blog post featured a 2010 position paper on international adoption and the crisis in Haiti. Referring to its social service experience throughout the twentieth century, the ISS-USA recalled that "in general, international adoption should not take place in a situation of war or natural disaster, given that these events make it impossible to verify the personal and family situation of children."[42] The organization acknowledged that multiple adoption dossiers were in the process of being finalized before the earthquake. Yet, remaining true to its social service principles, it encouraged the various actors involved in international adoption to exercise restraint and reflection, in particular, regarding the sensitive issue of the adoption of these children when managing the current crisis.

* * *

Given the vibrancy of the communities formed through Asian international adoption, the field of Asian American Studies must include adoptee experiences in its teaching, research, and professional service. From its historical origins in the late 1960s, Asian American Studies has focused on the histories, cultural expressions, and contemporary concerns of Asians in North America. Although seminal Asian American history texts to date have not included the history of Asian international adoption, an emergent critical mass of new scholarship is contesting this absence. Recent books and scholarly articles by Gregory Paul Choy, Sara Dorow, David Eng, Mark Jerng, Eleana Kim, Josephine Lee, Richard Lee, Andrea Louie, Jiannbin Lee Shiao, and Mia Tuan as well as my own work aim to reach audiences within Asian American Studies as well as adoption studies.[43]

In the 2011 anthology *Asian American Plays for a New Generation*, edited by Josephine Lee, Don Eitel, and R. A. Shiomi, plays about Korean adoptees that have been produced by Theatre Mu in Minneapolis, Minnesota, take center stage. As Lee writes in the introduction:

> The prevailing sensibility that Minnesota is "white" is belied by the large concentrations of Hmong and Korean adoptees, both constituencies fairly new to claiming "Asian American" identity. What is produced by way of theatre registers these distinctions. Mu's first production, *Mask Dance*, featured the stories of young Korean adoptees raised in Minnesota. This focus on adoptees, many of whom grew up as the only non-white individuals in their rural communities, departs radically from an understanding of Asian American stories as centered on immigrant families. These differences in the imagining of "Asian America" cannot be dismissed as just a set of quaint regional distinctions. Titling a play *Walleye Kid* has relevance beyond associating transracial adoption with

a notably Minnesota fish; it emphasizes the *prominence of the adoptee in refiguring what "Asian American" is*. Racial isolation is an experience familiar to many in the Midwest, so much so that it should be thought of as paradigmatic rather than a peripheral part of Asian American experience.[44]

In their 2011 book *Choosing Ethnicity, Negotiating Race: Korean Adoptees in America*, the education studies scholar Mia Tuan and the sociologist Jiannbin Lee Shiao compare the experience of Korean adoptees to the experience of Asian Americans. They conclude:

> A part and yet apart, Korean adoptees are bound to other Asian Americans because of their race and, as a result, have overlapping experiences. However, their unique life and family circumstances make them a different type of Asian American: they harbor greater expectations for social acceptance from white people and experience greater disappointment when that acceptance is not forthcoming.[45]

The leadership of Korean adoptee artists and scholars has been pivotal in making Asian adoptee concerns integral to the field of Asian American Studies. Deann Borshay Liem's former position as the executive director of the National Asian American Telecommunications Association (now named the Center for Asian American Media) undoubtedly contributed to the organization's showcasing of films about international adoption, such as *Wo Ai Ni Mommy*, *In the Matter of Cha Jung Hee*, and *Passing Through*, through development funding; screenings at its annual Asian American International Film Festival in San Francisco; and distribution to educational institutions as well as the general public. "Adoption" is a featured subject area of its catalog of videos and DVDs.

In sum, the crossover between Asian American Studies and adoption studies has begun, enriching Asian American Studies while insisting on and maintaining the unique and autonomous identity of Asian adoptees. The Association for Asian American Studies (AAAS) features an Asian Adoptee section. A Korean adoptee named Kim Park Nelson, the coauthor of *Here: A Visual History of Adopted Koreans in Minnesota* and a department chair of American Multicultural Studies at Minnesota

State University, Moorhead, founded the section in 2007. At the annual meetings of the AAAS, scholarly panels have featured recent research on Asian adoptee issues.

This scholarship should be used to expand as well as to complicate Asian American history's chronological and geographical scope and its major historical actors. Specifically, this book engages in that conversation by showcasing how the post–World War II and Cold War periods created the foundation for the multigenerational Asian adoptee community of the twenty-first century and why it is important to view this history from the perspectives of its diverse participants: international social workers in the receiving and sending countries, independent adoption advocates, adoptive and birth parents, and the adoptees themselves.

Finally, this learning process must go both ways. Adoptive parents, policy makers, and social welfare workers need not solely turn to Asian heritages as resources for adopted children. Like the Asian adoptee undergraduates who ventured into my Asian American Studies courses in the late 1990s, they should also consider how Asian adoptees in the United States are part of a growing and increasingly diverse Asian American community in the United States and a part of an Asian American history that is centuries old. As a result, their heritages are multiple. They are Asian adoptees, but they are also adopted Asian Americans.

INTRODUCTION

1. "International adoption" is the current popular term used to describe the phenomenon of adoption across national borders. In the 1950s and 1960s, social workers commonly referred to this phenomenon as "intercountry" adoption. Recently, some scholars of international adoption have preferred to use the term "transnational adoption" in order to emphasize the ways that the phenomenon creates a significant social field between two or more specific nation-states. See, for example, Barbara Yngvesson, *Belonging in an Adopted World: Race, Identity, and Transnational Adoption* (Chicago: University of Chicago Press, 2010); Eleana Kim, *Adopted Territory: Transnational Korean Adoptees and the Politics of Belonging* (Durham: Duke University Press, 2010); Sara K. Dorow, *Transnational Adoption: A Cultural Economy of Race, Gender, and Kinship* (New York: NYU Press, 2006); and Toby Alice Volkman, ed., *Cultures of Transnational Adoption* (Durham: Duke University Press, 2005).

2. Michelle Knoll and Nicole Muehlhausen, "Local Korean Adoptee Reunited with Birth Mother after 37 Years," KSTP-TV—Minneapolis and St. Paul, February 6, 2009, available at http://kstp.com/news/stories/S768458.shtml?cat=206 (accessed October 1, 2009). The author Jae Ran Kim writes that "while we do not have exact numbers of how many of us are adopted Koreans, we do know that since the mid-1950s, an estimated 13,000 to 15,000 South Korean children have been adopted to families in Minnesota." See Jae Ran Kim, "Foreword," in Kim Jackson and Heewon Lee with Jae Ran Kim, Kim Park Nelson, and Wing Young Huie, *Here: A Visual History of Adopted Koreans in Minnesota* (St. Paul, Minn.: Yeong & Yeong Book Company, 2010), 10. In her 2010 book *Adopted Territory*, Eleana Kim notes that "Minnesota is home to more than ten thousand Korean adoptees and has the highest number per capita of adoptees in the nation" (110). And, according to Erika Lee, the director of the University of Minnesota's Asian American Studies Program, "Minnesota social service agencies were very active in the adoption network through the state's missionary connections in Asia, and over 10,000 Korean adoptees came to the state. It is estimated that 50 percent or more of the Korean population in Minnesota is adopted." See Erika Lee, "Asian American Studies in the Midwest: New

Questions, Approaches, and Communities," *Journal of Asian American Studies* (October 2009): 247–273.

3. "International Adoption Facts," the Evan B. Donaldson Adoption Institute, available at http://www.adoptioninstitute.org/FactOverview/international.html (accessed May 16, 2012).

4. Michelle Tauber, "World's Most Beautiful Family: At Play in the Desert of Namibia, the Jolie-Pitt Clan (and Baby-to-Be!) Simply Dazzle," *People* 65, no. 18, May 8, 2006, available at http://www.people.com/people/archive/article/0,,20062187,00.html (accessed May 16, 2012).

5. Luchina Fisher, "Katherine Heigl Adopting Korean Girl: Heigl Joins Madonna and Angelina Jolie in Adopting Child Overseas," *ABC News*, September 10, 2009, available at http://abcnews.go.com/Entertainment/katherine-heigl-adopting-korean-girl/story?id=8536170 (accessed May 16, 2012).

6. Andy Newman, "Journey from a Chinese Orphanage to a Jewish Rite of Passage," *New York Times*, March 8, 2007, available at http://www.nytimes.com/2007/03/08/nyregion/08batmitzvah.html?_r=2&pagewanted=1 (accessed May 16, 2012).

7. Mi Ok Song Bruining, "A Few Words from Another Left-Handed Adopted Korean Lesbian," in *Seeds from a Silent Tree: An Anthology by Korean Adoptees*, ed. Tonya Bishoff and Jo Rankin (San Diego: Pandal Press, 1997), 66.

8. See Dorow, *Transnational Adoption*, 37–38.

9. Barbara Demick, "Some Chinese Parents Say Their Babies Were Stolen for Adoption," *Los Angeles Times*, September 20, 2009, available at http://articles.latimes.com/2009/sep/20/world/fg-china-adopt20 (accessed May 16, 2012).

10. For example, the Korean Studies scholar Tobias Hubinette writes that "contemporary international adoption, which has seen at least half a million children flown in to Western countries during a period of 50 years, has so many parallels to the transatlantic slave trade . . . and to present day's massive trafficking of non-Western women for international marriage and sexual exploitation" (Hubinette, *Comforting an Orphaned Nation: Representations of International Adoption and Adopted Koreans in Korean Popular Culture* [Jimoondang, Seoul: Korean Studies Series, No. 32, 2006], 17).

11. Adam Pertman, *Adoption Nation: How the Adoption Revolution Is Transforming America* (New York: Basic Books, 2000). In addition to Yngvesson, *Belonging in an Adopted World*; Kim, *Adopted Territory*; Dorow, *Transnational Adoption*; Hubinette, *Comforting an Orphaned Nation*; and Volkman, *Cultures of Transnational Adoption*, some of the recent book-length studies that document historical shifts in international adoption include Barbara Melosh, *Strangers and Kin: The American Way of Adoption* (Cambridge: Harvard University Press, 2002); Ellen Herman, *Kinship by Design: A History of Adoption in the Modern United States* (Chicago: University of Chicago Press, 2008); Heather Jacobson, *Culture Keeping: White Mothers, International Adoption, and the Negotiation of Family Difference* (Nashville, Tenn.: Vanderbilt University Press, 2008); Diana Marre and Laura Briggs, eds., *International Adoption: Global Inequalities and the*

Circulation of Children (New York: NYU Press, 2009); Karen Dubinsky, *Babies without Borders: Adoption and Migration across the Americas* (New York: NYU Press, 2010); and Laura Briggs, *Somebody's Children: The Politics of Transracial and Transnational Adoption* (Durham: Duke University Press, 2012).

In the study of the history of Asian international adoption, the exception in the scholarly literature is the emergent critical mass of research on the history of Korean international adoption. In addition to Kim's *Adopted Territory* and Hubinette's *Comforting an Orphaned Nation*, see Arissa Oh, "A New Kind of Missionary Work: Christians, Christian Americanists, and the Adoption of Korean GI Babies, 1955–1961," *Women's Studies Quarterly* 33, nos. 3 and 4 (Fall/Winter 2005): 161–188; Catherine Ceniza Choy, "Institutionalizing International Adoption: The Historical Origins of Korean Adoption in the United States," in *International Korean Adoption: A Fifty-Year History of Policy and Practice*, ed. Kathleen Ja Sook Bergquist, M. Elizabeth Vonk, Dong Soo Kim, and Marvin D. Feit (Binghamton, N.Y.: Haworth Press, 2007), 25–42; and Eleana Kim, "The Origins of Korean Adoption: Cold War Geopolitics and Intimate Diplomacy," WP 09-09 (Washington, D.C.: U.S.-Korea Institute at SAIS Working Paper Series, 2009), 1–26. Recent dissertations on the history of Korean international adoption include Arissa Hyun Jung Oh, "Into the Arms of America: The Korean Roots of International Adoption" (Ph.D. diss., University of Chicago, 2008); Susie Woo, "A New American Comes 'Home': Race, Nation, and the Immigration of Korean War Adoptees, 'GI Babies,' and Brides" (Ph.D. diss., Yale University, 2008); Soojin Pate, "Genealogies of Korean Adoption: American Empire, Militarization, and Yellow Desire," (Ph.D. diss., University of Minnesota, 2010); and Bongsoo Park, "Intimate Encounters, Racial Frontiers: Stateless GI Babies in South Korea and the United States, 1953–1965" (Ph.D. diss., University of Minnesota, 2010).

12. A notable exception is Mike Mullen, "Identity Development of Korean Adoptees," in *Reviewing Asian America: Locating Diversity*, ed. Wendy L. Ng, Soo-Young Chin, James S. Moy, and Gary Y. Okihiro (Pullman: Washington State University Press, 1995), 61–74.

13. See, for example, Nam Soon Huh and William J. Reid, "Intercountry, Transracial Adoption and Ethnic Identity: A Korean Example," *International Social Work* 43, no. 1 (2000): 75–87; Kevin L. Wickes and John R. Slate, "Transracial Adoption of Koreans: A Preliminary Study of Adjustment," *International Journal for the Advancement of Counselling* 19 (1996): 187–195; Herma J. M. Versluis-den Bieman and Frank C. Verhulst, "Self-Reported and Parent-Reported Problems in Adolescent International Adoptees," *Journal of Child Psychology and Psychiatry* 36, no. 8 (1995): 1411–1428; Wun Jung Kim, "International Adoption: A Case Review of Korean Children," *Child Psychiatry and Human Development* 25, no. 3 (Spring 1995): 141–154; and Nguyen My Lien, Knarig Katchadurian Meyer, and Myron Winick, "Early Malnutrition and 'Late' Adoption: A Study of Their Effects on the Development of Korean Orphans Adopted into American Families," *American Journal of Clinical Nutrition* 30 (October 1977): 1734–1739.

14. Eleana Kim further critiques psychology and social work outcome studies, which, she writes, "have thus far dominated transnational adoption as a field. These studies attempted to measure the mental health or 'adjustment' of children and adolescents adopted transracially and transnationally, and they are limited by their tendency to disembed the phenomenon of transnational adoption from its relevant historical, social, and political contexts. . . . The majority of these studies, for the most part based on samples of one hundred or fewer, determined that transnational adoptees are no different from and sometimes are better adjusted than domestic adoptees, as well as in comparison to nonadopted siblings. The power of these findings as 'expert knowledge' is often mobilized to support the so-called positive view of transracial adoption, despite problematic assumptions, methods, and measures" (Kim, *Adopted Territory*, 9). Kim cites Howard Altstein and Rita Simon's book *Adoption across Borders: Serving the Children in Transracial and Inter-country Adoptions* (published by Rowman and Littlefield in 2000) for an overview of these studies.

    In the past decade, Asian American Studies scholars have influenced the field of psychology by creating a new body of knowledge about international and transracial adoption that takes into account the unique racial and ethnic experiences of Asian Americans. A noteworthy example is the research of Richard Lee, a professor of psychology and Asian American Studies at the University of Minnesota. Some of his recent publications include R. M. Lee, K. O. Seol, M. Y. Sung, M. J. Miller, and the Minnesota International Adoption Project Team, "The Behavioral Development of Korean Children in Institutional Care and International Adoptive Families," *Developmental Psychology* 46 (2010): 468–478; R. M. Lee, A. B. Yun, H. C. Yoo, and K. Park Nelson, "Comparing the Ethnic Identity and Well-being of Adopted Korean Americans with Immigrant/U.S.-born Korean Americans and Korean International Students," *Adoption Quarterly* 13 (2010): 2–17; and R. M. Lee and the Minnesota International Adoption Project Team, "Perceived Parental Discrimination as a Post-Adoption Risk Factor in Internationally Adopted Children and Adolescents," *Cultural Diversity and Ethnic Minority Psychology* 16 (2010): 493–500.

15. The University of Minnesota Libraries' finding aid of the ISS-USA records, which was written by Jon Davidann and revised by Linnea M. Anderson, provides a collection summary and detailed descriptions of the records. It is available at http://special.lib.umn.edu/findaid/xml/sw0109.xml (accessed June 1, 2012).

16. In 1957, the letterhead of the ISS headquarters stationery read as follows: "For inter-country service in adoptions and individual and family problems." Kimi Tamura to Susan T. Pettiss, October 31, 1957, International Social Service, American branch (hereafter, ISS-USA) papers, Box 12, File 7, Social Welfare History Archives (hereafter, SWHA), Minneapolis, Minn.

17. Akira Iriye, "Internationalizing International History," in *Rethinking American History in a Global Age*, ed. Thomas Bender (Berkeley: University of California Press, 2002), 60.

18. Eleana Kim, "Wedding Citizenship and Culture: Korean Adoptees and the Global Family of Korea," in *Cultures of Transnational Adoption*, ed. Toby Alice Volkman (Durham: Duke University Press, 2005), 49–80.

19. On the history of matching in U.S. adoption, see chapter 5, " 'The Best' or 'Good Enough'? Child-Placing Professionals, Adoptive Parents, and Definitions of Family, 1920–1950," in Julie Berebitsky, *Like Our Very Own: Adoption and the Changing Culture of Motherhood, 1851–1950* (Lawrence: University of Kansas Press, 2000), 128–165; chapter 2, "Families by Design: 'Fitness' and 'Fit' in the Creation of Kin," in Melosh, *Strangers and Kin*, 51–104; and chapter 4, "Matching and the Mirror of Nature," in Herman, *Kinship by Design*, 121–154.

20. Hung Cam Thai, *For Better or for Worse: Vietnamese International Marriages in the New Global Economy* (New Brunswick: Rutgers University Press, 2008).

21. Felicity Amaya Schaeffer, *Love and Empire: Cybermarriage and Citizenship across the Americas* (New York: NYU Press, 2012).

22. Richard H. Weil, "International Adoptions: The Quiet Migration," *International Migration Review* 18, no. 2 (Summer 1984): 276–293. For a broad range of artistic work by and about Asian American international and transracial adoptees, see Jane Jeong Trenka, Julia Chinyere Oparah, and Sung Yung Shin, eds., *Outsiders Within: Writing on Transracial Adoption* (Cambridge, Mass.: South End Press, 2006). *Outsiders Within* was translated into Korean and published in Seoul by KoRoot Press in 2012. Most anthologies feature writing by and about Korean adoptees. In addition to the 1997 publication of *Seeds from a Silent Tree: An Anthology by Korean Adoptees*, edited by Tonya Bishoff and Jo Rankin, see Susan Soon-Keum Cox, ed., *Voices from Another Place: A Collection of Works from a Generation Born in Korea and Adopted to Other Countries* (St. Paul, Minn.: Yeong & Yeong Book Company, 1999); Dr. Sook Wilkinson and Nancy Fox, eds., *After the Morning Calm: Reflections of Korean Adoptees* (Bloomfield Hills, Mich.: Sunrise Ventures, 2002); and Ellen Lee, Marilyn Lammert, and Mary Anne Hess, *Once They Hear My Name: Korean Adoptees and Their Journeys toward Identity* (Silver Spring, Md.: Tamarisk, 2008).

CHAPTER 1

1. See E. Wayne Carp, *Family Matters: Secrecy and Disclosure in the History of Adoption* (Cambridge: Harvard University Press, 1998), 33–34; Christina Klein, *Cold War Orientalism: Asia in the Middlebrow Imagination, 1945–1961* (Berkeley: University of California Press, 2003), 174–179; and Ellen Herman, *Kinship by Design: A History of Adoption in the Modern United States* (Chicago: University of Chicago Press, 2008), 215–217. The Korean "mascots" refer to the children whom GI units took under their wings, providing them with clothing, food, and candy. For a discussion of the adoption of Korean War military mascots in relation to Korean international adoption, see Arissa Oh, "Into the Arms of America: The Korean Roots of International Adoption" (Ph.D. dissertation, University of Chicago, 2008), 62–78; Eleana Kim, *Adopted Territory: Transnational Korean Adoptees and the Politics of Belonging*

(Durham: Duke University Press, 2010), 45, 47–53; and Susie Woo, "A New American Comes 'Home': Race, Nation, and the Immigration of Korean War Adoptees, 'GI Babies,' and Brides" (Ph.D. dissertation, Yale University, 2010), 57–59, 68–69.

2. According to U.S. Immigration and Naturalization Service data, American families adopted 10,099 children from Europe between 1948 and 1962, including 3,116 children from Greece, 2,575 children from Italy, and 1,845 children from Germany. Richard H. Weil, "International Adoptions: The Quiet Migration," *International Migration Review* 18, no. 2 (Summer 1984): 280–281.

3. From D. Dodds, Hqs. to ISS-Austria, Far East (Japan and Korea), Germany, Greece, Italy—for replies, all other branches for information and comments, April 25, 1957, International Social Service, American branch (hereafter, ISS-USA) papers, Box 10, File on "Children 1954–62, Intercountry Adoption General," Social Welfare History Archives (hereafter, SWHA), Minneapolis, Minn.

4. International Social Service, American Branch, Inc., "Nationality and Location of Foreign Children in Need of Adoptive Homes in the U.S.," ISS-USA papers, Box 11, File on "Adoption Manual and Other Printed Material," SWHA.

5. For sociohistorical accounts of interracial romance and marriage, see Paul Spickard, *Mixed Blood : Intermarriage and Ethnic Identity in Twentieth-Century America* (Madison: University of Wisconsin Press, 1989); and Ji-Yeon Yuh, *Beyond the Shadow of Camptown: Korean Military Brides in America* (New York: NYU Press, 2002). See Gina Marchetti, *Romance and the "Yellow Peril": Race, Sex, and Discursive Strategies in Hollywood Fiction* (Berkeley: University of California Press, 1993); Klein, *Cold War Orientalism*; and Naoko Shibusawa, *America's Geisha Ally: Reimagining the Japanese Enemy* (Cambridge: Harvard University Press, 2006) on the theme of Asian-U.S. interracial intimacy in cultural productions.

6. *Sayonara*, videorecording, directed by Joshua Logan (Beverly Hills, Calif.: MGM Home Entertainment, 2001), 147 minutes.

7. Elizabeth Anne Hemphill, *The Least of These: Miki Sawada and Her Children* (New York: Weatherhill, 1980), 80. In her book *Trans-Pacific Racisms and the U.S. Occupation of Japan* (New York: Columbia University Press, 1999), the historian Yukiko Koshiro begins chapter 5 on "The Problem of Miscegenation" with a description of the same radio announcement. According to Koshiro, "The announcer called the baby a symbol of love and friendship between Japan and the United States: 'a rainbow across the Pacific' " (159).

8. The American media called babies born of American fathers and Japanese mothers "Occupation babies" and "half-half babies" (Koshiro, *Trans-Pacific Racisms*, 161). According to the historian Arissa Oh, the popularity of the term "GI babies" "reflected both the dominance of Americans in the Korean imagination after the Korean War and the fact that Americans represented the majority of the foreign troop presence in Korea" ("Into the Arms of America," 36).

9. Ruth Moynihan, "Inter-racial Adoption," *Marriage Magazine* (May 1965), p. 11, ISS-USA papers, Box 12, File on "Children: Newspaper Clippings of Child Welfare Issues," SWHA.

10. Kaji Onose, "Giving Children a New Start in Life," *Yomiuri Japan News*, May 10, 1958, p. 8, ISS-USA papers, Box 12, File on "Children: Newspaper Clippings of Child Welfare Issues," SWHA.

11. Norman M. Lobsenz, "The Sins of the Fathers," *Redbook* (April 1956), pp. 22, 26, ISS-USA papers, Box 12, File on "Children: Newspaper Clippings of Child Welfare Issues," SWHA. The exception to Lobsenz's observation about no external sign was the plight of mixed-race children who had been born to African American servicemen and German women. Yukiko Koshiro delineates similarities between the problems of miscegenation that West German and Japanese societies faced in the 1940s and 1950s. As in Japan, public attitudes toward mixed-race German and African American children displayed overlapping prejudices against the mothers' backgrounds, enemy occupation forces, and mixed-race people (Koshiro, *Trans-Pacific Racisms*, 183, 272).

12. Lobsenz, "The Sins of the Fathers," 22.

13. See Catherine Ceniza Choy, "Race at the Center: The History of American Cold War Asian Adoption," *Journal of American-East Asian Relations* 16, no. 3 (2009): 1–20. Susie Woo makes similar observations about the South Korean situation in Woo, "A New American Comes 'Home,' " 215–219.

14. These homes for mixed-race children were established in Japan in the late 1940s. Japanese welfare agencies and Japanese people sent mixed-race babies to these homes, which were mainly Christian institutions, believing that Occupation authorities and the "foreigners' religion" were responsible for these children (Koshiro, *Trans-Pacific Racisms*, 162–163). Robert A. Fish's dissertation provides a different perspective of the situation of mixed-race children in Japan. Fish attempts to dispel what he calls "the myth of mixed-blood children as an ostracized group" by tracing the life courses of the children who grew up in the home. According to Fish, "over one thousand of the children in the Home grew up to be productive, functioning adult members of Japanese society." He argues that "neither racism nor oppression defined the lives of this group." See Fish, "The Heiress and the Love Children: Sawada Miki and the Elizabeth Saunders Home for Mixed-Blood Orphans in Postwar Japan" (Ph.D. dissertation, University of Hawai'i, 2002), 3, xii.

15. Lobsenz, "The Sins of the Fathers," 30.

16. See Susan T. Pettiss to Rosalind Giles, April 5, 1957, ISS-USA papers, Box 10, File on "Children 1954–65, Adoption Plans of Racially Mixed Children," SWHA; International Social Service-American Branch, Inc., "Meeting of Child Welfare Expert, Intercountry Adoptions," January 31, 1963, pp. 1–6, ISS-USA papers, Box 10, File on "Children-Intercountry Adoption Conferences and Workshops," SWHA.

17. Susan T. Pettiss to Rosalind Giles, April 5, 1957, ISS-USA papers, Box 10, File on "Children 1954–65, Adoption Plans of Racially Mixed Children," SWHA.

18. Koshiro, *Trans-Pacific Racisms*, 178.

19. Era Bell Thompson, "Japan's Rejected," *Ebony* (1967), pp. 44, 46, ISS-USA papers, Box 12, File on "Children: Newspaper Clippings of Child Welfare Issues," SWHA. The actual numbers of mixed-race children in Japan and Korea were difficult to

obtain, and they fluctuated widely depending on who reported them. Sawada Miki of the Elizabeth Saunders Home estimated that the number was around two hundred thousand, while the estimate given by Takada Masami, the chief of the Children's Bureau of Japan's Welfare Ministry, was around one hundred fifty thousand. A 1952 census on the numbers of mixed-race children by the Children's Bureau gave a final, significantly smaller count, of 5,002. See Koshiro, *Trans-Pacific Racisms*, 164. Susie Woo writes that the U.S. media exaggerated the numbers of mixed-race children in Korea. In 1964, *Time* magazine estimated that 20,000 mixed-race children resided in South Korea, whereas the Korean newspaper *Chosun Shinmun* placed the number at 12,280. Culling statistics from various sources, Woo estimates that, between 1950 and 1965, 3,500 to 3,600 mixed-race Korean and American babies entered the United States as the sons and daughters of "predominantly white, middle-class families." See Woo, "A New American Comes 'Home,'" 16–17, 138, 152–153. However, the attention given to the mixed-race population exceeded its numerical significance because of its symbolic importance for U.S.-Asian foreign relations and Asian and American national identities.

20. Susan T. Pettiss to Rosalind Giles, April 5, 1957, ISS-USA papers, Box 10, File on "Children 1954–65, Adoption Plans of Racially Mixed Children," SWHA.

21. Daniel Quinn to Elizabeth Nicholky, Susan Pettiss, Ann Rabinowitz, Richard Smith, Ann S. Potluck, and Rita Deutsch, December 9, 1958, ISS-USA papers, Box 10, File on "Children-Intercountry Adoption Conferences and Workshops," SWHA.

22. Susan T. Pettiss, "Effect of Adoption of Foreign Children on U.S. Adoption Standards and Practices," *Child Welfare* (July 1958), ISS-USA papers, Box 11, File on "Adoption Manual and Other Printed Material," SWHA.

23. Department of Defense Office of Armed Forces Information and Education, "Manual on Intercountry Adoption," 1959, p. 4, ISS-USA papers, Box 12, File on "Children: Newspaper Clippings of Child Welfare Issues," SWHA.

24. Lobsenz, "The Sins of the Fathers," 22.

25. Thompson, "Japan's Rejected," 46.

26. Margaret A. Valk, "Adjustment of Korean-American Children in Their American Adoptive Homes," paper presented at the 1957 National Conference on Social Welfare, p. 2, ISS-USA papers, Box 10, File on "Adjustment of Foreign Children in Their Adoptive Homes," SWHA. Yukiko Koshiro notes that the U.S. ambassador to Japan Robert Murphy and the esteemed writer James Michener, author of *Sayonara*, shared similar views that attributed Japanese racism to primitive beliefs about Japanese homogeneity. See Koshiro, *Trans-Pacific Racisms*, 196–198. Susie Woo observes that publicized statements made by Harry Holt and Pearl Buck in the 1950s about the abysmal situation of mixed-race Korean and American children also presented Korean people as backwards and inhumane. See Woo, "A New American Comes 'Home,' " 151–152.

27. The historian Tara Zahra poignantly reminds us that the post–World War II reconstruction of Europe was comprised of nationalist movements that were

"brutally gendered." It entailed rituals of public humiliation and the passage of new crimes of "offending national honor" to discipline and punish these European women. See Zahra, " 'A Human Treasure': Europe's Displaced Children between Nationalism and Internationalism," *Past and Present* 210, supplement 6 (2011): 334. U.S. military attitudes as well as Japanese and Korean beliefs contributed to the moral condemnation and the destructive stereotyping of Japanese and Korean women as ignorant girls on the one hand or conniving prostitutes on the other. See Koshiro, *Trans-Pacific Racisms*, 161, 168, 177–178; and Woo, "A New American Comes 'Home,' " 71–75.

28. On the post–World War II controversy over French-German children, see Tara Zahra, *The Lost Children: Reconstructing Europe's Families after World War II* (Cambridge: Harvard University Press, 2011). On the plight of German–African American children, see Heide Fehrenbach, *Race after Hitler: Black Occupation Children in Postwar Germany and America* (Princeton, N.J.: Princeton University Press, 2005); and May Opitz, Katharina Oguntoye, and Dagmar Schultz, eds., *Showing Our Colors: Afro-German Women Speak Out* (Amherst: University of Massachusetts Press, 1992).

29. Koshiro, *Trans-Pacific Racisms*, 163–168.

30. Ibid., 181–183.

31. Ibid., 191–193.

32. Rachel F. Moran, *Interracial Intimacy: The Regulation of Race and Romance* (Chicago: University of Chicago Press, 2001), 17.

33. American chaplains counseled against intermarriage, and unit commanders separated American and Japanese couples through new assignments and transfers. U.S. military laws abrogated American servicemen's responsibility toward their mixed-race children unless they admitted paternity and registered their children's births with the U.S. Consulate. As enemy aliens, Japanese mothers were prohibited from pursuing paternity or child-support suits. See Koshiro, *Trans-Pacific Racisms*, 162, 198; and Herman, *Kinship by Design*, 216. For a detailed discussion of the attempt of the U.S. military to curtail marriages between American servicemen and Korean women, see Woo, "A New American Comes 'Home,' " 75–87.

34. John W. Dower, *Embracing Defeat: Japan in the Wake of World War II* (New York: Norton, 1999), 61.

35. Ibid., 112, 133.

36. Exceptional cases of success occurred in sports, such as basketball, baseball, and boxing. A 1971 *Korea Times* article featured Kang Yong-ho, a nineteen-year-old "half-blood" son of a black U.S. soldier and a Korean woman who was selected as one of the top eighteen cagers and who would represent South Korea in the Seventh Asian Basketball Championship. He stated, "I did not know how my face and physique were different from my friends when I was a child. I didn't understand even the reason why my friends made fun of me until I entered high school. . . . I don't mind being a half-blood any longer."

See Yun Yeo-Chun, "Mixed-Blood Athletes Emerging," *Korea Times*, July 18, 1971, ISS-USA papers, Box 12, File on "Children: Newspaper Clippings of Child Welfare Issues," SWHA.

37. Susan T. Pettiss to Rosalind Giles, April 5, 1957, ISS-USA papers, Box 10, File on "Children 1954–65, Adoption Plans of Racially Mixed Children," SWHA.

38. Susan T. Pettiss to Lois McCarthy, May 1, 1957, ISS-USA papers, Box 10, File on "Children 1954–65, Adoption Plans of Racially Mixed Children," SWHA. Arissa Oh observes that these dramatic assessments were "reiterated by every other observer of the orphan situation in Korea" (*Into the Arms of America*, 36–37).

39. "Results of Leadership, Demonstrations, and Training in South Korea by International Social Service, 1954–1966," December 1966, ISS-USA papers, Box 34, File on "Korea—Administrative Correspondence," SWHA.

40. "Korean-Negro Orphan L," October 7, 1958, ISS-USA papers, Box 12, File on "Contracts with Government: Contracts," SWHA.

41. See Richard H. Weil, "International Adoptions: The Quiet Migration," *International Migration Review* 18, no. 2 (Summer 1984): 276–293; and Kirsten Lovelock, "Intercountry Adoption as a Migratory Practice: A Comparative Analysis of Intercountry Adoption and Immigration Policy and Practice in the United States, Canada, and New Zealand in the Post WWII Period," *International Migration Review* 34, no. 3 (Fall 2000): 907–949.

42. Koshiro, *Trans-Pacific Racisms*, 183–184.

43. Lloyd Barner Graham, "The Adoption of Children from Japan by American Families, 1952–1955," Programme of the Final Oral Examination for the Degree of Doctor of Social Work, p. 5, ISS-USA papers, Box 17, File on "Report on Japanese-American Adoptions, 1954–61," SWHA.

44. Susan T. Pettiss to Helen M. Day, April 29, 1957, ISS-USA papers, Box 10, File on "Children 1954–65, Adoption Plans of Racially Mixed Children," SWHA.

45. M. A. Valk to S. T. Pettiss, October 7, 1957 (emphasis hers), ISS-USA papers, Box 34, File on "Korea-Adoptions, 1957," SWHA.

46. Evangeline Canonizado Buell, *Twenty-Five Chickens and a Pig for a Bride: Growing Up in a Filipino Immigrant Family* (San Francisco: T'Boli, 2006), 17.

47. Ibid., 18.

48. In addition to this early twentieth-century historical context, the ISS observed a cultural pattern in the Philippines in which children were rarely abandoned or given to strangers for adoption. See correspondence from Susan T. Pettiss to Miss Marie Youngberg, February 20, 1963, ISS-USA papers, Box 19, File on "American National Red Cross, 1946–80," SWHA. The persistence of a U.S. military presence in the archipelago and its resultant population of mixed-race Filipino and American children may partly explain why the Philippines was among the top twenty primary sending countries of adoptive children to the United States in the new millennium. According to the Evan B. Donaldson Adoption Institute, the Philippines was the thirteenth leading sending country of adoptive children to the United States in 2000 and 2001. However, the plight of mixed-race children

within the Philippines continues in more recent times. See Cecilia Gastardo-Conaco and Carolyn Israel Sobritchea, *Filipino Amerasians: Living in the Margins* (Quezon City, Philippines: University Center for Women's Studies Foundation in collaboration with the Pearl S. Buck International and Agencies Collaborating Together with Amerasians, 1999). See also Emma Rossi Landi and Alberto Vendemmiati's documentary film *Left by Ship*, which follows the lives of four Filipino Amerasians who struggle with discrimination, family, history, and identity. "Left by Ship," available at http://www.leftbytheship.com/home_2.html (accessed March 19, 2012), and *Left by Ship*, videorecording, directed by Emma Rossi Landi and Alberto Vendemmiati (Charleston, S.C.: CreateSpace, 2010), 79 minutes.

49. Mary Dudziak, *Cold War Civil Rights: Race and the Image of American Democracy* (Princeton, N.J.: Princeton University Press, 2000); Thomas Borstelmann, *The Cold War and the Color Line: American Race Relations in the Global Arena* (Cambridge: Harvard University Press, 2003); and Penny M. Von Eschen, *Satchmo Blows Up the World: Jazz Ambassadors Play the Cold War* (Cambridge: Harvard University Press, 2006).

50. Lobsenz, "The Sins of the Fathers," 22.

51. Ibid., 23.

52. Ibid., 24.

53. Ibid., 23.

54. Ibid., 85.

55. "5 Orphans from Japan Getting Homes in U.S.," *New York Times*, January 11 or 12, 1955, ISS-USA papers, Box 3, File on "Intercountry Adoptions Committee-ISS Records," SWHA.

56. "Hearts across the Sea: Korean Orphans Find Happy Homes Here," *Sacramento Bee*, September 17, 1963, ISS-USA papers, Box 10, File on "Children, Independent Adoption Schemes—Holt, Harry 1960–63," SWHA.

57. "Joy in Arrival of 5 Korean Orphans," *Kansas City Times*, December 20, 1956, ISS-USA papers, Box 10, File on "Children 1954–56, Proxy Adoptions," SWHA.

58. Dorothea Bump, "Reporter Meets Five Little Charmers at 3009 Torquay," *Muncie Evening Press*, February 19, 1964, pp. 1, 8, ISS-USA papers, Box 10, File on "Children 1954–65, Adoption Plans of Racially Mixed Children," SWHA.

59. A 1958 *Yomiuri Japan News* article praised the work of the ISS-Japan with facilitating the adoption of "GI babies": "From 1955 to 1957, the agency placed 279 children of mixed parentage in adopted homes, including James Eugene and Thomas Wayne, pictures of whose happy home life appear on this page." See Kaji Onose, "Giving Children a New Start in Life," *Yomiuri Japan News*, May 10, 1958, p. 9, ISS-USA papers, Box 12, File on "Children: Newspaper Clippings of Child Welfare Issues," SWHA.

60. "These Are Merely a Handful of Examples of How ISS Has Brought Children and Adoptive Families Together," November 9, 1956, ISS-USA papers, Box 20, File on "Church World Service, Requests for Renewal of Support from ISS, ca. 1962–1969," SWHA.

61. Margaret A. Valk, "Adjustment of Korean-American Children in Their Ameri-can Adoptive Homes," paper presented at the 1957 National Conference on Social Welfare, p. 2, ISS-USA papers, Box 10, File on "Adjustment of Foreign Children in Their Adoptive Homes," SWHA. See also S. Pettiss to Greta Frank, July 29, 1954, ISS-USA papers, Box 10, File on "Children 1954–62, Intercoun-try Adoption, General," SWHA. Pettiss wrote, "At the present time we are in the process of negotiating with interested groups and individuals in Japan and Korea about the placement of the Eurasian children in this country for adop-tion. . . . We understand that there are several hundred children (half American, half Korean or Japanese) in each country who, because of cultural attitudes could find more satisfactory adjustment in this country" (3).

62. Margaret A. Valk to Miriam Richardson, January 9, 1957, Case No. 40227, Box 52, Folder 15, ISS-USA case records, SWHA.

63. Laurin Hyde and Virginia P. Hyde, "A Study of Proxy Adoptions," June 1958, p. 5, ISS-USA papers, Box 13, File on "Intercountry Adoptions Committee-ISS Records," SWHA.

64. Vance Bourjaily, "Have Jacket, Will Travel," *Armstrong Circle Theatre* television program, directed by William Corrigan (originally aired in 1957), 60 minutes, 2 film reels, UCLA Film and Television Archive, Los Angeles, Calif.

65. Bruce Weber, "Vance Bourjaily, Novelist Exploring Postwar America, Dies at 87," *New York Times*, September 3, 2010, available at http://www.nytimes. com/2010/09/03/arts/03bourjaily.html (accessed March 19, 2012).

66. Having a news anchor serve as the host and narrator for the program enhanced the docudrama format. The original host was the NBC news anchorman John Cameron Swayze. When the series moved from NBC to CBS in 1957, Douglas Edwards replaced Swayze. Susan Gibberman, "Arm-strong Circle Theatre," The Museum of Broadcast Communications, available at http://www.museum.tv/eotvsection.php?entrycode=armstrongcir (accessed February 21, 2012).

67. Klein, *Cold War Orientalism*; Shibusawa, *America's Geisha Ally*. See also chapter 1, "Wartime Sentiment: American GI's and the Militarization of Korea's Women and Children," of Susie Woo's dissertation, "A New American Comes 'Home.'"

68. Margaret A. Valk to Willella Kennedy, March 14, 1955, Case No. 37217, Box 21, Folder 23, ISS-USA case records, SWHA.

69. Elsie Heller, "International Social Service Inter-Country Adoptions," March 1966, p. 5, ISS-USA papers, Box 12, File on "Children: Newspaper Clippings of Child Welfare Issues," SWHA.

70. Graham, "The Adoption of Children from Japan by American Families," 7.

71. "Recent Developments in Adoption between the United States and Other Coun-tries," 1957, p. 8, ISS-USA papers, Box 10, File on "Children 1954–62, Intercoun-try Adoption General," SWHA.

72. Susan Pettiss to Files, June 6, 1958, ISS-USA papers, Box 10, File on "Children Independent Adoption Schemes—Holt, Harry 1958–59, Vol. II," SWHA.

73. Margaret A. Valk to Willella Kennedy, March 14, 1955, Case No. 37217, Box 21, Folder 23, ISS-USA case records, SWHA.

74. ISS-Korea to ISS-New York, June 2, 1958, ISS-USA papers, Box 34, File on "Korea-Adoptions, 1958," SWHA.

75. Margaret Valk to Far Eastern Representative Miss Florence Boester, February 18, 1960, ISS-USA papers, Box 12, File on "Children: SOS Children's Village-Austria, 1960–66," SWHA.

76. "Recent Developments in Adoption between the United States and Other Countries," 1, 7.

77. Ibid., 8.

78. ISS, American branch, "Report on September 27, 1957 Workshop on Intercountry Adoptions," p. 2, ISS-USA papers, Box 10, File on "Children—Intercountry Adoption Conferences and Workshops," SWHA.

79. Ibid., 3.

80. Subcommittee on Procedures, Intercountry Adoption Committee, "Report of Visit to Korea," July 16, 1964, p. 1, ISS-USA papers, Box 10, File on "Children—Intercountry Adoption Conferences and Workshops," SWHA.

81. "International Social Service Newsletter," Fall 1964, ISS-USA papers, Box 16, File on "ISS/American Branch Publications," SWHA.

82. Paul R. Cherney to Mrs. Jerome Margulis, December 1, 1965, ISS-USA papers, Box 22, File on "Pearl Buck Foundation, 1965," SWHA.

83. Sidney Talisman, "Report on Visit to Korea—June 24 to July 2, 1968," p. 6, ISS-USA papers, Box 34, File on "Korea-Administrative-Correspondence, 1963–73," SWHA.

84. Ibid., 11.

85. Ibid., 16.

86. Gloria Emerson, "Part Vietnamese, Part Black—And Orphans," *New York Times*, February 7, 1972, p. 25, ISS-USA papers, Box 12, File on "Children: Newspaper Clippings of Child Welfare Issues," SWHA.

87. Loren Jenkins, "Vietnam's War-Torn Children," *Newsweek*, May 28, 1973, p. 56, ISS-USA papers, Box 17, File on "Regulations on Social Service, TAISSA action on, ca. 1973," SWHA.

88. Ibid., 61.

89. Wells Klein, "The Special Needs of Vietnamese Children—A Critique," September 1971, p. 2, ISS-USA papers, Box 20, File on "Church World Service, Requests for Renewal of Support from ISS, ca. 1962–1969," SWHA.

90. Ibid., 3.

91. Ibid.

92. Ibid., 4.

93. John Seabrook, "The Last Babylift: Adopting a Child in Haiti," *The New Yorker*, May 10, 2010, p. 48.

94. ISS, American branch, "Report on ISS Service in Korea," March 1967, ISS-USA papers, Box 10, File on "Adoption Correspondence," SWHA.

95. Heller, "International Social Service Inter-Country Adoptions," 8–9.

96. Ibid., 15.

97. Ibid., 18.

98. Group Chairmen, "Material for Group Discussion of Integration of Racially Mixed Children in the Asian and Oceanic Countries," p. 9, First Asia-Oceania Conference of the ISS, March 18–23, 1973, Tokyo, Japan, ISS-USA papers, Box 12, File on "Children: Children in Crisis throughout the World, Reports on Children as Refugees," SWHA.

99. Group Chairmen, "Statement for Workshop on Intercountry Adoptions, International Social Service Asia-Oceania Conference, Tokyo, Japan, March 1973," pp. 2–3, ISS-USA papers, Box 12, File on "Children: Children in Crisis throughout the World, Reports on Children as Refugees," SWHA.

100. Group Chairmen, "Material for Group Discussion," 12.

CHAPTER 2

1. Toby Alice Volkman, "Embodying Chinese Culture: Transnational Adoption in North America," in *Cultures of Transnational Adoption*, ed. Toby Alice Volkman (Durham: Duke University Press, 2005), 81–113; and David L. Eng, *The Feeling of Kinship: Queer Liberalism and the Racialization of Intimacy* (Durham: Duke University Press, 2010), 97–103.

2. Jennifer Wright, "There Is a Chinese Baby Adoption Barbie," *the gloss*, September 8, 2010, available at http://thegloss.com/odds-and-ends/there-is-a-chinese-baby-adoption-barbie/ (accessed April 24, 2012). Sara Dorow writes about the White Swan Hotel in her ethnography of contemporary Chinese international adoption, *Transnational Adoption: A Cultural Economy of Race, Gender, and Kinship* (New York: NYU Press, 2006), 152–162.

3. Beginning in 1979, the one-child policy "emerged from the belief that development would be compromised by rapid population growth and that the sheer size of China's population together with its young age structure presented a unique challenge." See Penny Kane and Ching Y. Choi, "China's One Child Family," *British Medical Journal* 319, no. 7215 (October 9, 1999): 992–994, available at http://www.ncbi.nlm.nih.gov/pmc/articles/PMC1116810/ (accessed June 16, 2011).

4. Kay Johnson's research points to the Chinese government's role in discouraging domestic adoption and its focus on international adopters to help solve the problem of child abandonment in order to explain the increasing popularity of Chinese international adoption in the late twentieth and early twenty-first centuries. Her research is highly critical of the stereotype that the Chinese are unwilling to adopt the children of those who are not blood relatives, especially girls. Kay Johnson, "*Chaobao*: The Plight of Chinese Adoptive Parents in the Era of the One-Child Policy," in Volkman, *Cultures of Transnational Adoption*, 117–141.

5. Sandra Patton, *Birthmarks: Transracial Adoption in Contemporary America* (New York: NYU Press, 2000); and Ana Teresa Ortiz and Laura Briggs, "Crack, Abortion, the Culture of Poverty, and Welfare Cheats: The Making of the 'Healthy White Baby Crisis,' " *Social Text* 75 (September 2003): 39–57.

6. See chapter 7, "The Difference Difference Makes," in Ellen Herman, *Kinship by Design: A History of Adoption in the Modern United States* (Chicago: University of Chicago Press, 2008), 229–252. See also the topics of "African-American Adoptions," "Indian Adoption Project," "Indian Child Welfare Act (ICWA)," and "Transracial Adoptions," in Ellen Herman, "The Adoption History Project," available at http://pages.uoregon.edu/adoption/ (accessed June 16, 2011).

7. "History of Adoption from Korea," POV's (Documentaries with a Point of View) online overview of the film "In the Matter of Cha Jung Hee," available at http://www.pbs.org/pov/chajunghee/background.php#identity (accessed August 10, 2011).

8. International Social Service, American branch (hereafter, ISS-USA), "Intercountry Adoption Program: January 1 through December 31, 1955," ISS-USA papers, Box 3, File on "Intercountry Adoptions Committee-ISS Records," Social Welfare History Archives (hereafter, SWHA), Minneapolis, Minn.

9. In 1958, fifty-seven children from Hong Kong emigrated to the United States under PL 414 (the regular immigration law) and PL 85–316 (the special orphans program). ISS-USA, "Intercountry Adoption Program Report for 1958," ISS-USA papers, Box 3, File on "Intercountry Adoptions Committee-ISS Records," SWHA.

10. The change can also be partly attributed to increased publicity. For example, in a 1959 manual on intercountry adoption published by the U.S. Department of Defense's Office of Armed Forces Information and Education, it is noted that adoptable children may be found "also in Hong Kong, where there are many orphaned Chinese children." Office of Armed Forces Information and Education, "Manual on Intercountry Adoption," Department of Defense, 1959, p. 4, ISS-USA papers, Box 12, File 38, SWHA.

11. "ISS, State Dept., Launch Program to Bring Hong Kong WAIFS to U.S. Homes," *ISS World News*, June 1958, ISS-USA papers, Box 16, File 21, SWHA.

12. Susan T. Pettiss, "Memorandum, Subject: Hong Kong Program," February 13, 1958, ISS-USA papers, Box 13, File 14, SWHA.

13. Chi-Kwan Mark has characterized the situation of Chinese refugees in Hong Kong from 1949 to 1962 as the "problem of people." See Chi-Kwan Mark, "The 'Problem of People': British Colonials, Cold War Powers, and the Chinese Refugees in Hong Kong," *Modern Asian Studies* 41, no. 6 (November 2007): 1145–1181.

14. Wynne Chan, "Ref. 115/58 Social History," May 6, 1958, Case No. 580255, Box 86, Folder 14, ISS-USA case records, SWHA.

15. Ho Kam Fai, "Social Study," May 21, 1962, Case No. 580255, 1958, Box 86, Folder 14, ISS-USA case records, SWHA.

16. Valeen Pon, "Social Study," July 8, 1959, Case No. 591014, 1959, Box 111, Folder 17, ISS-USA case records, SWHA.

17. "Recent Developments in Adoption between the United States and Other Countries," 1957, p. 8, ISS-USA papers, Box 10, File on "Children 1954–62, Intercountry Adoption General," SWHA.

18. See, for example, "Oriental Waifs Due Fast Help," *Oklahoma City Times*, June 1, 1962, and "Looking for a Home," *Evening Journal*, June 18, 1962, which

announced the availability of Hong Kong orphans for adoption. Both articles are in ISS-USA papers, Box 16, File 25, SWHA.

19. Memorandum to Mr. W. T. Kirk and Miss Emilie T. Strauss from Dorothy H. Sills, "Re: Request for Information on Hong Kong Adoption Case," June 30, 1958, Case No. 581388, 1958, Box 96, Folder 6, ISS-USA case records, SWHA.

20. Margaret A. Valk to Rose T. Wilbur, March 27, 1958, ISS-USA papers, Box 10, File on "Children—Adoption Plans of Racially Mixed Children, 1954–1965," SWHA.

21. "ISS, State Dept., Launch Program to Bring Hong Kong WAIFS to U.S. Homes," *ISS World News*, June 1958, ISS-USA papers, Box 16, File 21, SWHA.

22. "Hands across the Sea—#2," *Children's Aid Society Newsletter*, ISS-USA papers, Box 11, File on "Preparation Outlines-Adoption" (General), SWHA.

23. "500th Hong Kong Orphan Adopted through ISS," *International Social Service Newsletter*, June 1961, ISS-USA papers, Box 16, File 21, SWHA; "ISS, State Dept., Launch Program to Bring Hong Kong WAIFS to U.S. Homes," *ISS World News*, June 1958, ISS-USA papers Box 16, File 21, SWHA.

24. See Ellen Key Blunt, "Chinese WAIFs to Come to U.S.," *Washington Post*, June 19, 1962; "Bamboo Curtain Tots Arrive," *Los Angeles Herald-Examiner*, June 27, 1962; "Bob Kennedy Greets Orphan Arrivals Here," *Los Angeles Times*, June 28, 1962, pp. 1, 3; "Shy, Smiling Waif Captures Suburb," *Chicago Daily News*, June 28, 1962, p. 1; Howard James, "Hong Kong's Waifs Meet New Parents," *Chicago Daily Tribune*, June 28, 1962, p. 1; "An Orphan No Longer," Chicago's *American*, June 28, 1962; "10 Chinese Orphans in New Home," Chicago's *American*, June 28, 1962; "10 Chinese Orphans Arrive Here," *Chicago Sun-Times*, June 28, 1962; "Family Here Taking Hong Kong Orphan," Amarillo, Texas's *Globe-Times*, June 27, 1962; " 'Hello' Melts Fears of Chinese Orphan," Hammond, Indiana's *Times*, June 28, 1962; "Two Orphans Due Here," *Oregonian*, June 29, 1962; "48 Orphans Fly to U.S.," Cedar Rapids, Iowa's *Gazette*, June 27, 1962; "Chinese Orphans Leave Hong Kong by Air for Homes in U.S. Under New Social Setup," Boise, Idaho's *Statesman*, June 27, 1962; "Arkansas Couple Adopts Refugees," *Arkansas Democrat*, June 28, 1962; "Largest Group of Orphans Leaving Hong Kong for U.S.," Charleston, South Carolina's *News & Courier*, June 27, 1962; "American Families to Adopt 48 Chinese Orphans," Helena, Montana's *Independent Record*, June 27, 1962; "Fairborn Couple among Six Ohioans Adopting Chinese Orphans from Hong Kong," Springfield, Ohio's *News*, June 28, 1962; "Refugees Welcomed," Amarillo, Texas's *News*, June 28, 1962; "Hong Kong Orphans Find a Home in U.S.," *Pacific Stars & Stripes*, June 30, 1962; "Chinese Orphans Greeted in U.S. by Robert Kennedy," *New York Times*, June 28, 1962; "Mass of Chinese Orphans Being Adopted in U.S.," Chattanooga, Tennessee's *News-Free Press*, June 27, 1962; "Chinese Orphans Head Here," Las Vegas, Nevada's *Review Journal*, June 27, 1962; "Chinese Tot Finds Love in Mentor Village Home," Painesville, Ohio's *Telegraph*, June 29, 1962; Alan T. Lewin, "Emily Gets New Parents, a Name," St. Paul, Minnesota's *Pioneer Press*, July 2, 1962; "Young Newcomer

Meets His Family," Amarillo, Texas's *Globe-Times*, July 4, 1962; Howard James, "Adopted Chinese Child Is Really on the Ball," *Chicago Tribune*, July 5, 1962; Pat Connors, "Orphans from Hong Kong Look to U.S. for a Home," *New York World Telegram*, May 28, 1962. All of these articles are in ISS-USA papers, Box 16, File 25, SWHA. A document entitled "Stories or Pictures of the Hong Kong Orphan Flight" listed six newspapers in Alabama, eight in Arkansas, twenty-nine in California, six in Colorado, seven in Connecticut, one in Delaware, twelve in Florida, three in Georgia, six in Idaho, twelve in Illinois, twenty-three in Indiana, eleven in Iowa, ten in Kansas, six in Kentucky, eight in Louisiana, three in Maine, one in Maryland, six in Massachusetts, eight in Michigan, eleven in Minnesota, two in Mississippi, and two in Missouri in which more publicity appeared, ISS-USA papers, Box 16, File 25, SWHA.

25. ISS-USA, "Intercountry Adoption Program Report (January 1, 1962 through December 31, 1962)," ISS-USA papers, Box 10, File on "Children: Intercountry Adoption Conferences and Workshops," SWHA. According to this 1962 report, the largest group in process of emigrating but that had not yet arrived as of December 31, 1962, were ninety-four children from Hong Kong, with forty-three Korean children with the same status constituting the second largest group. The report also notes fifty home studies of American families desiring children from Hong Kong, the largest number of home studies desiring children from a specific place. According to a 1963 statistical summary by the ISS-Far East, their Hong Kong international adoption program had been in operation for five years since March 1958 and the ISS-Far East had completed 779 adoption placements from Hong Kong, the largest number of placements. The 716 completed placements from Japan composed the second highest number, followed by Korea and Okinawa. See ISS-Far East, "Statistical Summary," May 15, 1963, ISS-USA papers, Box 14, File 19, SWHA. An ISS-Hong Kong statistical report with data from June 1958 through March 1962 points to the year 1960 as a high point for adoption placements from Hong Kong. That year, there were 203 placements completed. The vast majority (163) of adoptees were placed in the U.S. mainland, but 15 went to Great Britain and 9 to the U.S. (Hawaii). Canada, New Zealand, France, Honduras, Japan, Panama, and the Netherlands were among the other destinations for adoption placements. See ISS-Hong Kong, "Statistical Report (1st quarter June 1958 through 20th quarter March 1963)," ISS-USA papers, Box 14, File 19, SWHA.

26. Elsie L. Heller, Special Assistant, Adoption Division to Adoption Supervisor, December 9, 1965, ISS-USA papers, Box 20, File 15, SWHA.

27. Wayne E. Hinrichs to Mr. and Mrs. D [pseudonym], January 27, 1976, ISS-USA papers, Box 11, File on "Adoption Programs TAISSA," SWHA. Hinrichs wrote to these potential adoptive parents that "in March we hope to expand the Korean program and again open our adoption program with Hong Kong."

28. ISS-USA, "A Year of International Social Service," 1963, ISS-USA papers, Box 16, File 21, SWHA.

29. Florence Boester, "International Social Service: A Brief Study of the Inter-Country Adoption Program in the Far East," May 1, 1959, p. 2, ISS-USA papers, Box 14, File 19, SWHA.

30. "Group Consultation Meeting, Subject: Placement Plans for Hong Kong Children Living with Relatives," December 22, 1959, p. 1, ISS-USA papers, Box 12, File 29, SWHA.

31. Ibid., 3.

32. Wynne Chan, "Ref. 115/58 Social History on [Eldest Brother]," May 6, 1958, Case No. 580255, Box 86, Folder 14, ISS-USA case records, SWHA.

33. Patricia Seavers to Susan T. Pettiss, March 25, 1959, letter from Case No. 580255, Box 86, Folder 14, ISS-USA case records, SWHA.

34. Mary E. Sullivan and Elizabeth Many to Andree Laurent, February 2, 1960, Case No. 592079, Box 118, Folder 20, ISS-USA case records, SWHA.

35. Margaret U to ISS-USA, May 11, 1960, Case No. 600644, Box 127, Folder 18, ISS-USA case records, SWHA.

36. Madeline Hsu, *Dreaming of Gold, Dreaming of Home: Transnationalism and Migration between the United States and South China, 1882–1943* (Stanford: Stanford University Press, 2000), 121.

37. Boester, "International Social Service," 3. Approximately 25 percent of the sixty-six known adoptive Chinese children in the 1958–1959 study were girls.

38. Ibid.

39. Lois T. McKethan, "Supervisory Visit," March 27, 1962, Case No. 590666, Box 108, Folder 30, ISS-USA case records, SWHA.

40. Grace C. Beals to Susan T. Pettiss, July 3, 1963, Case No. 610303, Box 140, Folder 31, ISS-USA case records, SWHA.

41. Crystal D. Breeding to Althea B. Knickerbocker, December 15, 1959, Case No. 581388, Box 96, Folder 6, ISS-USA case records, SWHA.

42. Crystal D. Breeding to Althea B. Knickerbocker, April 21, 1960, Case No. 581388, Box 96, Folder 6, ISS-USA case records, SWHA.

43. Crystal D. Breeding to Althea B. Knickerbocker, May 25, 1960, Case No. 581388, Box 96, Folder 6, ISS-USA case records, SWHA.

44. Althea Knickerbocker to Ho Kam Fai, September 6, 1960, Case No. 581388, Box 96, Folder 6, ISS-USA case records, SWHA.

45. "A Free Translation (from a letter in Chinese)," September 14, 1960, Case No. 581388, Box 96, Folder 6, ISS-USA case records, SWHA.

46. Susan T. Pettiss, "Invoice," April 25, 1957, ISS-USA papers, Box 12, File 17, SWHA.

47. "Chinese Orphans Need Adoptive Homes in the U.S.A.," circa 1950s (emphasis mine), ISS-USA papers, Box 11, File on "Adoption Manual and Other Printed Material," SWHA.

48. "ISS Group Back from Far East Inspection," *ISS World News*, February 1959 (emphasis mine), ISS-USA papers, Box 16, File 21, SWHA.

49. Ibid.

50. Ibid.

51. Ibid.

52. The photograph appears below the article "World Church Body, ISS Plan Joint Adoption Project," *ISS World News*, Summer 1959, ISS-USA papers, Box 16, File 21, SWHA.

53. Mollie J. Strickland and Helen L. Springer to Margaret A. Valk, August 15, 1958, Case No. 581125, Box 93, Folder 20, ISS-USA case records, SWHA.

54. [Mr. and Mrs. Cheng] to Margaret A. Valk, May 14, 1958, Case No. 580311, 1958, Box 87, Folder 2, ISS-USA case records, SWHA.

55. Patricia Seavers to Susan T. Pettiss, January 7, 1960, Case No. 580561, Box 89, Folder 16, ISS-USA case records, SWHA.

56. Ibid.

57. "Adoption of Oriental Children by American White Families: An Edited Transcript of a Symposium Held under the Auspices of International Social Service on May 1, 1959" (New York: Child Welfare League of America, Inc., 1960), p. 5, ISS-USA papers, Box 11, File on "Adoption Manual and Other Printed Material," SWHA.

58. Ibid., 11.

59. Ibid., 16–17.

60. Ibid., 23.

61. Ibid., 24–25.

62. Ibid., 28–29.

63. Ibid., 34–35.

64. Pat Connors, "Orphans from Hong Kong Look to U.S. for a Home," *New York World-Telegram and Sun*, May 28, 1962, ISS-USA papers, Box 12, File 7, SWHA. Another copy of the article appears in Box 16, File 25, SWHA.

65. Margaret A. Valk to [Mr. and Mrs. Cheng], April 7, 1958, Case No. 580311, Box 87, Folder 2, ISS-USA case records, SWHA.

66. Ibid.

CHAPTER 3

1. Michael T. Johnson, "Strange Korean Operations of the Pearl Buck Foundation," extracted from *An Asian Notebook* (October–December 1968), International Social Service, American branch (hereafter, ISS-USA) papers, Box 19, File 34, Social Welfare History Archives (hereafter, SWHA), Minneapolis, Minn.

2. See Richard H. Weil, "International Adoptions: The Quiet Migration," *International Migration Review* 18, no. 2 (Summer 1984): 276–293; and Kirsten Lovelock, "Intercountry Adoption as a Migratory Practice: A Comparative Analysis of Intercountry Adoption and Immigration Policy and Practice in the United States, Canada and New Zealand in the Post WW II Period," *International Migration Review* 34, no. 3 (2000): 907–949.

3. Bob Pierce, "Dear Friend," World Vision, Inc., brochure, ISS-USA papers, Box 10, File 29, SWHA.

4. "Christian Social Welfare Service," World Vision, Inc., brochure, ISS-USA papers, Box 10, File 29, SWHA.

5. Christina Klein, "Family Ties and Political Obligation: The Discourse of Adoption and the Cold War Commitment to Asia," in *Cold War Constructions: The Political Culture of United States Imperialism, 1945–1966,* ed. Christian Appy (Amherst: University of Massachusetts Press, 2000), 35–66.

6. Margaret Leal to Susan T. Pettiss, August 17, 1955, ISS-USA papers, Box 10, File 29, SWHA.

7. Excerpt from Multnomah County Public Welfare Commission letter, May 31, 1955, ISS-USA papers, Box 10, File 29, SWHA.

8. Erwin W. Raetz to Richard Neuberger, June 30, 1955, ISS-USA papers, Box 10, File on "Children-Independent Adoption Schemes, Harry Holt, 1955–1957, Vol. 1," SWHA.

9. "Excerpt from *Congressional Record* of July 30, 1955," ISS-USA papers, Box 10, File on "Children-Independent Adoption Schemes, Harry Holt, 1955–1957, Vol. 1," SWHA.

10. Gene Kramer, " 'Pied Piper' Corrals 12 Korean Babies, Flies Them to America for Adoption," *Washington Post,* October 14, 1955, ISS-USA papers, Box 10, File on "Children-Independent Adoption Schemes, Harry Holt, 1955–1957, Vol. 1," SWHA.

11. "Mr. Holt 'Moves the World,' " *Oregonian,* April 9, 1956, ISS-USA papers, Box 10, File on "Children-Independent Adoption Schemes, Harry Holt, 1955–1957, Vol. 1," SWHA.

12. Erwin W. Raetz to Office of the Governor in the State of Wisconsin, August 1, 1955; and Erwin W. Raetz to Office of the Governor in the State of Nevada, August 1, 1955, ISS-USA papers, Box 10, File 29, SWHA.

13. Susan T. Pettiss to Andrew F. Juras, August 19, 1955, ISS-USA papers, Box 10, File 29, SWHA.

14. Susan T. Pettiss to Bob Pierce, November 22, 1955, ISS-USA papers, Box 10, File 29, SWHA.

15. Florence Boester, "ISS in Asia and Oceania: The Pioneer Days," in *First Asia-Oceania Conference of International Social Service Report,* Tokyo, March 18–23, 1973 (Tokyo, Japan: International Social Service of Japan, Inc.), p. 44, ISS-USA papers, Box 34, File on "ISS-Japan-Report," SWHA.

16. Susan Pettiss to ISS HQ and branches from ISS-USA, "Re: Proxy Adoptions, July 28, 1958," p. 2, ISS-USA papers, Box 10, File on "Children-Intercountry, Adoption Seminar, Leysin, Suisse (May 22–31, 1960), " SWHA.

17. Matthew Pratt Guterl, "Josephine Baker's 'Rainbow Tribe': Radical Motherhood in the South of France," *Journal of Women's History* 21, no. 4 (Winter 2009): 45.

18. William T. Kirk to Antonio A. Micocci, September 8, 1954, p. 1, ISS-USA papers, Box 12, File 12, SWHA.

19. Harry Holt, "Dear Friends," December 14, 1955, ISS-USA papers, Box 10, File on "Children-Independent Adoption Schemes, Harry Holt, 1955–1957, Vol. 1," SWHA.

20. Harry Holt, "Dear Friends," no date given, ISS-USA papers, Box 10, File on "Children-Independent Adoption Schemes, Harry Holt, 1955–1957, Vol. 1," SWHA.

21. Ibid.

22. Sibyl Thompson to William T. Kirk, April 11, 1956, ISS-USA papers, Box 10, File on "Children-Independent Adoption Schemes, Harry Holt, 1955–1957, Vol. 1,"

SWHA; Harry Holt, "Dear Friends," no date given, ISS-USA papers, Box 10, File on "Children-Independent Adoption Schemes, Harry Holt, 1955–1957, Vol. 1," SWHA.

23. Lucile Kennedy to Susan T. Pettiss, April 26, 1956, ISS-USA papers, Box 10, File on "Children-Independent Adoption Schemes, Harry Holt, 1955–1957, Vol. 1," SWHA.

24. Harry Holt, "Dear Friends," December 27, 1956, ISS-USA papers, Box 10, File on "Children-Independent Adoption Schemes, Harry Holt, 1955–1957, Vol. 1," SWHA.

25. Heber W. Robertson to ISS-USA, February 1, 1957, ISS-USA papers, Box 10, File on "Children-Independent Adoption Schemes, Harry Holt, 1955–1957, Vol. 1," SWHA.

26. Susan T. Pettiss to Ralph W. Collins, April 23, 1956, ISS-USA papers, Box 10, File 29, SWHA.

27. Susan T. Pettiss, "Report: Trip to the West Coast and Ohio," March 11, 1956, ISS-USA papers, Box 10, File 29, SWHA.

28. Susan T. Pettiss to Lucile L. Chamberlin, April 30, 1956, ISS-USA papers, Box 10, File 29, SWHA.

29. Lynne Taylor, "Foreword," in Susan T. Pettiss with Lynne Taylor, *After the Shooting Stopped: The Story of an UNRRA Welfare Worker in Germany, 1945–1947* (Victoria, B.C.: Trafford, 2004), i–iv.

30. Nadine Brozan, "Caseworker to History's Victims," *New York Times*, May 23, 1982, available at http://www.nytimes.com/1982/05/23/style/caseworker-to-history-s-victims.html?pagewanted=all (accessed May 24, 2012).

31. Boester, "ISS in Asia and Oceania," 43.

32. Ibid., 44.

33. Lucile L. Chamberlin to Susan Pettiss, March 23, 1956, ISS-USA papers, Box 10, File 29, SWHA.

34. John Braxton to Rev. Norman Minard, August 20, 1963, ISS-USA papers, Box 10, File 26, SWHA.

35. Lillian M. Lewis to Eugenie Hochfeld, January 22, 1963, ISS-USA papers, Box 13, File 9, SWHA.

36. Laurin Hyde and Virginia P. Hyde, "A Study of Proxy Adoptions," June 1958, pp. 8–9, ISS-USA papers, Box 13, File on "Intercountry Adoptions Committee-ISS Records," SWHA.

37. "Woman Accused by Jury of Killing Korea Orphan," newspaper clipping, ISS-USA papers, Box 10, File on "Children-Independent Adoption Schemes, Harry Holt, 1955–1957, Vol. 1," SWHA.

38. Margaret A. Valk to Willella Kennedy, March 14, 1955, Case No. 37217, Box 21, Folder 23, ISS-USA case records, SWHA.

39. From Mrs. Douglass A. Young to Mrs. Webb, March 25, 1958, and from Susan T. Pettiss to Muriel S. Webb, April 18, 1958, ISS-USA papers, Box 10, File on "Children Independent Adoption Schemes—Holt, Harry 1958–59, Vol. II," SWHA.

40. Letitia Di Virgilio, "Adjustment of Foreign Children in Their Adoptive Homes," *Child Welfare*, November 1956, p. 17, ISS-USA papers, Box 10, File on "Adjustment of Foreign Children in Their Adoptive Homes," SWHA.

41. D. Adjemovitch to Ruth Elsenraat, December 23, 1959, ISS-USA papers, Box 10, File 15, SWHA.

42. Virginia Baumgartner to Susan T. Pettiss, July 11, 1958, ISS-USA papers, Box 10, File 15, SWHA.

43. Lillie Reed Smith to ISS-USA, March 22, 1960, ISS-USA papers, Box 10, File on "Children-Adoption Independent Schemes, Miscellaneous, 1955–," SWHA.

44. Susan T. Pettiss to Lillie Reed Smith, May 16, 1960, ISS-USA papers, Box 10, File on "Children-Adoption Independent Schemes, Miscellaneous, 1955–," SWHA.

45. Susan T. Pettiss to John H. Winters, May 16, 1960, ISS-USA papers, Box 10, File on "Children-Adoption Independent Schemes, Miscellaneous, 1955–," SWHA.

46. "Help Heal a Child's Broken Heart," Everett Swanson Evangelistic Association, Inc., advertisement, ISS-USA papers, Box 10, File 28, SWHA.

47. Susan T. Pettiss to Garner J. Cline, April 29, 1963, ISS-USA papers, Box 10, File 28, SWHA.

48. Herman, *Kinship by Design*, 222.

49. Pearl S. Buck and Theodore F. Harris to Republic of Korea Ministry of Health and Social Affairs, December 21, 1965, ISS-USA papers, Box 22, File on "Pearl Buck Foundation," SWHA.

50. Carol W. Johnson to the *Milwaukee Journal*, October 12, 1965, ISS-USA papers, Box 22, File on "Pearl Buck Foundation," SWHA.

51. Paul R. Cherney to Mrs. J. Cabell Johnson, November 15, 1965, ISS-USA papers, Box 22, File on "Pearl Buck Foundation," SWHA.

52. Jane Russell, *My Paths and My Detours: An Autobiography* (New York: Franklin Watts, 1985).

53. Ibid., 134.

54. Ibid., 135.

55. Ibid., 141.

56. Ibid., 142.

57. Ibid., 171.

CHAPTER 4

1. Karl Kohrs, "An Orphan Boy Comes 'Home' to America," *Parade*, April 27, 1958, pp. 10–11, International Social Service, American branch (hereafter, ISS-USA) papers, Box 11, File on "Adoption Manual and Other Printed Material," Social Welfare History Archives (hereafter, SWHA), Minneapolis, Minn.

2. Ibid., 10.

3. Ibid.

4. Ibid.

5. Ibid.

6. Ibid. See also the story from pages 80–81 of chapter 3 about Mr. and Mrs. Carter who, after seeing the Korean mixed-race infant Rebecca's picture, "sponsored" her by sending her money and clothing. After several months of sponsorship, they contacted the county's public welfare commission to discuss the possibility

of bringing her to the United States for legal adoption. Laura Briggs, a gender and women's studies scholar, wrote the article "Mother, Child, Race, Nation: The Visual Iconography of Rescue and the Politics of Transnational and Transracial Adoption" to show how visual culture, specifically photographs of the "Madonna" and "child-waif," enabled a mass public understanding of the rescue of Asian women and children from World War II through the Cold War. Even international agencies that did not focus on mother-and-child programs, such as the United Nations Korea Reconstruction Agency, which after 1953 worked on agricultural development programs, featured Asian women and street children in their public relations campaigns. The communications and science studies scholar Lisa Cartwright has studied the role of visual documentation, specifically the television news media show, in the emergence of a global social movement dedicated to the care of the social orphan (a child with living parents who were unable to support him or her) in the 1990s. Her essay "Images of 'Waiting Children': Spectatorship and Pity in the Representation of the Global Social Orphan in the 1990s" critically analyzes Western media reports about human rights violations in Romanian state orphanages, though she notes that these reports also targeted the Chinese government.

7. In her study of the adoption of Korean GI babies from 1955 to 1961, the historian Arissa Oh argues that two groups—Christians and Christian Americanists—conceptualized Korean international adoption in the United States as a "new kind of missionary work." Oh distinguishes the first group of Christians who were motivated by their faith to adopt Korean children in contrast to the larger group of Christian Americanists in Congress and the mass media who intertwined nationalism and religiously motivated adoptions, using the "color blindness of the Christian adoptive families to support Cold War claims of racial democracy" (163). See Oh, "A New Kind of Missionary Work: Christians, Christian Americanists, and the Adoption of Korean GI Babies, 1955–1961," *Women's Studies Quarterly* 33, nos. 3/4 (Fall/Winter 2005): 161–188.

8. Kohrs, "An Orphan Boy Comes 'Home' to America," 10. A 1964 article in *Chicago's American* entitled "Charity Can Begin at Home, Couple Happily Learns" features the Cloonan family, who adopt a three-year-old Korean girl, Mia, and it similarly describes the warm welcome of Mia in their American family: " 'Mia loves black raspberry ice cream and tea,' said her stepsister, Michele. 'I have this way of pushing her in the buggy and she just loves it and gives me a big smile. I'm glad we're keeping this starving orphan.' Michele plays with Mia as though she were a favorite doll. Children in the neighborhood flock around Mia and try to play with her. Already she is less shy, surrounded by affection." See Sybil Lillie, "Charity Can Begin at Home, Couple Happily Learns," *Chicago's American*, May 28, 1964, reprinted by WAIF Adoption Division, ISS-USA papers, Box 12, File 7, SWHA.

9. See Oh, "A New Kind of Missionary Work." For the intersections of U.S. domestic concerns with international Cold War politics, see Elaine Tyler May,

Homeward Bound: American Families in the Cold War Era, fully revised and updated twentieth anniversary edition (New York: Basic Books, 2008); and Mary Dudziak, *Cold War Civil Rights: Race and the Image of American Democracy* (Princeton, N.J.: Princeton University Press, 2000).

10. ISS-USA, "Minutes, Group Consultation, Subject: Replacement of Children and the Extent of ISS Responsibility in Cases of Matched Children," June 18, 1957, p. 1, ISS-USA papers, Box 12, File 29, SWHA.
11. Ibid., 2.
12. Ibid., 1.
13. Ibid., 2.
14. Ibid.
15. Susan T. Pettiss to John F. Rieger, December 31, 1956. Pettiss signed five invoices dated September 1, 1956; sixteen invoices dated December 31, 1956; three dated January 11, 1957; two dated January 31, 1957; one dated February 5, 1957; four dated February 28, 1957; three dated March 29, 1957; and one dated April 25, 1957. All are located within ISS-USA papers, Box 12, File 17 on "Contracts with Governments: Contracts," SWHA.
16. Susan T. Pettiss to John F. Rieger, December 31, 1956, ISS-USA papers, Box 12, File 17 on "Contracts with Governments: Contracts," SWHA.
17. Susan T. Pettiss, "Invoice, Case #38751/MAV," December 31, 1956, ISS-USA papers, Box 12, File 17 on "Contracts with Governments: Contracts," SWHA.
18. Susan T. Pettiss, "Invoice, Case #37163/MAV," February 28, 1957, ISS-USA papers, Box 12, File 17 on "Contracts with Governments: Contracts," SWHA.
19. Susan T. Pettiss, "Invoice, Case #38522/MAV," December 31, 1956, ISS-USA papers, Box 12, File 17 on "Contracts with Governments: Contracts," SWHA.
20. Susan T. Pettiss, "Invoice, Case #39992/MAV," December 31, 1956, ISS-USA papers, Box 12, File 17 on "Contracts with Governments: Contracts," SWHA.
21. Susan T. Pettiss, "Invoice, Case #57–203/MAV," April 25, 1957, ISS-USA papers, Box 12, File 17 on "Contracts with Governments: Contracts," SWHA.
22. W. C. Klein to Staff, "Administrative Memorandum #6, Re: Revision of Adoption Schedule," June 16, 1970, ISS-USA papers, Box 12, File 27, SWHA.
23. Ibid.
24. Bertha Holt as told to David Wisner, *The Seed from the East* (Los Angeles: Oxford Press, 1956).
25. Ibid., 239.
26. Ibid., 240 (emphasis hers).
27. Jan de Hartog, *The Children: A Personal Record for the Use of Adoptive Parents* (New York: Atheneum, 1969).
28. Ibid., xiii.
29. Althea B. Knickerbocker to Elizabeth Maney, February 1, 1961, ISS-USA papers, Box 34, File on "Korea-Adoptions, Questions," SWHA.
30. Although the letter is signed by both parents, in the body of the letter, the father refers to himself as "I" and refers to his wife in the third person. Evelyn and

Adam Thayer, "Theresa and the United States," no date, ISS-USA papers, Box 34, File 26 on "Korea-Adoptions, Questions, 1958–1962," SWHA.

31. Ibid., 1.
32. Ibid.
33. Ibid.
34. Ibid.
35. Ibid.
36. See, for example, ISS-USA, "Practical Hints about Your Child from Japan," no date, ISS-USA papers, Box 16, File 18, SWHA.
37. Evelyn and Adam Thayer, "Theresa and the United States."
38. Ibid.
39. Ibid., 2.
40. Ibid., 1.
41. Ibid., 2.
42. The historian Ellen Herman explains that the Child Citizenship Act of 2000 "amended the Immigration and Nationality Act to make citizenship automatic for many children adopted by (as well as born to) U.S. citizens outside the United States. Such children, who are not granted citizenship by birth, enter the United States as lawful permanent residents. The Act also extended protections related to deportation, to findings of 'bad moral character,' and to criminal penalties associated with voting illegally and making false claims of citizenship. The law became effective on February 27, 2001. Children who met the requirements on that date, including thousands of foreign-born adoptees already in the United States, became automatic citizens, greatly streamlining one aspect of international adoptions." See Herman, "Child Citizenship Act of 2000," in "The Adoption History Project," available at http://pages.uoregon.edu/adoption/archive/ChildCitizenshipAct.htm (accessed June 13, 2011). To be eligible for automatic citizenship, the child must meet the following requirements: "The child has at least one United States citizen parent (by birth or naturalization); [t]he child is under 18 years of age; [t]he child is currently residing permanently in the United States in the legal and physical custody of the United States citizen parent; [t]he child has been admitted to the United States as a lawful permanent resident or has been adjusted to this status; [a]n adopted child must also meet the requirements applicable to the particular provision under which they qualified for admission as an adopted child under immigration law." See U.S. Citizenship and Immigration Services, "Fact Sheet: The Child Citizenship Act of 2000," October 25, 2004, U.S. Department of Homeland Security Press Office.
43. Leonard Shecter, "My Friend the Brother," publication name and date are not available on the article photocopy in the archival records, pp. 38–43, ISS-USA papers, Box 12, File 7, SWHA. In an email message from Jim Bouton, dated May 11, 2011, he recollected that the article was published in *Signature* magazine in late 1968 or 1969. He also mentions that the article about Kyong Jo's adoption appeared briefly in *Ball Four*. See Jim Bouton, *Ball Four*, twentieth anniversary

edition, edited by Leonard Shecter (New York: Wiley, 1990), 119. Even with advances in information technology and with the astute assistance of university librarians, I have been unable to locate the original magazine issue, which contains Shecter's article.

44. Shecter, "My Friend the Brother," 40.
45. "Jim Bouton Biography," in *NOW* with David Brancaccio, Politics and Economy, November 28, 2003, available at http://www.pbs.org/now/politics/bouton.html (accessed June 7, 2011). A fascinating transcript of Bill Moyers's interview with Jim Bouton about his crusade to save a historic baseball park in Massachusetts follows the biography, illustrating that Bouton's political activism and social commentary continued into the twenty-first century.
46. Shecter, "My Friend the Brother," 38.
47. Ibid.
48. Ibid., 40.
49. Ibid., 43.
50. Ibid., 42.
51. Ibid.
52. See Barbara Yngvesson, *Belonging in an Adopted World: Race, Identity, and Transnational Adoption* (Chicago: University of Chicago Press, 2010), 18–26.
53. Ibid., 1–2.
54. Shecter, "My Friend the Brother," 40.
55. Ibid.
56. Ibid.
57. Ibid.
58. Ibid., 42.
59. Ibid.
60. Jim Bouton, "One Man's Family Planning," in Paul Gillette, *The Vasectomy Informational Manual* (New York: Outerbridge & Lazard, 1972), and reprinted in *New York Magazine*, April 10, 1972.
61. Douglas Hartmann, *Race, Culture, and the Revolt of the Black Athlete: The 1968 Olympic Protests and Their Aftermath* (Chicago: University of Chicago Press, 2003), 296.
62. ISS-USA, "Request for Renewal of Support from Church World Service for the Year 1965," September 1, 1964, p. 4, ISS-USA papers, Box 20, File 15, SWHA.
63. "Third WAIF Leadership Conference, New York City," April 27–29, 1965, p. 2, ISS-USA papers, Box 17, File on "WAIF—conferences, reports, and correspondence," SWHA.
64. John Molleson, " 'So We Could Have a Family,' " *New York Herald Tribune*, May 10, 1961, ISS-USA papers, Box 12, File 7, SWHA.
65. Ibid.
66. See chapter 7, "The Difference Difference Makes," in Ellen Herman, *Kinship by Design: A History of Adoption in the Modern United States* (Chicago: University of Chicago Press, 2008), 229–252. See also the topics of "African-American

Adoptions," "Indian Adoption Project," "Indian Child Welfare Act (ICWA),"
and "Transracial Adoptions," in Herman, "The Adoption History Project," available at http://pages.uoregon.edu/adoption/topics/index.html (accessed June 16,
2011).

67. Shecter, "My Friend the Brother," 42.

68. Ibid.

69. See Jean Pfaelzer, *Driven Out: The Forgotten War against Chinese Americans*
(Berkeley: University of California Press, 2008).

70. For comprehensive historical overviews of Asian American history, see Ronald
Takaki, *Strangers from a Different Shore: A History of Asian Americans*, updated
and rev. ed. (Boston: Little, Brown, 1998), and Sucheng Chan, *Asian Americans:
An Interpretive History* (Boston: Twayne, 1991). For a collection of recent Asian
American historical scholarship, see Lon Kurashige and Alice Yang Murray,
eds., *Major Problems in Asian American History: Documents and Essays* (Boston:
Houghton Mifflin, 2003).

71. See Roger Daniels, "No Lamps Were Lit for Them: Angel Island and the Historiography of Asian American Immigration," *Journal of American Ethnic History* 17,
no. 1 (1997): 10–17; and Sucheng Chan, "Asian American Historiography," *Pacific
Historical Review* 65, no. 3 (August 1996): 363–399.

72. See Mia Tuan, *Forever Foreigners or Honorary Whites? The Asian Ethnic Experi-
ence Today* (New Brunswick: Rutgers University Press, 1998) and Sara Dorow,
Transnational Adoption: A Cultural Economy of Race, Gender, and Kinship (New
York: NYU Press, 2006), 37–38.

73. See Keith Osajima, "Asian Americans as the Model Minority: An Analysis of the
Popular Press Image in the 1960s and 1980s," in Kent A. Ono, ed., *A Companion
to Asian American Studies* (Oxford, U.K.: Blackwell, 2007), 215–225.

74. Shecter, "My Friend the Brother," 43.

75. Ibid.

76. Ibid.

77. Ibid.

78. Ibid.

CHAPTER 5

This chapter is based on a conference paper coauthored with Gregory Paul Choy
that was presented at the Second International Symposium on Korean Adoption
Studies in Seoul, South Korea, on August 3, 2010, and published in the symposium
proceedings. See Catherine Ceniza Choy and Gregory Paul Choy, "Memory Works:
Re-imagining Loss in *First Person Plural, Bontoc Eulogy*, and *History and Memory*,"
in *Second International Symposium on Korean Adoption Studies*, ed. Kim Park Nelson
with Tobias Hubinette, Eleana Kim, Jennifer Kwon Dobbs, Kim Langrehr and Lene
Myong (Seoul, Korea, August 2010), 129–145. I am indebted to Gregory Paul Choy's
contributions to this chapter, especially his insightful analysis of Rea Tajiri's film *History and Memory*.

1. See Richard H. Weil, "International Adoptions: The Quiet Migration," *International Migration Review* 18, no. 2 (Summer 1984): 276–293.
2. Tonya Bishoff and Jo Rankin, eds., *Seeds from a Silent Tree: An Anthology by Korean Adoptees* (San Diego: Pandal Press, 1997).
3. In addition to Tonya Bishoff and Jo Rankin's edited anthology *Seeds from a Silent Tree*, other anthologies featuring writing by and about Korean adoptees include, but are not limited to, Susan Soon-Keum Cox, ed., *Voices from Another Place* (St. Paul, Minn.: Yeong & Yeong Book Company, 1999); Dr. Sook Wilkinson and Nancy Fox, eds., *After the Morning Calm: Reflections of Korean Adoptees* (Bloomfield Hills, Mich.: Sunrise Ventures, 2002); and Ellen Lee, Marilyn Lammert, and Mary Anne Hess, eds., *Once They Hear My Name: Korean Adoptees and Their Journeys toward Identity* (Silver Spring, Md.: Tamarisk, 2008). Examples of memoirs include Elizabeth Kim, *Ten Thousand Sorrows: The Extraordinary Journey of a Korean War Orphan* (New York: Doubleday, 2000); Katy Robinson, *A Single Square Picture: A Korean Adoptee's Search for Her Roots* (New York: Berkley, 2002); Jane Jeong Trenka, *The Language of Blood: A Memoir* (St. Paul, Minn.: Minnesota Historical Society, 2003); and Jane Jeong Trenka, *Fugitive Visions: An Adoptee's Return to Korea* (St. Paul, Minn.: Graywolf Press, 2009).
4. See Eleana Kim, "Korean Adoptee Auto-Ethnography: Refashioning Self, Family, and Finding Community," *Visual Anthropology Review* 16, no. 1 (Spring–Summer 2000): 43–70.
5. The Center for Asian American Media is formerly known as the National Asian American Telecommunications Association. *First Person Plural*, DVD, directed by Deann Borshay Liem (San Francisco: Center for Asian American Media, 2000), 59 minutes.
6. *In the Matter of Cha Jung Hee*, DVD, directed by Deann Borshay Liem (Harriman, N.Y.: New Day Films, 2010), 62 minutes. I am deeply grateful to the literary scholar Mark Jerng for his suggestion that I incorporate an analysis of *In the Matter of Cha Jung Hee* in this chapter. Jerng's first book focuses on transracial adoption. See Jerng, *Claiming Others: Transracial Adoption and National Belonging* (Minneapolis: University of Minnesota Press, 2010).
7. Frustrated attempts of corporeal assimilation are part of the collective experience of being Korean and adopted in the United States. In our analysis of the pioneering 1997 anthology by and about Korean adoptees, *Seeds from a Silent Tree*, we argued that, despite having been raised in white adoptive families, many of the Korean adoptee authors emphasized the ways in which the racialized foreignness inscribed on their bodies, and in particular their faces, negated their Americanness. For example, in the creative nonfiction piece "New Beginnings," Sherilyn Cockroft reflects on the ways in which her facial differences prevented her from having a "normal" American childhood: "I didn't have a 'normal' childhood. Not that I had a bad childhood, but I always felt different and inferior. . . . Even going to the mall, people would sometimes stare at me because I looked different. On one occasion in my early teens, I remember an

innocent child said to me, 'How come your face is so flat?' Even though the child asked an innocent question, I felt very uncomfortable with my appearance." Catherine Ceniza Choy and Gregory Paul Choy, "Transformative Terrains: Korean American Adoptees and the Social Constructions of an American Childhood," in *The American Child*, ed. Caroline Levander and Carol Singley (New Brunswick: Rutgers University Press, 2003), 267.

8. Ji-Yeon Yuh, "Moved by War: Migration, Diaspora, and the Korean War," *Journal of Asian American Studies* 8, no. 3 (October 2005): 279.

9. See Catherine Ceniza Choy, "Race at the Center: The History of American Cold War Asian Adoption," *Journal of American-East Asian Relations* 16, no. 3 (Fall 2009): 1–20; and Eleana Kim, "The Origins of Korean Adoption: Cold War Geopolitics and Intimate Diplomacy," Working Paper Series, U.S.-Korea Institute, October 2009, WP 09-09, pp. 3–26.

10. David L. Eng, "Transnational Adoption and Queer Diasporas," *Social Text* 21, no. 3 (Fall 2003): 1–37; and David L. Eng, *The Feeling of Kinship: Queer Liberalism and the Racialization of Intimacy* (Durham: Duke University Press, 2010).

11. The scholar Jodi Kim argues that when the adoptee has at least one living birth parent, the production of the adoptee as a legal orphan creates a "conjoined 'social death' of the adoptee and the birth mother." She analyzes representations of international and transracial adoption in *First Person Plural* and *Daughter from Danang* in Jodi Kim, "An 'Orphan' with Two Mothers: Transnational and Transracial Adoption, the Cold War, and Contemporary Asian American Cultural Politics," *American Quarterly* 61, no. 4 (December 2009): 856–857.

12. *Bontoc Eulogy*, DVD, directed by Marlon Fuentes (New York: Cinema Guild, 2007), 56 minutes.

13. "Interview with Robert Rydell," *RACE—The Power of an Illusion*, California Newsreel, 2003, PBS.org, http://www.pbs.org/race/000_About/002_04-background-02-11.htm (accessed March 13, 2010).

14. As Victor Bascara writes, "An object's having been 'labeled but nameless' means that it has been categorized, but not individuated. Fuentes articulates a liminal category that is not really invisible, but not quite functional either." See Victor Bascara, *Model-Minority Imperialism* (Minneapolis: University of Minnesota Press, 2006), 110.

15. Tim Dirks, "Meet Me in St. Louis (1944)," http://www.filmsite.org/meetm.html (accessed March 5, 2010).

16. Mia Blumentritt, "*Bontoc Eulogy*, History, and the Craft of Memory: An Extended Conversation with Marlon E. Fuentes," *Amerasia Journal* 24, no. 3 (1998): 84.

17. *History and Memory*, DVD, directed by Rea Tajiri (New York: Women Make Movies, 2008), 30 minutes.

18. Lisa Lowe, "The Power of Culture," *Journal of Asian American Studies* 1, no. 1 (1998): 20 n. 4.

19. Ibid., 9.

206 << NOTES TO CONCLUSION

20. Ibid., 7.

21. Gloria Anzaldúa, *Borderlands/La Frontera: The New Mestiza* (San Francisco: Spinsters Aunt Lute, 1987), 78.

22. Lowe, "The Power of Culture," 17.

CONCLUSION

1. Peter Selman, "The Movement of Children for International Adoption: Developments and Trends in Receiving States and States of Origin, 1998–2004," in *International Adoption: Global Inequalities and the Circulation of Children*, ed. Diana Marre and Laura Briggs (New York: NYU Press, 2009), 33.

2. Heather Jacobson, *Culture Keeping: White Mothers, International Adoption, and the Negotiation of Family Difference* (Nashville, Tenn.: Vanderbilt University Press, 2008), 21–26.

3. Karen Dubinsky, *Babies without Borders: Adoption and Migration across the Americas* (New York: NYU Press, 2010), 108.

4. "Adoption Stories: Background," *POV: Documentaries with a Point of View*, updated on April 28, 2011, PBS.org, available at http://www.pbs.org/pov/adoption/background.php (accessed July 26, 2012).

5. "forOne license: A Social License of Enterprise and Product for the Underprivileged," updated June 18, 2011, available at http://www.for1.com (accessed July 26, 2012).

6. "Featured Film: Geographies of Kinship—The Korean Adoption Story," available at http://www.mufilms.org (accessed July 26, 2012).

7. Selman, "The Movement of Children for International Adoption," 32, 34.

8. Sara Dorow, *Transnational Adoption: A Cultural Economy of Race, Gender, and Kinship* (New York: NYU Press, 2006), 82, 290–291 n. 11.

9. Ibid., 82.

10. Laura Briggs and Diana Marre, "Introduction: The Circulation of Children," in *International Adoption: Global Inequalities and the Circulation of Children*, ed. Diana Marre and Laura Briggs (New York: NYU Press, 2009), 19.

11. Barbara Yngvesson, *Belonging in an Adopted World: Race, Identity, and Transnational Adoption* (Chicago: University of Chicago Press, 2010).

12. My book review of Yngvesson's *Belonging in an Adopted World* was published in *Adoption Quarterly* 14, no. 3 (2011): 218–220.

13. Diana Marre, " 'We Do Not Have Immigrant Children at This School, We Just Have Children Adopted from Abroad': Flexible Understandings of Children's 'Origins,' " in *International Adoption: Global Inequalities and the Circulation of Children*, ed. Diana Marre and Laura Briggs (New York: NYU Press, 2009), 231.

14. Ibid., 228.

15. Ibid.

16. Selman, "The Movement of Children for International Adoption," 34.

17. "Foreign Adoptions in U.S. Decline for Third Year," *MSNBC.com*, November 30, 2007, available at http://www.msnbc.msn.com/id/22045640/ns/

health-childrens_health/t/foreign-adoptions-us-decline-third-year/#.TuBE-BUb8zrg (accessed December 7, 2011).

18. David Crary, "Foreign Adoptions by Americans Drop Sharply," *USA Today*, November 17, 2008, available at http://www.usatoday.com/news/nation/2008–11–17–3481490130_x.htm (accessed December 7, 2011).

19. "About Families with Children from China (FCC)," Families with Children from China, September 20, 2009, available at http://fwcc.org/index.php?option=com_content&view=article&id=3&Itemid=10 (accessed December 5, 2011).

20. Toby Alice Volkman, "Embodying Chinese Culture: Transnational Adoption in North America," in *Cultures of Transnational Adoption*, ed. Toby Alice Volkman (Durham: Duke University Press, 2005), 87.

21. "Families with Children from Viet Nam," Families with Children from Viet Nam, available at http://www.fcvn.org/ (accessed December 5, 2011).

22. Eleana Kim, *Adopted Territory: Transnational Korean Adoptees and the Politics of Belonging* (Durham: Duke University Press, 2012), 106–107.

23. Ibid., 110.

24. "About Us," Association of Korean Adoptees—San Francisco (AKASF), available at http://www.akasf.com/about-us (accessed December 5, 2011).

25. "About KAHI," KAHI (Korean Adoptees of Hawai'i), available at http://www.kahawaii.org/about.html (accessed December 5, 2011).

26. "History," Also-Known-As, available at http://www.alsoknownas.org/organization/history.html (accessed December 5, 2011).

27. "About AAAW," Asian Adult Adoptees of Washington, November 22, 2007, available at http://aaawashington.org/wpress/about/ (accessed December 5, 2011).

28. Volkman, "Embodying Chinese Culture," 87.

29. Kim, *Adopted Territory*, 110–114.

30. "About FAN," Filipino Adoptees Network, September 15, 2009, available at http://www.filipino-adoptees-network.org/?page_id=2 (accessed December 5, 2011).

31. "About Us," *Korean Quarterly*, available at http://www.koreanquarterly.org/About.html (accessed December 5, 2011).

32. "About Us," Yeong & Yeong Book Company, available at http://www.yeongandyeong.com/about_us.php (accessed December 5, 2011).

33. "Homepage," *Mei Magazine*, available at http://www.meimagazine.com/ (accessed December 5, 2011).

34. A. L. Baden, "From Hong Kong with Love: The Life of a Chinese Adoptee," *Transcultured Magazine* 2 (2000): 17–18.

35. "About Us," 1st Chinese Adult Adoptee Worldwide Reunion (CAAWR) 2010 Hong Kong, available at http://www.caawr.com/about/ (accessed July 26, 2012).

36. Jacobson, *Culture Keeping*, 1–2.

37. Ibid., 2.

38. "KAAN: Korean Cultural Programs—Culture Camps," Korean American Adoptee Adoptive Family Network, available at http://www.kaanet.com/korean_cultural_programs/camps.php (accessed December 5, 2011).

39. "History," Heritage Camps for Adoptive Families, available at http://heritage-camps.org/what-we-do/the-camps.html (accessed December 5, 2011).

40. Kate Mee-Hee Sands, Jennifer Kwon Dobbs, and Bert Ballard to President Barack Obama, June 12, 2012, available at http://adopsource.org/Shepherd_Community_Letter_%20final.pdf (accessed July 26, 2012).

41. Ibid.

42. International Reference Centre for the Rights of Children Deprived of their Family (ISS/IRC), "Position Paper on International Adoption and the Crisis in Haiti," January 18, 2009, *ISS-USA Blog*, posted June 12, 2010, available at http://iss-blog.iss-usa.org/earthquake-in-haiti-intercountry-adoption-cases/ (accessed July 26, 2012).

43. See Catherine Ceniza Choy and Gregory Paul Choy, "Transformative Terrains: Korean American Adoptees and the Social Constructions of an American Childhood," in *The American Child*, ed. Caroline Levander and Carol Singley (New Brunswick: Rutgers University Press, 2003), 262–279; Catherine Ceniza Choy, "Race at the Center: The History of American Cold War Asian Adoption," *Journal of American-East Asian Relations* 16, no. 3 (2009): 1–20; Dorow, *Transnational Adoption*; David L. Eng, *The Feeling of Kinship: Queer Liberalism and the Racialization of Intimacy* (Durham: Duke University Press, 2010); Mark Jerng, *Claiming Others: Transracial Adoption and National Belonging* (Minneapolis: University of Minnesota Press, 2010); Kim, *Adopted Territory*; Josephine Lee, Don Eitel, and R. A. Shiomi, eds., *Asian American Plays for a New Generation* (Philadelphia: Temple University Press, 2011); Richard Lee, "The Transracial Adoption Paradox: History, Research, and Counseling Implications of Cultural Socialization," *Counseling Psychologist* 31, no. 3 (2003): 711–744; Andrea Louie, "'Pandas, Lions, and Dragons, Oh My!': How White Adoptive Parents Construct Chineseness," *Journal of Asian American Studies* 12, no. 3 (2009): 285–320; and Mia Tuan and Jiannbin Lee Shiao, *Choosing Ethnicity, Negotiating Race: Korean Adoptees in America* (New York: Russell Sage Foundation, 2011).

44. Josephine Lee, "Introduction," in *Asian American Plays for a New Generation*, 5 (emphasis mine).

45. Tuan and Shiao, *Choosing Ethnicity, Negotiating Race*, 145–146.

BIBLIOGRAPHY

ARCHIVAL COLLECTIONS

Friends Meeting for the Sufferings of Vietnamese Children, Records, Swarthmore College Peace Collection, Swarthmore, Pa.

International Social Service, United States of America Branch, Records, Social Welfare History Archives, University of Minnesota Libraries, University of Minnesota, Minneapolis.

UCLA Film and Television Archive, Los Angeles, Calif.

NEWSPAPERS AND MAGAZINES

Amarillo (Texas) *Globe-Times*

Amarillo (Texas) *News*

Arkansas Democrat

Boise (Idaho) *Statesman*

Cedar Rapids (Iowa) *Gazette*

Charleston (S.C.) *News & Courier*

Chattanooga (Tenn.) *News-Free Press*

Chicago Daily News

Chicago Daily Tribune

Chicago Sun-Times

Chicago Tribune

Chicago's American

Ebony

Evening Journal

Hammond (Ind.) *Times*

Helena (Mont.) *Independent Record*

Kansas City Times

Korea Times

Las Vegas (Nev.) *Review Journal*

Los Angeles Herald-Examiner

Los Angeles Times

Marriage Magazine

Muncie Evening Press

New York Herald Tribune
New York Magazine
New York Times
New York World Telegram and Sun
Newsweek
New Yorker
Oklahoma City Times
Oregonian (Portland, Ore.)
Pacific Stars & Stripes
Painesville (Ohio) *Telegraph*
Parade
People
Redbook
Sacramento Bee
St. Paul (Minn.) *Pioneer Press*
Springfield (Ohio) *News*
Transcultured Magazine
USA Today
Washington Post
Yomiuri Japan News

BOOKS AND ARTICLES

Altstein, Howard, and Rita J. Simon, eds. *Intercountry Adoption: A Multinational Per-spective*. New York: Praeger, 1991.

Anzaldúa, Gloria. *Borderlands/La Frontera: The New Mestiza*. San Francisco: Spinsters Aunt Lute, 1987.

Bascara, Victor. *Model-Minority Imperialism*. Minneapolis: University of Minnesota Press, 2006.

Berebitsky, Julie. *Like Our Very Own: Adoption and the Changing Culture of Mother-hood, 1851–1950*. Lawrence: University of Kansas Press, 2000.

Bergquist, Kathleen Ja Sook, and M. Elizabeth Vonk, Dong Soo Kim, and Marvin D. Feit, eds. *International Korean Adoption: A Fifty-Year History of Policy and Practice*. Binghamton, N.Y.: Haworth Press, 2007.

Bishoff, Tonya, and Jo Rankin, eds. *Seeds from a Silent Tree: An Anthology by Korean Adoptees*. San Diego: Pandal Press, 1997.

Blumentritt, Mia. "*Bontoc Eulogy*, History, and the Craft of Memory: An Extended Conversation with Marlon E. Fuentes." *Amerasia Journal* 24, no. 3 (1998): 75–91.

Borstelmann, Thomas. *The Cold War and the Color Line: American Race Relations in the Global Arena*. Cambridge: Harvard University Press, 2003.

Bouton, Jim. *Ball Four*. Twentieth anniversary edition. Edited by Leonard Shecter. New York: Wiley, 1990.

Briggs, Laura. "Mother, Child, Race, Nation: The Visual Iconography of Rescue and the Politics of Transnational and Transracial Adoption." *Gender and History* 15, no. 2 (August 2003): 179–200.

———. *Somebody's Children: The Politics of Transracial and Transnational Adoption.* Durham: Duke University Press, 2012.

Briggs, Laura, and Diana Marre. "Introduction: The Circulation of Children." In *International Adoption: Global Inequalities and the Circulation of Children,* edited by Diana Marre and Laura Briggs, 1–28. New York: NYU Press, 2009.

Bruining, Mi Ok Song. "A Few Words from Another Left-handed Adopted Korean Lesbian." In *Seeds from a Silent Tree: An Anthology by Korean Adoptees,* edited by Tonya Bishoff and Jo Rankin, 64–72. San Diego: Pandal Press, 1997.

Buell, Evangeline Canonizado. *Twenty-Five Chickens and a Pig for a Bride: Growing Up in a Filipino Immigrant Family.* San Francisco: T'Boli, 2006.

Carp, E. Wayne. *Family Matters: Secrecy and Disclosure in the History of Adoption.* Cambridge: Harvard University Press, 1998.

Cartwright, Lisa. "Images of 'Waiting Children': Spectatorship and Pity in the Representation of the Global Social Orphan in the 1990s." In *Cultures of Transnational Adoption,* edited by Toby Alice Volkman, 185–212. Durham: Duke University Press, 2005.

Chan, Sucheng. "Asian American Historiography." *Pacific Historical Review* 65, no. 3 (August 1996): 363–399.

———. *Asian Americans: An Interpretive History.* Boston: Twayne, 1991.

Choy, Catherine Ceniza. "Institutionalizing International Adoption: The Historical Origins of Korean Adoption in the United States." In *International Korean Adoption: A Fifty-Year History of Policy and Practice,* edited by Kathleen Ja Sook Bergquist, M. Elizabeth Vonk, Dong Soo Kim, and Marvin D. Feit, 25–42. Binghamton, N.Y.: Haworth Press, 2007.

———. "Race at the Center: The History of American Cold War Asian Adoption." *Journal of American-East Asian Relations* 16, no. 3 (2009): 1–20.

———. Review of *Belonging in an Adopted World,* by Barbara Yngvesson. *Adoption Quarterly* 14, no. 3 (2011): 218–220.

Choy, Catherine Ceniza, and Gregory Paul Choy. "Memory Works: Re-imagining Loss in *First Person Plural, Bontoc Eulogy,* and *History and Memory.*" In *Second International Symposium on Korean Adoption Studies,* edited by Kim Park Nelson with Tobias Hubinette, Eleana Kim, Jennifer Kwon Dobbs, Kim Langrehr, and Lene Myong, 129–145. Seoul, Korea, August 2010.

———. "Transformative Terrains: Korean American Adoptees and the Social Constructions of an American Childhood." In *The American Child,* edited by Caroline Levander and Carol Singley, 262–297. New Brunswick: Rutgers University Press, 2003.

Cox, Susan Soon-Keum, ed. *Voices from Another Place.* St. Paul, Minn.: Yeong & Yeong Book Company, 1999.

Daniels, Roger. "No Lamps Were Lit for Them: Angel Island and the Historiography of Asian American Immigration." *Journal of American Ethnic History* 17, no. 1 (1997): 10–17.

de Hartog, Jan. *The Children: A Personal Record for the Use of Adoptive Parents*. New York: Atheneum, 1969.

Dorow, Sara K. *Transnational Adoption: A Cultural Economy of Race, Gender, and Kinship*. New York: NYU Press, 2006.

Dower, John W. *Embracing Defeat: Japan in the Wake of World War II*. New York: Norton, 1999.

Dubinsky, Karen. *Babies without Borders: Adoption and Migration across the Americas*. New York: NYU Press, 2010.

Dudziak, Mary. *Cold War Civil Rights: Race and the Image of American Democracy*. Princeton, N.J.: Princeton University Press, 2000.

Eng, David L. *The Feeling of Kinship: Queer Liberalism and the Racialization of Intimacy*. Durham: Duke University Press, 2010.

———. "Transnational Adoption and Queer Diasporas." *Social Text* 21, no. 3 (Fall 2003): 1–37.

Fehrenbach, Heide. *Race after Hitler: Black Occupation Children in Postwar Germany and America*. Princeton, N.J.: Princeton University Press, 2005.

Gastardo-Conaco, Cecilia, and Carolyn Israel Sobritchea. *Filipino Amerasians: Living in the Margins*. Quezon City, Philippines: University Center for Women's Studies Foundation in collaboration with Pearl S. Buck International and Agencies Collaborating Together with Amerasians, 1999.

Guterl, Matthew Pratt. "Josephine Baker's 'Rainbow Tribe': Radical Motherhood in the South of France." *Journal of Women's History* 21, no. 4 (Winter 2009): 38–58.

Hartmann, Douglas. *Race, Culture, and the Revolt of the Black Athlete: The 1968 Olympic Protests and Their Aftermath*. Chicago: University of Chicago Press, 2003.

Hemphill, Elizabeth Anne. *The Least of These: Miki Sawada and Her Children*. New York: Weatherhill, 1980.

Herman, Ellen. *Kinship by Design: A History of Adoption in the Modern United States*. Chicago: University of Chicago Press, 2008.

Holt, Bertha, as told to David Wisner. *The Seed from the East*. Los Angeles: Oxford Press, 1956.

Hubinette, Tobias. *Comforting an Orphaned Nation: Representations of International Adoption and Adopted Koreans in Korean Popular Culture*. Seoul, South Korea: Jimoondang, 2006.

Huh, Nam Soon, and William J. Reid. "Intercountry, Transracial Adoption and Ethnic Identity: A Korean Example." *International Social Work* 43, no. 1 (2000): 75–87.

Jackson, Kim, and Heewon Lee with Jae Ran Kim, Kim Park Nelson, and Wing Young Huie. *Here: A Visual History of Adopted Koreans in Minnesota*. St. Paul, Minn.: Yeong & Yeong Book Company, 2010.

Jacobson, Heather. *Culture Keeping: White Mothers, International Adoption, and the Negotiation of Family Difference*. Nashville, Tenn.: Vanderbilt University Press, 2008.

Jerng, Mark. *Claiming Others: Transracial Adoption and National Belonging*. Minneapolis: University of Minnesota Press, 2010.

Johnson, Kay. "Chaobao: The Plight of Chinese Adoptive Parents in the Era of the One-Child Policy." In *Cultures of Transnational Adoption*, edited by Toby Alice Volkman, 117–141. Durham: Duke University Press, 2005.

Kane, Penny, and Ching Y. Choi. "China's One Child Family." *British Medical Journal* 319, no. 7215 (October 9, 1999): 992–994. Accessed June 16, 2011. http://www.ncbi.nlm.nih.gov/pmc/articles/PMC1116810/.

Kim, Eleana. *Adopted Territory: Transnational Korean Adoptees and the Politics of Belonging*. Durham: Duke University Press, 2010.

———. "Korean Adoptee Auto-Ethnography: Refashioning Self, Family, and Finding Community." *Visual Anthropology Review* 16, no. 1 (Spring–Summer 2000): 43–70.

———. "The Origins of Korean Adoption: Cold War Geopolitics and Intimate Diplomacy." WP 09-09. Washington, D.C.: U.S.-Korea Institute at SAIS Working Paper Series, 2009, 1–26.

———. "Wedding Citizenship and Culture: Korean Adoptees and the Global Family of Korea." In *Cultures of Transnational Adoption*, edited by Toby Alice Volkman, 49–80. Durham: Duke University Press, 2005.

Kim, Elizabeth. *Ten Thousand Sorrows: The Extraordinary Journey of a Korean War Orphan*. New York: Doubleday, 2000.

Kim, Jodi. "An 'Orphan' with Two Mothers: Transnational and Transracial Adoption, the Cold War, and Contemporary Asian American Cultural Politics." *American Quarterly* 61, no. 4 (December 2009): 855–880.

Kim, Wun Jung. "International Adoption: A Case Review of Korean Children." *Child Psychiatry and Human Development* 25, no. 3 (Spring 1995): 141–154.

Klein, Christina. *Cold War Orientalism: Asia in the Middlebrow Imagination, 1945–1961*. Berkeley: University of California Press, 2003.

———. "Family Ties and Political Obligation: The Discourse of Adoption and the Cold War Commitment to Asia." In *Cold War Constructions: The Political Culture of United States Imperialism, 1945–1966*, edited by Christian Appy, 35–66. Amherst: University of Massachusetts Press, 2000.

Koshiro, Yukiko. *Trans-Pacific Racisms and the U.S. Occupation of Japan*. New York: Columbia University Press, 1999.

Kurashige, Lon, and Alice Yang Murray, eds. *Major Problems in Asian American History: Documents and Essays*. Boston: Houghton Mifflin, 2003.

Lee, Ellen, Marilyn Lammert, and Mary Anne Hess, eds. *Once They Hear My Name: Korean Adoptees and Their Journeys toward Identity*. Silver Spring, Md.: Tamarisk, 2008.

Lee, Erika. "Asian American Studies in the Midwest: New Questions, Approaches, and Communities." *Journal of Asian American Studies* 12 (October 2009): 247–273.

Lee, Josephine. "Introduction." In *Asian American Plays for a New Generation*, edited by Josephine Lee, Don Eitel, and R. A. Shiomi, 1–10. Philadelphia: Temple University Press, 2011.

Lee, Richard M. "The Transracial Adoption Paradox: History, Research, and Counseling Implications of Cultural Socialization." *Counseling Psychologist* 31, no. 3 (2003): 711–744.

Lee, R. M., and the Minnesota International Adoption Project Team. "Perceived Parental Discrimination as a Post-Adoption Risk Factor in Internationally Adopted Children and Adolescents." *Cultural Diversity and Ethnic Minority Psychology* 16 (2010): 493–500.

Lee, R. M., K. O. Seol, M. Y. Sung, M. J. Miller, and the Minnesota International Adoption Project Team. "The Behavioral Development of Korean Children in Institutional Care and International Adoptive Families." *Developmental Psychology* 46 (2010): 468–478.

Lee, R. M., A. B. Yun, H. C. Yoo, and K. Park Nelson. "Comparing the Ethnic Identity and Well-being of Adopted Korean Americans with Immigrant/U.S.-born Korean Americans and Korean International Students." *Adoption Quarterly* 13 (2010): 2–17.

Lien, Nguyen My, Knarig Katchadurian Meyer, and Myron Winick. "Early Malnutrition and 'Late' Adoption: A Study of Their Effects on the Development of Korean Orphans Adopted into American Families." *American Journal of Clinical Nutrition* 30 (October 1977): 1734–1739.

Louie, Andrea. " 'Pandas, Lions, and Dragons, Oh My!': How White Adoptive Parents Construct Chineseness." *Journal of Asian American Studies* 12, no. 3 (2009): 285–320.

Lovelock, Kirsten. "Intercountry Adoption as a Migratory Practice: A Comparative Analysis of Intercountry Adoption and Immigration Policy and Practice in the United States, Canada, and New Zealand in the Post WWII Period." *International Migration Review* 34, no. 3 (Fall 2000): 907–949.

Lowe, Lisa. "The Power of Culture." *Journal of Asian American Studies* 1, no. 1 (1998): 5–29.

Marchetti, Gina. *Romance and the "Yellow Peril": Race, Sex, and Discursive Strategies in Hollywood Fiction.* Berkeley: University of California Press, 1993.

Mark, Chi-Kwan. "The 'Problem of People': British Colonials, Cold War Powers, and the Chinese Refugees in Hong Kong." *Modern Asian Studies* 41, no. 6 (November 2007): 1145–1181.

Marre, Diana. " 'We Do Not Have Immigrant Children at This School, We Just Have Children Adopted from Abroad': Flexible Understandings of Children's 'Origins.' " In *International Adoption: Global Inequalities and the Circulation of Children*, edited by Diana Marre and Laura Briggs, 226–243. New York: NYU Press, 2009.

Marre, Diana, and Laura Briggs, eds. *International Adoption: Global Inequalities and the Circulation of Children.* New York: NYU Press, 2009.

May, Elaine Tyler. *Homeward Bound: American Families in the Cold War Era.* Fully revised and updated twentieth anniversary edition. New York: Basic Books, 2008.

Melosh, Barbara. *Strangers and Kin: The American Way of Adoption.* Cambridge: Harvard University Press, 2002.

Moran, Rachel F. *Interracial Intimacy: The Regulation of Race and Romance.* Chicago: University of Chicago Press, 2001.

Mullen, Mike. "Identity Development of Korean Adoptees." In *Reviewing Asian America: Locating Diversity*, edited by Wendy L. Ng, Soo-Young Chin, James S. Moy, and Gary Y. Okihiro, 61–74. Pullman: Washington State University Press, 1995.

Oh, Arissa. "A New Kind of Missionary Work: Christians, Christian Americanists, and the Adoption of Korean GI Babies, 1955–1961." *Women's Studies Quarterly* 33, nos. 3/4 (Fall/Winter 2005): 161–188.

Opitz, May, Katharina Oguntoye, and Dagmar Schultz, eds. *Showing Our Colors: Afro-German Women Speak Out.* Translated by Anne V. Adams, in cooperation with Tina Campt, May Opitz, and Dagmar Schultz. Amherst: University of Massachusetts Press, 1992.

Ortiz, Ana Teresa, and Laura Briggs. "Crack, Abortion, the Culture of Poverty, and Welfare Cheats: The Making of the 'Healthy White Baby Crisis.'" *Social Text* 75 (September 2003): 39–57.

Osajima, Keith. "Asian Americans as the Model Minority: An Analysis of the Popular Press Image in the 1960s and 1980s." In *A Companion to Asian American Studies,* edited by Kent A. Ono, 215–225. Oxford, U.K.: Blackwell, 2007.

Patton, Sandra. *Birthmarks: Transracial Adoption in Contemporary America.* New York: NYU Press, 2000.

Pettiss, Susan T. "Effect of Adoption of Foreign Children on U.S. Adoption Standards and Practices." *Child Welfare* 37 (July 1958): 27–33.

Pettiss, Susan T., with Lynne Taylor. *After the Shooting Stopped: The Story of an UNRRA Welfare Worker in Germany, 1945–1947.* Victoria, B.C.: Trafford, 2004.

Pfaelzer, Jean. *Driven Out: The Forgotten War against Chinese Americans.* Berkeley: University of California Press, 2008.

Robinson, Katy. *A Single Square Picture: A Korean Adoptee's Search for Her Roots.* New York: Berkley, 2002.

Russell, Jane. *My Paths and My Detours: An Autobiography.* New York: Franklin Watts, 1985.

Schaeffer, Felicity Amaya. *Love and Empire: Cybermarriage and Citizenship across the Americas.* New York: NYU Press, 2012.

Selman, Peter. "The Movement of Children for International Adoption: Developments and Trends in Receiving States and States of Origin, 1998–2004." In *International Adoption: Global Inequalities and the Circulation of Children,* edited by Diana Marre and Laura Briggs, 32–51. New York: NYU Press, 2009.

Shibusawa, Naoko. *America's Geisha Ally: Reimagining the Japanese Enemy.* Cambridge: Harvard University Press, 2006.

Spickard, Paul. *Mixed Blood: Intermarriage and Ethnic Identity in Twentieth-Century America.* Madison: University of Wisconsin Press, 1989.

Takaki, Ronald. *Strangers from a Different Shore: A History of Asian Americans.* Updated and revised edition. Boston: Little, Brown, 1998.

Thai, Hung Cam. *For Better or for Worse: Vietnamese International Marriages in the New Global Economy.* New Brunswick: Rutgers University Press, 2008.

Trenka, Jane Jeong. *Fugitive Visions: An Adoptee's Return to Korea.* St. Paul, Minn.: Graywolf Press, 2009.

———. *The Language of Blood: A Memoir.* St. Paul, Minn.: Minnesota Historical Society, 2003.

Trenka, Jane Jeong, Julia Chinyere Oparah, and Sung Yung Shin, eds. *Outsiders Within: Writing on Transracial Adoption.* Cambridge, Mass.: South End Press, 2006.

Tuan, Mia. *Forever Foreigners or Honorary Whites? The Asian Ethnic Experience Today.* New Brunswick: Rutgers University Press, 1998.

Tuan, Mia, and Jiannbin Lee Shiao. *Choosing Ethnicity, Negotiating Race: Korean Adoptees in America*. New York: Russell Sage Foundation, 2011.

Versluis-den Bieman, Herma J. M., and Frank C. Verhulst. "Self-Reported and Parent Reported Problems in Adolescent International Adoptees." *Journal of Child Psychology and Psychiatry* 36, no. 8 (1995): 1411–1428.

Volkman, Toby Alice, ed. *Cultures of Transnational Adoption*. Durham: Duke University Press, 2005.

———. "Embodying Chinese Culture: Transnational Adoption in North America." In *Cultures of Transnational Adoption*, edited by Toby Alice Volkman, 81–115. Durham: Duke University Press, 2005.

Von Eschen, Penny M. *Satchmo Blows Up the World: Jazz Ambassadors Play the Cold War*. Cambridge: Harvard University Press, 2006.

Weil, Richard H. "International Adoptions: The Quiet Migration." *International Migration Review* 18, no. 2 (Summer 1984): 276–293.

Wickes, Kevin L., and John R. Slate. "Transracial Adoption of Koreans: A Preliminary Study of Adjustment." *International Journal for the Advancement of Counselling* 19 (1996): 187–195.

Wilkinson, Dr. Sook, and Nancy Fox, eds. *After the Morning Calm: Reflections of Korean Adoptees*. Bloomfield Hills, Mich.: Sunrise Ventures, 2002.

Yngvesson, Barbara. *Belonging in an Adopted World: Race, Identity, and Transnational Adoption*. Chicago: University of Chicago Press, 2010.

Yuh, Ji-Yeon. *Beyond the Shadow of Camptown: Korean Military Brides in America*. New York: NYU Press, 2002.

———. "Moved by War: Migration, Diaspora, and the Korean War." *Journal of Asian American Studies* 8, no. 3 (October 2005): 277–291.

Zahra, Tara. " 'A Human Treasure': Europe's Displaced Children between Nationalism and Internationalism." *Past and Present* 210, supplement 6 (2011): 332–350.

———. *The Lost Children: Reconstructing Europe's Families after World War II*. Cambridge: Harvard University Press, 2011.

DISSERTATIONS

Fish, Robert A. "The Heiress and the Love Children: Sawada Miki and the Elizabeth Saunders Home for Mixed-Blood Orphans in Postwar Japan." Ph.D. diss., University of Hawai'i, 2002.

Hurdis, Rebecca Lynne. "Love's Limitations: Imagining and Negotiating Racial Difference in Korean Adoptee Families." Ph.D. diss., University of California, Berkeley, 2009.

Oh, Arissa Hyun Jung. "Into the Arms of America: The Korean Roots of International Adoption." Ph.D. diss., University of Chicago, 2008.

Park, Bongsoo. "Intimate Encounters, Racial Frontiers: Stateless GI Babies in South Korea and the United States, 1953–1965." Ph.D. diss., University of Minnesota, 2010.

Pate, Soojin. "Genealogies of Korean Adoption: American Empire, Militarization, and Yellow Desire." Ph.D. diss., University of Minnesota, 2010.

Woo, Susie. "A New American Comes 'Home': Race, Nation, and the Immigration of Korean War Adoptees, 'GI Babies,' and Brides." Ph.D. diss., Yale University, 2010.

TELEVISION AND FILM

Bontoc Eulogy. Directed by Marlon Fuentes. New York: Cinema Guild, 2007. DVD.

Bourjaily, Vance. "Have Jacket, Will Travel." *Armstrong Circle Theatre* television program. Directed by William Corrigan. 1957. Los Angeles, Calif.: UCLA Film and Television Archive. Two film reels.

First Person Plural. Directed by Deann Borshay Liem. San Francisco: Center for Asian American Media, 2000. DVD.

History and Memory. Directed by Rea Tajiri. New York: Women Make Movies, 2008. DVD.

In the Matter of Cha Jung Hee. Directed by Deann Borshay Liem. Harriman, N.Y.: New Day Films, 2010. DVD.

Left by Ship. Directed by Emma Rossi Landi and Alberto Vendemmiati. Charleston, S.C.: CreateSpace, 2010. DVD.

Sayonara. Directed by Joshua Logan. Beverly Hills, Calif.: MGM Home Entertainment, 2001. DVD.

WEBSITES

"About AAAW." Asian Adult Adoptees of Washington, November 22, 2007. Accessed December 5, 2011. http://aaawashington.org/wpress/about/.

"About Families with Children from China (FCC)." Families with Children from China, September 20, 2009. Accessed December 5, 2011. http://fwcc.org/index.php?option=com_content&view=article&id=3&Itemid=10.

"About FAN." Filipino Adoptees Network, September 15, 2009. Accessed December 5, 2011. http://www.filipino-adoptees-network.org/?page_id=2.

"About KAHI." Korean Adoptees of Hawai'i. Accessed December 5, 2011. http://www.kahawaii.org/about.html.

"About Us." Association of Korean Adoptees—San Francisco. Accessed December 5, 2011. http://www.akasf.com/about-us.

"About Us." 1st Chinese Adult Adoptee Worldwide Reunion (CAAWR) 2010 Hong Kong. Accessed July 26, 2012. http://www.caawr.com/about/.

"About Us." *Korean Quarterly.* Accessed December 5, 2011. http://www.koreanquarterly.org/About.html.

"About Us." Yeong & Yeong Book Company. Accessed December 5, 2011. http://www.yeongandyeong.com/about_us.php.

"Adoption Stories: Background." *POV: Documentaries with a Point of View.* Updated on April 28, 2011. PBS.org. Accessed July 26, 2012. http://www.pbs.org/pov/adoption/background.php.

Aslanian, Sasha, Ellen Guettler, and Michael Montgomery. "Finding Home: Fifty Years of International Adoption." American RadioWorks. Accessed March 7, 2013. http://americanradioworks.publicradio.org/features/adoption/.

Davidann, Jon and revised by Linnea M. Anderson. "International Social Service United States of America Branch Records Finding Aid." Social Welfare History Archives. Accessed June 1, 2012. http://special.lib.umn.edu/findaid/xml/sw0109.xml.

Dirks, Tim. "Meet Me in St. Louis (1944)." AMC Filmsite. Accessed March 5, 2010. http://www.filmsite.org/meetm.html.

"Families with Children from Viet Nam." Families with Children from Viet Nam. Accessed December 5, 2011. http://www.fcvn.org/.

"Featured Film: Geographies of Kinship—The Korean Adoption Story." Mu Films. Accessed July 26, 2012. http://www.mufilms.org.

Fisher, Luchina. "Katherine Heigl Adopting Korean Girl: Heigl Joins Madonna and Angelina Jolie in Adopting Child Overseas." ABC News, September 10, 2009. Accessed May 16, 2012. http://abcnews.go.com/Entertainment/katherine-heigl-adopting-korean-girl/story?id=8536170.

"Foreign Adoptions in U.S. Decline for Third Year." MSNBC.com, November 30, 2007. Accessed December 7, 2011. http://www.msnbc.msn.com/id/22045640/ns/health-childrens_health/t/foreign-adoptions-us-decline-third-year/#.TuBEBUb8zrg.

"forOne license: A Social License of Enterprise and Product for the Underprivileged." Updated June 18, 2011. Accessed July 26, 2012. http://www.for1.com.

Gibberman, Susan. "Armstrong Circle Theatre." The Museum of Broadcast Communications. Accessed February 21, 2012. http://www.museum.tv/eotvsection.php?entrycode=armstrongcir.

Herman, Ellen. "The Adoption History Project." Last modified February 24, 2012. http://pages.uoregon.edu/adoption/topics/index.html.

"History." Also-Known-As. Accessed December 5, 2011. http://www.alsoknownas.org/organization/history.html.

"History." Heritage Camps for Adoptive Families. Accessed December 5, 2011. http://heritagecamps.org/what-we-do/the-camps.html.

"History of Adoption from Korea." POV: Documentaries with a Point of View, on-line overview of the film In the Matter of Cha Jung Hee. Accessed August 10, 2011. http://www.pbs.org/pov/chajunghee/background.php#identity.

"Homepage." Mei Magazine. Accessed December 5, 2011. http://www.meimagazine.com/.

"International Adoption Facts." Evan B. Donaldson Adoption Institute. Accessed May 16, 2012. http://www.adoptioninstitute.org/FactOverview/international.html.

International Reference Centre for the Rights of Children Deprived of their Family (ISS/IRC). "Position Paper on International Adoption and the Crisis in Haiti." January 18, 2009. ISS-USA Blog. Posted June 12, 2010. Accessed July 26, 2012. http://iss-blog.iss-usa.org/earthquake-in-haiti-intercountry-adoption-cases/.

"Interview with Robert Rydell." RACE—The Power of an Illusion. California Newsreel, 2003. PBS.org. Accessed March 13, 2010. http://www.pbs.org/race/000_About/002_04-background-02–11.htm.

"Jim Bouton Biography." *NOW* with David Brancaccio, Politics and Economy 28 (November 2003). Accessed June 7, 2011. http://www.pbs.org/now/politics/bouton.html.

"KAAN: Korean Cultural Programs-Culture Camps." Korean American Adoptee Adoptive Family Network. Accessed December 5, 2011. http://www.kaanet.com/korean_cultural_programs/camps.php.

Knoll, Michelle, and Nicole Muehlhausen. "Local Korean Adoptee Reunited with Birth Mother after 37 Years." KSTP-TV (Minneapolis and St. Paul), February 6, 2009. Accessed October 1, 2009. http://kstp.com/news/stories/S768458.shtml?cat=206.

Sands, Kate Mee-Hee, Jennifer Kwon Dobbs, and Bert Ballard to President Barack Obama, June 12, 2012. Accessed July 26, 2012. http://adopsource.org/Shepherd_Community_Letter_%20final.pdf.

U.S. Department of Homeland Security Press Office. "Fact Sheet: The Child Citizenship Act of 2000." U.S. Citizenship and Immigration Services. October 25, 2004. Accessed July 5, 2012. http://www.uscis.gov/files/pressrelease/CCA_102504.pdf.

Wright, Jennifer. "There Is a Chinese Baby Adoption Barbie." *the gloss*, September 8, 2010. Accessed April 24, 2012. http://thegloss.com/odds-and-ends/there-is-a-chinese-baby-adoption-barbie/.

Page references in italics indicate illustrations.

AAAS (Association for Asian American Studies), 174–75
AAAW (Asian Adult Adoptees of Washington), 167
abortion, legalization of, 48
Adams, Ansel, 156–57
AdopSource, 171
Adoptee Rights and Equality, 171
Adopterade Koreaners Förening (Association of Adopted Koreans; AKF; Stockholm), 166
Adoption Centre (Sweden), 164
African American children adopted by white families, 48, 125–26
AKConnection, 168
Also-Known-As, 167
American Committee on Africa, 124–25
American Joint Committee for Assisting Japanese-American Orphans, 90
American-Korean Foundation, 83, 91
Andros, Petro, 30
antimiscegenation laws, 4, 22, 78
Anzaldúa, Gloria, 160
apartheid, 124–25
Armstrong Circle Theatre, 30–31, 188n66. *See also* "Have Jacket, Will Travel"
Asian Adult Adoptees of Washington (AAAW), 167
Asian American culture, 158–59
Asian American history, 127–28, 149–59, 175. *See also* narratives of adoptees
Asian American International Film Festival (San Francisco), 174
Asian American Plays for a New Generation, 173–74
Asian Americans as model minority, 128
Asian American Studies, 6, 173–75, 180n14

Asian international adoption: agencies involved in (*see* ISS-USA; labor of Asian international adoption); from China, 2–3, 47-48, 167–68 (*see also* China; Hong Kong Project); and East vs. West, 27; as exploitive, 5–6, 178n10; via global family making, 9; by Jewish couples, 3; from Korea, 4; Korean adoptees, number of, 1–2, 138, 177n2; as multiculturalism in the U.S., 2, 5, 11, 47; race's role in history of, 10, 17 (*see also* race and rescue); research on, 6; as social norm, 1; as transracial, 2–4, 47
Asia-Oceania Conference, First (ISS, Tokyo, 1973), 44–45
Asiatic Barred Zone, 24n
assimilation: in adoptees' narratives, 132; in adoptive families' narratives, 106–7, 122, 128–29, 199n8; barriers to, 38–39; as benevolent, 133; coerciveness of, 150; by Korean adoptees, 204–5n17
Association for Asian American Studies (AAAS), 174–75
Association of Korean Adoptees—San Francisco, 167

Baden, Amanda, 169
Baker, Josephine, 84, *85*
Ball Four (Bouton), 108, 119
Ballard, Bert, 171–72
Barroga, Jeannie: *Walls*, 159
Bascara, Victor, 205n14
Battle Hymn, 138
Baumgartner, Virginia, 37
Beals, Grace C., 62
Biko, Gina, 30
Bing family, 52, 59–60
birth control pills, 48

Catherine Ceniza Choy is Professor of Ethnic Studies at the University of California, Berkeley. Prior to coming to Berkeley, she was an assistant professor of American Studies and a cofounding member of the Asian American Studies Initiative at the University of Minnesota, Twin Cities. She is the author of the award-winning book *Empire of Care: Nursing and Migration in Filipino American History.*